ALASKA ON THE GO

ALASKA ON THE GO

EXPLORING THE 49TH STATE WITH CHILDREN

Erin Kirkland

University of Alaska Press
Fairbanks

University of Alaska Press
P.O. Box 756240
Fairbanks, AK 99775-6240

Library of Congress Cataloging-in-Publication Data

Kirkland, Erin.
 Alaska on the go : exploring the 49th state with children / by Erin Kirkland.
    page cm
 Includes index.
 ISBN 978-1-60223-221-1 (pbk. : alk. paper)—ISBN 978-1-60223-222-8
 1. Alaska—Guidebooks. 2. Family recreation—Alaska—Guidebooks.
 3. Children—Travel—Alaska—Guidebooks. I. Title.
 F902.3.K57 2014
 917.98'052—dc23
                        2013022119

Cover and text design by Paula Elmes,
ImageCraft Publications & Design

♾ This paper meets the requirements for ANSI / NISO Z39.48-1992 (R2002)
(Permanence of Paper).

Printed in the United States

Humbly dedicated to the individuals who taught me about living, loving, writing, and parenting. Bless your patience, genes, and gritty honesty.

Alaska's Flag

Eight stars of gold on a field of blue,
Alaska's flag, may it mean to you,
The blue of the sea, the evening sky,
The mountain lakes, and the flowers nearby,
The gold of the early sourdough's dreams,
The precious gold of the hills and streams,
The brilliant stars in the northern sky,
The "Bear," the "Dipper," and shining high
The great North Star with its steady light,
Over land and sea a beacon bright,
Alaska's flag to Alaskans dear,
The simple flag of a last frontier.

CONTENTS

ACKNOWLEDGMENTS

This book would not be possible without the generous support of many, many Alaskans. Professionally, special thanks are due to Michelle Theriault Boots, who helped me develop the concept of a family travel guide over cup after cup of coffee; Jamie Gonzales, a dedicated editor who brought me back from the edge of word panic, time after time; James Engelhardt and the entire University of Alaska Press editing and production team, who helped this new author navigate the publishing process start to finish. Additional thanks to Justin Matley for his excellent illustrations and Scott McMurren for constant family-travel evangelism. Gratitude is also owed to those within the travel and tourism industry, whose time and energy toward embracing the concept of family travel has made such a difference for parents choosing to bring children into the Last Frontier; I am proud to know you.

Personally, the children who contributed adorable quotes and the parents who offered practical suggestions and photos deserve my thanks. Sometimes travel is best accomplished as a village, and your honest appraisals of Alaska's communities and environment were indeed valuable. Thanks to the J. Williams, Keller, Roll, Knechtel, Manning, Field, Musselman, McGovern, Bauer-Lundberg, Timms, Whitt, Aist, Newell, Gonzales, Tyler, Thompson, Van Doorne, Mund, R. Williams, Zadra, and Lang families.

Finally, I could not have written one word of this book without three guys in my life who schlepped every mile of this journey by my side, all in the name of *Alaska on the Go*. James, Matt, and Owen—thank you for putting up with late nights, frenetic tours, and leftover meals. I owe you all a month in Hawaii.

INTRODUCTION

Our family moved to Anchorage, Alaska, three days after Christmas 2005. The day was so cold I could see frost on the mustache of a ground crew member who patiently waited near the aircraft's door while I struggled to stuff my squirming youngest child into fleece overalls, snowsuit, boots, hat, and mittens to walk 50 feet into the terminal of Ted Stevens International Airport. We slogged our overheated selves into the airport's depths, where a mountain of suitcases and boxes waited as a sobering reminder of our new permanent-resident status. Unlike the 1.5 million annual visitors who spend a week or two in the Last Frontier, Alaska was now our home, for better or worse. We watched wearily as the sun set, coloring the Chugach Mountains to the east a delicate shade of pink, offering promise of certain good fortune in this cold new place. That is, until our 11-year-old shouted from his perch atop a Samsonite, "Hey! It's only three o'clock! What's wrong with this place?" Welcome to Alaska.

In the eight years since, our entire family learned to love the 49th state, to embrace even its frigid winters and sometimes-rainy summers. We camp, hike, fish, and gaze daily upon a landscape that fits perfectly, as if Alaska was made specifically for us. It is and always will be home.

I've had this book in mind ever since my feet hit the frozen sidewalks of Anchorage back in 2005. As mothers often do, I created a mental list of things I wish someone had told me, vowing to make these nuggets of information available to other parents before they decide to pack up kids and caboodle and head north for the trip of a lifetime.

It took time, effort, and a whole lot of travel on our part to bring you this comprehensive, investigative, and, we hope, interesting Alaska family travel guide. It's full of honest reviews, hot tips, and easily found facts to impress your spouse and wow your kids (maybe even the teenagers) as you drive, fly, or sail your way around the Last Frontier. It's meant to be used. Scribble in the margins. Fold down the pages. Use it for a pillow. But above all, enjoy this unique corner of the world. We're glad you came.

Note: By nature, tourism is a fluid industry, with ebb and flow as consistent as an Alaska tide; attractions, hotels, transportation, and their pricing or availability may change with little notice. While I have made every effort to make certain the information contained in this book is timely and accurate, please contact business owners before you embark upon your Alaska adventure.

PLANNING YOUR ALASKA ADVENTURE

"To the lover of wilderness,
Alaska is one of the most wonderful
countries in the world."

—John Muir

Let's be honest. Preparing a trip across town with children can sometimes be difficult, never mind planning a vacation to a state twice the size of Texas. With almost 587,000 square miles of real estate, Alaska is a vast environmental presence that requires respectful attention to detail. No matter where you are coming from, a trek to the 49th state requires more forethought and planning than many other destinations. In this section you will find bits of wisdom gleaned by those who have gone before you in the holy name of family travel, including tips on seasonal advantages, modes of transportation, and our all-important packing list for parents who may be wondering (or worrying) about Alaska's oft-confusing climate.

1 WHEN TO GO

I am a firm believer in four-season travel with kids, especially in Alaska, where each month has its own personality and unique activities. That said, certain times of the year are definitely more challenging to manage with children than others. Here is an overview of Alaska's seasons, and the pros and cons of visiting during each.

Summer

Without a doubt, summer reigns in Alaska for access to attractions and ease of travel. The infamous "midnight sun" and plethora of activities mean tons of fun for the entire family, but at a price.

⬆ PROS

- Seasonal activities like flightseeing, fishing, and glacier/wildlife cruising are in full swing.
- Airlines beef up route schedules, offering frequent flights to/from Alaska on a daily basis.
- Weather is usually warmer, ranging from 80°F in Fairbanks to 58°F in southeast Alaska.
- Animals are more active during the summer months.
- Best availability for airfares, hotels, and attractions can be found mid-May through late August. Summer is also an excellent time to consider a road trip to, from, or around Alaska.

⇩ CONS

- Expect to pay premium rates for all aspects of your trip, including airfare.
- Popular attractions and areas of interest are extremely crowded, especially on days when large cruise ships visit port cities of southeast Alaska or the Alaska Railroad delivers those same cruise-tour passengers to areas like Denali National Park.
- Reservations for many hotels, tours, and car rental agencies must be made early in the season, with little wiggle room for changing plans.

Alaska Fact — Alaska's highest recorded temperature was taken at Fort Yukon in 1915. The thermometer registered a blistering 100°F that day, probably causing a minor stampede to the local creek.

Autumn

Crisp nights, changing leaves, and active wildlife hold much appeal for many Alaska visitors. Autumn actually shows up near the end of August, and hot deals often appear at the same time.

⇧ PROS

- Excellent end-of-season airfares offer relief from high-priced travel to and from Alaska.
- Some popular attractions remain open for residents and autumn travelers, featuring uncrowded boats, buses, and trains around the state.
- Scenery features colorful landscapes and opportunities to view moose, bears, and other wildlife.

⇩ CONS

- Many attractions do shut down after Labor Day, necessitating more independent travel planning. Travelers who thrive on guided tours may not find fall visits a good fit.
- Weather is unpredictable: warm and sunnyish one day, snowing the next. Prepare for the latter and cheer when daybreak brings

the former. Look for temperatures around 45–50°F during the day, dropping down to 32–40°F at night for most of Alaska.

- Some wildlife, especially moose, are busy with mating season. Parents should heed all warnings to avoid "the Rut," when male moose are cranky and possess big attitudes and enormous antlers called racks.

Winter

Winter travel, an evolving niche market in Alaska, requires a lot of planning. However, winter can also be the most authentic time to visit, with sled dogs, northern lights, and lots of snow. Winter usually arrives in full force around mid-November and sticks around until at least April.

⬆ PROS

- Airfare is at its most reasonable, save for the weeks surrounding Thanksgiving and Christmas.
- Families who participate in snow sports at home will revel in the abundance of kid-friendly alpine and Nordic skiing, snowshoeing, dog mushing, and snowmobiling.
- The aurora borealis, or northern lights, can dominate the night sky, offering a swirling, multicolored experience until very early in the morning.
- Admission to attractions like museums and cultural centers is often bargain-priced to encourage visitors.
- Community carnivals, festivals, and events related to winter are great ways to engage with residents.

⬇ CONS

- It's cold—sometimes really, really cold—and families will likely need to invest in quality gear to fully reap the benefits of outdoor fun.
- Expect temperatures to range from 45°F in southeast Alaska to −45°F in interior areas like Fairbanks.
- Short, dark days can be difficult for some families. On a December day in Anchorage, sunrise can arrive around 10 a.m. and sunset can begin around 3 p.m.

- The most popular and best-known attractions will be closed. Southeast Alaska in particular is quiet during the winter months, with limited hours at many museums and visitor centers.

Alaska Fact

Alaska schoolchildren go outside for recess nearly every day, unless outside temperatures reach –10°F (–20°F or so in the Interior). Otherwise, they bundle up, head out, and usually don't even notice the cold as they sled, ski, or skate during daily outdoor time. How awesome is that?

What's the Real Deal with the Daylight/Darkness?

It's a common question among visitors, and one of the most unique aspects of inhabiting a state so far north. Alaska sits near the top of our planet, and the Arctic Circle, at 66° 33´ latitude north, crosses the state 125 miles north of Fairbanks in the interior region of the state. The "circle" is the point at which the sun doesn't rise for a day in the winter (winter solstice) and doesn't set for a day in the summer (summer solstice). For arctic communities, this means a winter of almost total darkness, since the farther north one goes, the less the sun rises above or sets below the horizon. For most of Alaska, though, the winter and summer solstice events mean long stretches of daylight and/or darkness, but the sun *does* rise and set, albeit later or earlier, depending upon the season.

While it's kind of cool to stay up late during a summer vacation, I caution that while your family might be okay with a late-night free-for-all through a campground or hotel property, the rest of the visiting population might not appreciate it. Allow plenty of time for settling down; shut off electronics, read a book, sing songs around the campfire, and get ready for bed just like you would at home. Ask your hotel if blackout shades are available (most rooms have them) or use that extra blanket in the closet as a curtain. If traveling in an RV or sleeping in a tent, bedtime might not be so simple. Try the above tricks, but also add the caveat that an MP3 player may be used for a listening session of quiet music or a story as long

Spring

Alaskans go slightly bonkers in springtime, reveling in daylight and jumping about in their rubber boots through the slush. Everybody, from mama bears to tour companies, takes advantage of the warming weather to get the heck outdoors.

⬆ PROS

- While tours and attractions are not yet in full swing, a variety of options are available, including gray whale tours, ferry trips, museums, and excellent spring skiing.

Hours of Daylight

CITY	Jan.	Feb.	Mar.	Apr.	May	June	July	Aug.	Sept.	Oct.	Nov.	Dec.
Anchorage	5:41	7:50	10:27	13:25	16:16	18:45	19:10	17:04	14:12	11:22	8:28	6:05
Barrow	0:00	4:17	9:26	14:18	19:38	24:00	24:00	24:00	15:38	10:57	5:46	0:00
Fairbanks	4:03	6:60	10:10	13:39	17:06	20:31	21:28	18:08	14:35	11:16	7:48	4:39
Juneau	6:33	8:20	10:38	13:16	15:45	17:49	18:08	16:26	13:58	11:27	8:54	6:53

Times represent **hours:minutes** (rounded to nearest minute) for the first day of each month.

Daylight data researched on www.timeanddate.com.

as kids stay in their sleeping bags. Above all, remain calm and remember the mantra repeated by thousands of Alaska parents: *They can always sleep later.*

During an Alaska winter, the opposite strategy must sometimes be employed, especially with respect to babies and younger children who are still under the spell of darkness-equals-bedtime. If yawns start appearing around 5 p.m. and your family hasn't even had dinner, try taking the kids outside for a ski or snowshoe, or visit a sledding hill between dinner and bedtime. The golden rule of maintaining your family's routine pays off in Alaska during these crazy seasons of darkness or light—and might just save your sanity.

- Airfares and attractions are affordable during this shoulder season of travel. Some airlines begin seasonal service in April, so do your homework.
- Daylight arrives rapidly, animals begin to emerge from winter hiding places, and humans are outside almost constantly. May and June are known as springtime in Alaska.

⇩ CONS

- Spring is also known as breakup, meaning slush, mud, and road grit are everywhere. Trees are not yet bearing leaves, and the landscape is generally brown or gray.
- Weather can be a bit bipolar, with late snowstorms blowing in from the north or warm, strong Chinook (wind) storms rushing up from the south.
- Later in the spring, bears and moose bring out their babies, so these mamas are on high watch for threats. It is imperative to watch out for the new families, even to the detour of a favorite hiking trail or attraction.

HOW TO GET HERE

Once your family has reached agreement about when to visit Alaska, the next important question is how to get here: by airplane, boat, or automobile. Due to its location near the top of planet Earth, Alaska is relatively difficult to reach and always expensive no matter which option you choose, especially during the popular summer months. For parents traveling with children, getting to Alaska can be half the fun or provide all the stress, depending upon your family's personality and expectations.

As you research potential destinations, always keep Alaska's size in mind. The state is twice the size of Texas, and, in fact, if you were to place a map of Alaska over a map of the contiguous United States, it is quickly obvious that the Last Frontier stretches across most of America, sea to shining sea.

Alaska is also a state of roads and waterways that don't always connect where you want them to, or even where it might seem logical. Additionally, multilane highways and bustling airports are noticeably absent, save for Anchorage, and thus moving between cities during a typical weeklong vacation can result in more time on the road or in the air than actual boots-on-the-ground experiences. Knowing how to get to Alaska is as crucial as determining what your family will do once you arrive, and parents should always keep travel time in mind when making plans.

Below is a description of the various transportation options available in Alaska, with pros and cons for each. In many cases, however, one way will be the *only* way, and therefore visitors should budget accordingly.

Alaska Fact

Alaska residents refer to the contiguous United States as "Outside" or the "Lower 48." You might even encounter folks who speak of "the States," depending upon how long they have lived here.

By Air

Alaska Airlines is top dog among air transport to Alaska from the Lower 48. With a fleet of hundreds of planes whisking people and tons of cargo

Fly Friendly Skies!

Major airlines serving Alaska:

Alaska Airlines (www.alaskaair.com): Year-round service to/from many Alaska cities

JetBlue (www.jetblue.com): May–October service to Anchorage from Seattle and Long Beach, California

Frontier (www.flyfrontier.com): May–October service to/from Anchorage and Fairbanks

United (www.united.com): Year-round and seasonal service from various cities nationwide

Delta (www.delta.com): Year-round and seasonal service from various cities nationwide

Sun Country (www.suncountry.com): Summertime service to Anchorage from Los Angeles, Minneapolis, or San Francisco

Virgin America (www.virginamerica.com): Seasonal service to/from Anchorage and San Francisco

⬆ **Pros:** Faster, ultimately cheaper than driving or taking the ferry.

⬇ **Cons:** Can be an immediately expensive outlay for larger families. Consider mileage plans in advance to mitigate ticket prices.

Resources: Alaska Travelgram (www.alaskatravelgram.com) offers regular updates on reasonable airfares to and from Alaska. Hipmunk (www.hipmunk .com) is a low-fare search tool with reliable, timely airfare information.

throughout the state, Alaska Airlines will likely be your air carrier. However, during the busy summer months, other airlines seize the opportunity to give Alaska Airlines a run for its money, and thus fly to and from Anchorage quite frequently between the months of May and October. This active competition

Tips: Consider flying midweek, when prices can be a bit lower. Remember, too, that low prices might mean odd hours for arrival or departure; plan carefully for those middle-of-the-night experiences.

Stop and Go on the Milk Run

The "milk run" on Alaska Airlines is an interesting route to Alaska from Seattle. Usually more affordable, it involves frequent stops at southeast Alaska cities like Ketchikan, Wrangell, Petersburg, and Sitka. For some families, the up-down-up-down takeoff and landings are aggravating, but for many, the milk run is a fun way to arrive in the state. Just be sure you're prepared for the process.

Weather and Travel

Weather can complicate air travel in Alaska, especially in southeast Alaska, where low clouds and fog shroud mountains and make takeoff and landing on such days a bit tricky. Weather delays can occur at any time and screw up an itinerary faster than you can say "Winnie the Pooh and the Blustery Day." Parents flying to or from southeast Alaska should be prepared with *a full day* of snacks, diapers, and kid-friendly activities as ammunition against a day of disaster. Keep tabs on Alaska weather through the National Oceanic and Atmospheric Administration website (www.weather.gov). For detailed regional weather, the Weather Underground is a great resource (www .wunderground.com).

occasionally can provide travelers with more options to secure the flights they wish at closer to a price they can afford. That said, it is not unusual to spend $700 on a round-trip ticket for one person. For some smaller communities, like Sitka, Wrangell, and Ketchikan in southeast Alaska, Alaska Airlines is the *only* air carrier available, so do your homework when researching flights, especially if your final destination is not Anchorage.

By Car

Oh, to be on a freewheeling road trip with the kids happily singing in the backseat, playing automobile bingo, sharing chocolate-chip cookies, and writing journal entries at roadside rest stops. *Riiiight.*

Traveling to Alaska by car is great if your family has (a) the time and (b) the moxie to drive for hours and hours on a two-lane road with few services or attractions. While people have been driving the Alaska-Canada Highway since the 1930s, when Chevy station wagons were packed to the ceiling with kids, dogs, camping gear, and spare tires, a road trip north still requires meticulous preplanning and an independent spirit. At a distance of 2,638 miles from the Washington-Canada border to Anchorage, driving the famous Alcan will surely be an unforgettable trip for your kids.

⬆ PROS: Great for families using the journey as the vacation. Driving also offers a chance to travel more independently, stopping when and where you want. Plus, the scenery is pretty cool.

⬇ CONS: The rising cost of fuel means driving is more expensive every year. Services are also sparse along some portions of the route. Drivers must be alert and able to solve problems, both big and small, on their own. For those with limited time in Alaska itself, driving can be limiting.

Tips: Buy *The Milepost* (www.milepost.com), a click-by-click diary of all things highway from the Pacific Northwest and Montana to Deadhorse up on the North Slope of the Arctic, and every place in between. A must-have for anyone driving to or from Alaska via Canada. It's an interesting read as well, and my kids love to navigate by its colorful, engaging pages.

Mulling a road trip to Alaska? Here are more important considerations:

SEASON

As stated previously, summer is the most advantageous time to drive to Alaska. Roads are (hopefully) snow free, the weather is more manageable, and daylight is near continuous the farther north you travel. Summertime is also short, so plan to drive between late May and mid-August, when snowstorms or other nasty weather surprises are less likely to occur. That said, summer is also construction time (Alaskans joke that the state has but two seasons: winter and construction). Hours-long delays are not at all unusual, turning a 10-hour drive into a 14- or even 16-hour slog, so factor such into your driving itinerary.

VEHICLE

Many families drive their own vehicles, laden like pack mules with spare tires, tents, and extra gasoline. Alaska can be brutal on an automobile, even in these modern times of asphalt and wide shoulders. You see, Alaska's wildly swinging temperatures have created potholes, gravel washes, and something called a "frost heave," a ribbon-candy effect on an otherwise lovely stretch of road, causing a car to bounce higher than a super ball if the driver is caught unaware. Roadside repair is difficult to find, with little cell-phone service and only a handful of AAA-approved towing shops

> ### KIDSPEAK
> My mom always makes me take a bag whenever we drive to Haines, because I always get carsick. That's not the fun part.
> —Jimmy, age 13

available way out in the wilderness. (By the way, if you do have AAA, consider the extra dollars for extended service, like towing. It is likely that if your car breaks down, it will be a lengthy tow.) So, when driving a personal vehicle, pack a tool kit, the car's manual, a full-size spare tire, and extra gas, just in case. It doesn't hurt, either, to carry extra water, food, sleeping bags, and toys, even if you are not camping.

A popular way to experience the back roads of Canada and Alaska and burn up the miles is aboard an RV, rented at either end of the journey or on a round-trip basis. For those comfortable driving such vehicles, an RV can be the perfect compromise between road tripping and sightseeing—and it provides a comfy place to stay along the way. Indeed, one of the most popular ways to see Alaska is via RV, with many companies offering one-way deals from Anchorage to sister outfits in the Lower 48. Some families choose to spin around the state for a while before returning the RV and flying home while others opt for a ferry trip one way, driving the other. Whatever your desire, RV travel can be a great way to provide some extra family time without the burden of seeking overbooked hotels/motels or eating in restaurants every night. *The Milepost* provides helpful listings of campgrounds and pull-outs suitable for RV travelers within its pages. I'll talk more about RVs and driving in "Road Tripping with the Fam."

CANADA

All roads to Alaska pass through Canada and, thanks to a 2007 international law that says all travelers to and from Canada via the United States need to provide a passport, it behooves you to begin planning now if you want to drive to Alaska. You may want to give your car insurance carrier a call to find out options for coverage on your own vehicle or a rented vehicle while within the borders of our neighboring country. Be aware, too, that should only one parent be crossing the border into Canada, a signed, notarized note must accompany that child's passport. I found this out the hard way one summer at Beaver Creek, Yukon Territory, when taking our youngest to Haines, Alaska, with a friend and her three kids. Let's just say the resulting conversation nearly

> ### PARENT PRO TIP
>
> Our family loves the drive between Haines and Anchorage. While it is indeed long (two full days), we break up the hours with fun time at school playgrounds in Tok and Glenallen for a little exercise and fresh air. Our kids also appreciate a stop in Whitehorse, Yukon Territory, where all the Canadian coins they've saved up since our last visit come in handy at an ice cream and sweet treat shop just off the highway.
>
> —Jennifer, Anchorage mother of three

ended badly, with me finally offering to leave said preschooler in the agent's office, to be retrieved on the return trip.

Those travelers with prior felony convictions in the United States may be denied entry into Canada, and both countries have strict rules for firearms, explosives, and the like. Check the U.S. Department of State website for an exhaustive list of what one can or cannot bring back and forth (help.cbp.gov/app/answers/detail/a_id/737/kw/canada/sno/1).

By Ferry

Our family's favorite trip thus far was a two-week excursion aboard the Alaska Marine Highway System (AMHS) ferries. A state-operated, well-managed transportation option that carries as many locals as it does visitors all year long, AMHS is a fabulous way to show your kids the "real" Alaska. With a variety of itineraries, vessels, and ports of call both large and small, a vacation aboard the ferry will not only satisfy the need for adventure but also offer your children a healthy dose of Alaska culture along the way.

An actual designated Scenic Byway (the only one of its kind), the Alaska Marine Highway System stretches all the way from Bellingham, Washington, to the Aleutian Islands, a distance of around 1,500 miles. While it is possible to book passage along the entire distance, most visitors focus on the beautiful and placid Inside Passage of southeast Alaska, where scenery, activities, and wildlife capture the spirit of our state.

⬆ PROS: Many destinations mean lots of opportunities for disembarking and exploring independently. Families who love adventure will enjoy the ferry, especially those with a penchant toward kayaking, hiking, or camping, as these activities are popular with indie ferry travelers. Kids under six travel for free, and kids six to 12 travel for half-price. Seasonal specials are also available, so check the ferry website for information (www.ferryalaska.com).

⬇ CONS: The ferry can cost a lot, especially if bringing a car on board. Budget carefully. Random sailing times can mean very early or late departures/arrivals, and unless you book a stateroom, the kids (and you) will sleep on the floor, in your seats, or on the deck outside.

Tips: Make reservations as far in advance as possible; most ferries are very crowded between May and September. Reserve a stateroom with kids to allow for restful nights and space to decompress after busy days.

AMHS staff keep the staterooms in spit-spot condition, and all linens are provided. Some staterooms offer private baths, but the shared bathrooms are also maintained with the highest degree of cleanliness. Ask for a tour of the bridge—some captains love showing off their kingdom.

KIDSPEAK

My favorite part about taking the ferry was visiting the captain as he steered the boat. He let us look at a map of where to go!

—Owen, age seven

Alaska Fact

The Alaska Marine Highway was officially founded in 1963, and the first run of the MV *Malaspina* caused a traffic jam in southeast city Ketchikan as hundreds of people scrambled to the waterfront to catch a glimpse of the vessel.

IF YOU CRUISE

"But so seldom is Nature marred by the hand of man, so impressive the solitude, that you can stand at the bow of one of these steamers and imagine yourself the original explorer, the first man ever to have passed this way."

—Harry A. Franck, *The Lure of Alaska* (1943)

Cruising is big business in Alaska, especially for southeast communities. Each year, hundreds of thousands of passengers channel their inner explorer during a week (or more) of far northern adventures. From large, luxurious ships to smaller companies, cruising offers the best of Alaska in a rather short amount of time. Cruising is so popular that in 2011, nearly one million passengers sailed up and down Alaska's coasts, many with children in tow. While the typical cruise passenger's age hovers around 50, cruise lines are recognizing the desire of parents to expose their kids to Alaska and have responded with opportunities for the entire family.

This section is designed to remove some mystery about cruising Alaska with children. Here you'll find a short description of cruise lines catering to children and discern which type of cruise might fit your family's lifestyle. Pricing is included in each company's description, along with any specific kid-friendly services.

Our family has cruised both large and small ships around Alaska's southeastern section, and along the way we've learned some valuable lessons.

Note: Alaska boasts 11 cruise lines with itineraries in Alaska. I will discuss those companies that offer children's programs or itineraries best suited for families.

When to Go

The cruise ship season in Alaska operates from May to October, with special rates available for early- or late-season sailings.

Mid-May: Earliest departure/arrival date for Alaska cruising. Weather can be cool, windy, rainy, or even a bit snowy. Animals are emerging after a long winter, and viewing opportunities can be good, including migrating gray whales from Mexico. Port communities are quieter, offering good deals on attractions and tours. Many kids are still in school, so ships' activities may be less crowded.

Summer (June–August): High season for cruising and cruise tours. Port cities are teeming with people, but all attractions and sights are open and in full swing. Weather can range from rain to blue skies. Most expensive time to cruise, and most crowded.

Autumn (late August–early October): Colorful leaves, snow-capped mountains, and majestic animals. Great deals on shoulder-season cruising and cruise tours. Children have returned to school, and many families find access to many onboard activities. Weather can be cold and rainy, or even snowy.

How Shall We Sail?

The options for cruising Alaska range from luxury ships carrying more than 2,000 passengers to small boats playing host to a mere 75 individuals (or less). The choice lies with your family's desired level of activity.

In general, large cruise lines offer the same basic services, but each has programs and activities unique to the company. It can be confusing to navigate choosing, then booking, so I've outlined several cruise lines catering to the whole family, along with their basic information, price range, and style of cruising.

Arriving in Haines, Alaska, via Holland America Lines.

If you want more information about Alaska's seasonal cruise ships, contact the Alaska Cruise Association, an Alaska-based nonprofit organization that endeavors to establish workable relationships among cruise lines and the communities they visit (www.alaskacruise.org, 907-743-4529).

THE LARGE SHIPS

When most people envision themselves on a cruise, the big boats take center stage. Serving anywhere from 1,000 to 3,000 passengers, large cruise ships generally offer similar activities but differ widely when it comes to children's programming. Today, both lavish and more casual atmospheres rule onboard, and larger cruise lines appeal to many families because of their affordability, wide range of activities, and interesting entertainment.

Large cruise lines provide the added bonus of cruise tours that extend Alaska experiences by a few days or a few weeks, depending upon the company. For people who want to see as much of Alaska as possible, sometimes the guided-every-second tours operated by the larger companies can be arranged, right down to meal service and daily activities.

Holland America Line
(877) 932-4259
www.hollandamerica.com

Full of classic European tradition since 1873, when it was the Netherlands-America Steamship Company, Holland America is considered midsize by cruise line industry standards, serving around 1,300 passengers aboard its fleet of ships with names like the *Veendam*, *Oosterdam*, and *Amsterdam*. Holland America prides itself on classic service with lots of unruffled ambiance and, while not as flashy as some other large cruise lines, still delivers stellar programming for children and teens.

Staterooms range from small inside cabins to the fancy, Euro-style veranda suites. Shipboard life is definitely more subdued. While the average age of a Holland America cruiser is typically around 50, more families are taking advantage of great prices and a little less party atmosphere in which to show their kids Alaska. I found Holland America a great choice for our first cruise experience: casual and fine dining, activities that did not overwhelm us, and stellar service.

Sailing from Seattle or Vancouver, British Columbia, Holland America ships offer seven- or 14-day cruises to and from Alaska, depending upon the route, and include a number of shore excursions classified as kid-friendly. Aboard ship, children can participate in one of three programs, based upon age. Club HAL, designated for kids ages three through seven, is a solid day camp experience, with crafts, music, games, and special theme nights. Club HAL kids are sent back to their families during mealtimes, unless previous arrangements have been made, and during the evening hours before theme nights. Children in Club HAL must be out of diapers or pull-ups. Tween passengers between eight and 12 will enjoy time just for them, with games, more sophisticated activities, and some outdoor sporting time, weather permitting. Teenagers hang out in the Loft or Oasis area, depending upon the ship, and kids from 13 to 17 will find tons of electronic friends, in addition to new human ones.

Dances, mocktail mixing, and theme nights are just a few teen activities available.

Kids can also participate in HAL's Culinary Arts Program, learning hands-on cooking skills from the ship's kitchen staff. Children ages three through seven cook simple, kid-pleasing menu items, while those ages eight and older can prepare a full meal under the direction of professional chefs, receiving a copy of the recipes (and a tasting) upon completion.

Babysitting in your stateroom is available on a limited basis; inquire at the front office when you board. Club HAL babysitting for those enrolled in the program is available during port days and after hours in the evening for $5 per hour per child.

Cruises begin at around $500 per person, which includes stateroom, meals in most of the dining areas, some shipboard activities (including children's programs), and entertainment. Holland America also offers cruise-tour excursions at the beginning or end of your cruise, traveling by rail or motorcoach to places like Fairbanks, Denali National Park, and Skagway. Keep in mind, though, these trips are designed to see as much Alaska real estate as possible in a very short amount of time, often difficult for kids.

Princess Cruises
(800) 774-6237
www.princess.com

Somewhere in between the classic styling of Holland America and the faster-paced, dance-party cruise lines we'll mention later is Princess Cruises. Solid service, an ever-increasing fleet of large ships, and a diverse docket of activities mean many happy cruising families.

Sailing from San Francisco, Seattle, or Vancouver, British Columbia, Princess offers seven-, 10-, and 14-day cruises and a special "Alaska Sampler" cruise from Vancouver, Ketchikan, and Seattle, perfect for those with limited time.

Offering similar stateroom options to other large ships, Princess provides inside, outside, and veranda cabins, the benefits of which lie in their larger capacity of almost 3,000 passengers. There are two dining options:

traditional or anytime, the latter forgoing the reserved seating time in the formal dining room. In addition, Princess ships offer a wide variety of casual dining options that appeal to children, with pizza, burgers, and the like.

Princess ships and related motor coaches, lodges, and railroad cars are common sights around the state; shore excursions arranged through the cruise line are many and varied.

Children are treated well aboard Princess ships, with three age-appropriate options from which to choose. Those ages three through seven enjoy activities with the Pelicans, engaging in Alaska-themed crafts, games, and activities. The Shockwaves capture the 8–12 age group, keeping these tweens energized and engaged through hands-on activities, game rooms, and other "edutainment" options, like the weekly talent show. Teen Lounges are for 13–17-year-olds and offer late-night hangout time where pizza and movie nights and jam sessions are common. All age groups receive heavy science emphasis, from physics to biology and everything in between, presented in an age-appropriate format.

Shore Excursions: A Great Deal or Not?

DURING OUR FAMILY'S FIRST CRUISE, we were a bit confused about the extracurricular activities at each port of call. Cruise staff warned us ahead of time that should we decide to explore on our own and become delayed, the boat could depart at sailing time and leave us, stranded and friendless, in a strange Alaska city. Out of fear, we promptly signed up for shore excursions.

The term *shore excursion* merely means a guided tour or activity agreed upon between the cruise line and a private tour operator, who receives a portion of the day's income. Passengers are not required to book such activities, but the cruise line can guarantee the boat will wait for you should a delay occur (not likely, but possible). Shore excursion operators will pick you up at the end of the gangplank and provide transportation, activities, and in some cases a meal before delivering you back to the dock in time for departure. A shore excursion is for many a way to see as

Princess also values environmental learning while kids sail. Pete's Pals, a marine science stewardship program, provides insight into the marine life below and above the ship.

Babysitting is available for kids ages three through 12, with after-hours care in the children's clubs at the rate of $5 per hour per child. Port-day care is also available at no extra fee. Meals are served with parental consent.

Cruises are available starting at around $500 per person, with additional cruise tours and land/rail excursions offered as well, taking passengers on an extended visit through Alaska, including designated rail cars on the Alaska Railroad to Denali National Park, Seward, and Whittier.

Disney Cruise Line
(800) 951-3532
www.disneycruise.disney.go.com

Disney does big business in the family cruising world, with lots of entertaining characters, activities, and parental-free exploration. Offering seven- or nine-night cruises in Alaska, both departing from Vancouver,

much of Alaska as possible in a short amount of time—great if you don't think you'll ever visit again, but sometimes frenetic in pace.

Our recommendation? Spend some time reading this book, research activities ahead of your departure date for Alaska, then book directly with the tour operator or activity vendor. If you establish a line of communication well in advance, ask the questions, and clearly state that your mode of travel is via cruise ship, there is no reason why your family cannot save a bundle of cash (and energy) for other things.

Note: You must, however, know the length of time your ship will be docked, what time passengers are expected to be on board, and what time the ship sails. This is a nonnegotiable aspect of cruising about which all passengers (including children) must be aware. Every morning, cruise directors send all passengers a short newsletter about the port of call, arrival and departure times, etc.

British Columbia, the *Disney Wonder* stops in Ketchikan, Juneau, and Skagway (adding Sitka on the longer trip).

In typical Disney fashion, kids are treated to lots of special touches while aboard, including stateroom wake-up or goodnight calls, meals with all the favorite Disney characters, and special age-appropriate kids' clubs. Younger school-agers meet at the Oceaneer Club, tweens hang out at the Edge, and teenagers have their own space in the Vibe. Family common areas include Studio Sea and the D Lounge, with music, dancing, and lots of entertainment for each age group.

For families with children three and under, Founder's Reef Nursery provides activities designed for preschoolers. There is no nursery care on the *Disney Wonder*.

As an added bonus for entertainment, kids can enjoy daily movies, shows, and opportunities for family-friendly shore excursions designed especially for Disney cruise passengers. Oh, and listen for the nightly rendition of "When You Wish Upon a Star," blown by the ship's whistle.

Cruises on the *Disney Wonder* begin at around $1,400 per person for adults, and slightly less for children. Cruises include accommodations, meals, general entertainment, character interactions, and select activities.

THE SMALL SHIPS

Looking for a more intimate Alaska cruising experience? Small-ship cruising is hot right now, thanks to an increasing number of visitors wanting more from their vacation. Small ships regularly cruise the Inside Passage of Alaska, leaving from Seattle, Juneau, Sitka, or Ketchikan, and are able to sail into the nooks and crannies of remote waterways the big boats

The *Wilderness Discoverer*, operated by Un-Cruise Adventures, anchors near a glacier.

can't touch. A few companies operate out of Whittier or Seward and limit itineraries to Resurrection Bay or the greater Prince William Sound area. Most small-ship cruises board fewer than 200 passengers per sailing, with some maxing out at 20 or even 10 guests and offer almost one-to-one crew service for an outstanding docket of activities. Naturalist crew members lead hikes and kayak trips, present lectures, and even offer photography advice during a trip, but all this attention comes at a price. The average small-ship cruise starts at around $1,300 per person for a seven-day trip and travels upward depending upon cabin size and the type of boat.

If your family is adventurous and desires an authentic, hands-on week upon the briny waters of Alaska, this might just be the trip of a lifetime. Not every small-ship company is equipped to host children, however, so do your homework with our listings below. Very small children may not enjoy the experience as much as older, school-aged kids, but knowing your child's personality and outdoor interest level will help you determine his or her readiness for such an excursion.

Un-Cruise Adventures
(877) 901-1009
www.un-cruise.com

This innovative company operates under a strict policy of not being too strict when it comes to schedules. Flexibility is key during a cruise with this Seattle-based company, and passengers reap the rewards of sailing through the hidden coves and secluded waterways of southeast Alaska. Itineraries range from seven to 21 days and originate in Seattle, Ketchikan, Sitka, or Juneau.

Active cruisers will enjoy two ships, the *Wilderness Explorer* and the *Wilderness Discovery*, both accommodating around 75 passengers. A select number of itineraries in Alaska are designated as Kids in Nature sailings, offering age-appropriate activities and adventures just for children. Kids will hike, take a kayak float or stand-up paddleboard ride, listen for whales with the on-board hydrophones, and generally stay busy from dawn to dusk. The atmosphere is decidedly casual, with family-style meals and lots of meeting and greeting among passengers. Cabins are comfortable and are configured to accommodate up to three passengers each, but crew members are well versed in larger groups and families.

Those more comfortable with luxury cruising will enjoy experiences on board the *Safari Endeavor*, an 86-passenger vessel, or the *Safari Explorer*, a 36-passenger yacht. Both offer the same excellent service as the Adventure trips, but with an upscale attitude. Massages, free cocktails, and more personal attention define these cruises. Fares begin around $3,695 for a late-season cruise, with the same inclusive meals and activities as the adventure cruising boats.

Families participating in Kids in Nature sailings receive 25 percent off fares for children 12 and younger on all Un-Cruise trips.

Lindblad Expeditions
(800) 397-3348
www.expeditions.com

Working in partnership with the National Geographic Society, Lindblad Expeditions combines the intimacy of a small ship with the scientific exploration by which the National Geographic brand is known. Sailing

Alaska's Inside Passage between Juneau and Sitka, Lindblad's focus on marine science is attractive to active parents whose offspring desire more than a superficial view of Alaska's waterways and wildlife. Lindblad Expedition cruises are staffed by crew with extensive knowledge of both environment and ship, and all passengers aboard—including the kids—will receive in-depth experiences.

Children receive special attention aboard Lindblad trips, with kid-friendly meals, a special pizza and movie night, and tons of opportunities for hands-on marine science. Scavenger hunts, daily journaling, photo workshops, and learning how to drive the company's Zodiac rafts (complete with a certificate of achievement) are just a few kid-pleasing activities.

Fares begin near $5,990 per person, double occupancy, with $500 taken off the double occupancy rate for passengers 17 and under.

Cruising Accommodations for Families

Cabins aboard larger cruise ships range from teeny-tiny rooms no bigger than a walk-in closet to suites with spacious balconies and sitting rooms. Depending upon your family's budget, options include inside (no window or porthole) or outside (some sort of window or porthole, classified further as view-obstructed or nonobstructed). Extra-fancy accommodations are called veranda cabins and usually feature a lanai and all sorts of furniture configurations in their suites (deluxe, superior, etc.).

A family must keep in mind that cruise lines, in a brilliant marketing move, purposely designed cabins to be small so passengers will spend the majority of their on-board time (and money) taking part in activities in other areas of the ship. That said, if you are cruising with a small child or infant and need some extra space for naps, feedings, and/or sleeping arrangements, it might be prudent to shell out the extra money for a larger cabin, since you might well be spending more time within. Larger families might consider booking two cabins across the hall from each other, one inside, one outside, using the former for sleeping and the latter for hanging out during the day.

Alaska's scenery is also a major factor in cabin selection. Except for a brief amount of time spent sailing across the Gulf of Alaska, every minute of your cruise will be within a stunning line of sight for glaciers, wildlife, forested hillsides, and myriad other marine sights. If your budget allows for an outside cabin, book one. During our first cruise, our son, then four, spent a part of every day reclining in the large sill of our cabin window, counting wildlife on his fingers and reminiscing about the day's adventures.

Eating Well While Cruising

The stories are legendary: cruise ship passengers gaining 10 or more pounds after gorging at the never-ending chocolate buffet. Don't believe what you read—it's all in your mind. Cruise ships serve mountains of goodies at all hours, to be sure, but the larger ships have 2,000 or more people to feed, and all of them, including you, are on vacation.

The allure of every single plated meal, be it at the no-reservations buffet line or in the grand dining room, does indeed have the potential to bust even the most stalwart of diets. Children are no exception to this either, with enormous pudding parfaits and endless cookie trays of their favorites within an easy arm's reach.

We found mealtime to be less stressful once we figured out the mechanics of dining rooms, menus, and room service. Cruise lines have

A Kid's Day Onboard Ship

Our first cruise was a seven-day trip aboard Holland America's *MS Veendam* from Seward to Vancouver, British Columbia. Our son was registered in Club HAL, which served the preschool/kindergarten set. With a bubbly teacher at the helm, our youngster spent three daily chunks of time in Club HAL, doing crafts, exploring the ship, and learning about the landscape and environment of Glacier Bay National Park with an excellent Junior Ranger program, a requirement of all cruise ships passing through the park. Mealtimes and early-evening hours were designated as "family time" by Holland America, but kids reconvened every night for special events.

Evenings meant theme nights for kids, with Pirate Night, Cowboy Night, and Movie Hero Night of particular interest to our kiddo. When we finally also responded well to the cry for more flexibility, thus relaxing everything from dress codes to strict mealtimes. Depending upon your selected cruise, you may choose from a more casual experience where the kids can feast on pizza, burgers, and the like or opt for one or more days of formal, black-tie and fancy-dress-up dining. Inquire with your cruise line at the time of booking. Whatever you choose,

be sure to rehearse manners with your kids well prior to dining, since it's the perfect venue to teach about "please," "thank you," and "pass the butter."

With allergy awareness on the rise in all forms of vacationing, cruise lines will do what they can to spare your body from potentially threatening ingredients but must be made aware of any modifications well before your sailing date. Remember, cruise ship cooks can't just run out to Safeway if

made it back to our stateroom around 10 p.m., the exhausted child fell asleep immediately, quite thrilled at his newfound independence and ability to make friends with peers from all over the world.

Port days meant a lighter schedule in the club, with the obvious intention of encouraging families to spend time together.

Club HAL was well stocked with toys, games, crafts, and sports equipment, and kids seemed happy with the offerings. Teenagers were provided their own hangout with ample space, music, and plug-ins for various media devices. As parents, we enjoyed the balance the program offered: we had enough grownup time but still retained the essence of our trip, a family vacation.

a particular ingredient is not available. Carry your own allergy medication and make the ship's medical team aware of any severe allergies at the time of booking and again upon embarkation.

Children's Programs and Activities

Some cruise lines are better than others when it comes to providing activities and programs aboard ship for kids. Thus, you'll want to ask a few questions when perusing the list of companies sailing in Alaska. Take into consideration your child's age, interests, and ability to participate in activities away from you with kids he/she has never met before. Depending upon the cruise line, children have the option of attending a program for a few hours or all day, with themes and special events.

Of paramount importance are the qualifications of staff who interact on a daily basis with their young charges. Are counselors and staff certified/trained appropriately to deal with children of specific ages? Are background checks performed? What security measures are taken for children's safety while they are in the program?

In addition to the necessary safety considerations, also ask to view a typical daily schedule of activities to see if your child(ren) are interested and ask about age ranges of each group. Many cruise lines take children ages three through 18, and some take kids as young as two, depending upon the company and its penchant for entertaining or educating children.

4 PACKING FOR ALASKA

Traveling to Alaska requires more gear than the typical family vacation. The combination of variant weather patterns and a multitude of outdoor activities means parents must consider clothing, shoes, and outerwear for maximum enjoyment of Alaska experiences in every condition.

Layering is key, and even if changing weather necessitates adding or removing one or more layers throughout the day, kids will retain comfort and safety as they move about their activities. These layers need not be expensive, but they should be of quality materials designed to wick moisture away from the skin and trap warmth to prevent hypothermia (even in the summertime).

Shoes should be durable enough to survive a dunking in the ocean or muddy stomp on a hiking trail and light enough to dry out quickly at the end of both. Casual hiking shoes or sturdy tennis shoes should suffice unless your family is planning on a serious backcountry adventure, in which case hiking boots with lug soles are a good idea. Sandals may seem odd in a place like Alaska, but they can be incredibly convenient for traversing campgrounds or wearing inside hotels or cabins. Rubber boots arc great if you have room; otherwise, many parents bring two pairs of shoes and let kids wade away.

Clothing

Always pack extra clothing. So much outdoor fun means dirty, wet duds will be a sure thing. Below is a comprehensive list showing suggested clothing items for a typical seven-day trip to Alaska.

BASE

- Long underwear of polypropylene or wool, depending upon your child's tolerance (one set with long-sleeved top/pants)
- Hiking/outdoor socks (three pairs)
- Socks for day wear, casual hiking/walking (seven pairs)
- Underwear/diapers, etc. If you are a cloth-diapering family, check out Happy Bottoms Diaper Service (www.happybottomsdiaperservice.com) and their delivery options for visiting babies.

MIDLAYER

- Pants (REI conversion pants work great; legs zip off for shorts) (three pairs)
- Shirts (long- and short-sleeved for layering) (four)
- Fleece top (one)

What Alaskans Wear

We're not kidding when we say Alaska is a casual sort of place. Probably no other vacation destination in the United States is quite so nonchalant about attire. We do have our favorites, though, and if you really want to look like an Alaskan, consider the following items for your trip:

Sweatshirt, preferably the hoodie type. Thick, warm, and sporting a deep hood to keep off all manner of sun, rain, bugs, or salt spray, the hoodie is a handy item of clothing to have in Alaska. Bonus points awarded for a sweatshirt that looks like it has survived a thousand washings and at least one dunking in seawater.

Carhartt pants. Durable, heavy canvas material that sheds most adverse weather conditions gives Carhartts a decided leg up on blue jeans. Found in most Alaska retail outlets, Carhartts are worn by everyone, infants to grandparents, and they come in a variety of shapes and colors, from overalls to women-specific cuts. A recent change in design now has Carhartts sporting a handy buttoned, inner-elastic waistband in children's pants, so we buy a size up and wait for our son to grow into them.

Dress for fun in all types of Alaska weather!

TOP LAYER/OUTERWEAR
- Rain gear (consisting of pants and jacket, Gore-Tex or other waterproof material)
- Mittens/gloves (one pair of lighter-weight wool or wool blend)
- Hat with brim to shield from sun, plus a warm hat (one each)

FOOTWEAR
- Sturdy sneakers or hiking boots
- Sturdy sandals (we like Keen or Teva)
- Rubber boots

Not cheap (near the $40 mark for a pair) but extremely hardy, Carhartts are great for explorers of any age.

Xtratufs or rubber boots. Also known as "Alaska sneakers," Xtratufs are brown, knee-high rubber boots designed for cannery workers who stand around all day in fish guts or spend time in skiffs, hauling in soaking-wet nets. With their thick soles and leg-clinging fit, Xtratufs are the coolest footwear in every coastal community of Alaska. Costing around $85 for adult sizes and near $30 for kids, Xtratufs are completely waterproof and perfect for southeast Alaska adventures. Plus, they'll be a hot topic of discussion when you return home, since all your friends will want some. Don't want to pay that much? Rubber boots of any make or model will serve you well.

Hat. Ball cap, stocking hat, cute little beanie—it's all good in Alaska. Hats provide protection from the elements, including sun, and help keep pesky mosquitoes from noshing on your scalp. As is the case with most Alaska gear, the older the better and extra kudos to those who display their favorite outdoor recreation outfit across the brow.

MISCELLANEOUS
- Sunglasses
- Sunblock (really)
- Swimsuit
- Plastic bags for wet/dirty shoes and clothes
- Small, packable, quick-drying towels
- Family first-aid kit for minor ailments and regular medication

Unsure about the quality of your family's stuff? Visit a local outdoor retailer to check on the latest in children's clothing and gear. REI (www.rei .com) offers advice both in stores and online and can be a valuable resource.

Other Gear

Fortunately for parents of small children, Alaska is a pretty accessible place. Most local families navigate both sidewalks and trails easily with a jogging stroller and/or child carrier. Parents of very young children rely on front packs and backpacks that strap babies close to their bodies and

Help Is Here for Parents!

Alaska Baby Rentals (www.alaskababyrentals.com, info@alaskababyrentals .com, 907-240-RENT) rents gear, bedding, high chairs, carriers, joggers, car seats, and the like with a single phone call. Whether you're staying at a hotel or grandma's house, Alaska Baby Rentals takes the stress out of packing a ton of gear for babies and small children.

Diapering a baby or toddler in Alaska is fairly simple if you use disposables. Do carry a stash of plastic, zip-type bags with you if camping or adventuring out into the great Alaska wilderness, as bears can be attracted to the, er, contents. If you are a cloth-diapering family, you have the option of breaking down and going the disposable route for the length of your trip, bringing your own stash of diapers, or utilizing a company like Happy Bottoms Diaper Service (www.happybottomsdiaperservice.com, 907-903-2229) in Anchorage. A welcome addition to the ecotourism movement in Alaska, Happy Bottoms can arrange for a drop-off of diapers and covers for the duration of your vacation.

allow for safe, comfortable transport to and from just about any outdoor adventure.

When it comes to sleep-related equipment, many travel-savvy parents turn to creativity rather than sacrificing dollars at the airline ticketing counter or space in a vehicle for the mountains of gear young children can require. A few families, ours included, pack a sleeping bag, pad, and travel pillow for smaller kids who enjoy slumber parties on the floor, on a couch, or in a hotel closet (don't laugh, it was a favorite of our youngest for years). Babies and children under two often rest easier in a portable crib, offered by many resorts, hotels, and cabins. Ask well in advance during the busy summer months, however, since this is considered premium equipment.

Car seats are required in Alaska for children under 80 pounds and 57 inches in height, even in RVs, so be sure to either bring a car seat for your child or inquire about renting one upon arrival.

What to Leave at Home

Alaska is decidedly less urban than other outdoor destinations, and most residents don't care a whit about what folks wear. Function definitely trumps fashion here, and we like it that way. So, leave at home the fancy princess shoes and button-down shirts. You won't need 'em. Restaurants welcoming kids are casual and they certainly won't worry about what you're wearing.

ALASKA'S WILDLIFE

Alaska is just one big wildlife playground. Moose, lynx, wolves, caribou, Dall sheep, mountain goats, eagles, and brown, black, and polar bears make up the bulk of Alaska's land-based creature features. While some animals, like the lynx, are a bit elusive, many of the aforementioned critters happily reside in the same breathing space as we humans, making a vacation to Alaska ideal for families wanting to observe wildlife far from the confines of their local zoo. There is nothing quite so thrilling as the opportunity to spot a moose munching on tender grasses right outside the hotel room or being the first to catch a glimpse of an eagle sitting high atop a tree. It's an adventure, indeed, to be immersed in such wildness, especially with your children in tow.

PARENT PRO TIP

Parents need to remember to teach kids the basics of wildlife safety with a matter-of-fact approach that doesn't create fear, but encourages caution. My husband and I will turn bear or moose safety into a game: "Who can tell me one thing we could do if a moose won't get off the trail?" It's always a process, though, and we are constantly reminding our sons to be aware. Framing that awareness into the fact that all mothers want their young to be safe helps them tremendously, too.

—Elizabeth, biologist for Alaska Department of Fish and Game and mother of two

KIDSPEAK

I like to see the bears and moose in Alaska. We see moose on our street and in our backyard, too. One day there was a moose that climbed over our fence and was eating the leaves and branches from our tree. It was so funny!

—Susannah, age four and a half

That said, of course, Alaska's wildlife is, well, *wild*, and visitors should take heed before marching their brood along a local trail or following a set of tracks in the mud.

Moose

The wild critter you are most likely to spy is the moose, mostly because our neighborhood trails, parks, yards, and shrubbery are very much to their liking. The largest member of the deer family, moose are big creatures weighing nearly 1,000 pounds. Their bulbous noses and enormous, bulky frames make them easy

Where to Find Information About Animal Safety in Alaska

Informed visitors are less likely to panic should a wild animal encounter occur. Animals are one of the main reasons people travel to Alaska, and yet many people still operate under the assumption that animals do not venture close to tourist attractions or visitor centers. Alaska children are taught from an early age to be stewards of their valuable land and its priceless inhabitants; they learn in school how to respect animals and behave accordingly, and your kids can, too.

The Alaska Department of Fish and Game works hard to educate all residents and visitors about the risks and benefits of recreating in Alaska alongside a few thousand wild critters. All year, employees visit schools and attend fairs and festivals across the state with hopes of providing useful and, in some cases, life-saving information. Their comprehensive website (www.adfg.alaska.gov/index.cfm?adfg=livewith.main) offers a wealth of practical tips for sharing the outdoors with bears, moose, and other Alaska animals.

Moose

The Bureau of Land Management's Campbell Creek Science Center, located on 760 forested acres in southeast Anchorage, also offers many opportunities to learn about wild Alaska creatures. Staff often lead discussions throughout the summer months to encourage active participation in personal safety, and a class is held each June to teach parents how to recreate in bear country with their children. Visit their website (www .blm.gov/ak/st/en/prog/sciencecenter.html) for class descriptions and locations.

For a basic understanding of Alaska's large animals, a visit to the Alaska Zoo (www.alaskazoo.com) is a good option for families with limited time. Weekly programs and special events at the zoo also provide learning opportunities about facts of a particular Alaska animal and some strategies for safe recreation.

for kids to identify, as do the large racks of antlers that appear on males in August. Not at all like their shy, Lower 48 deer cousins, moose can be cranky creatures, especially during spring calving and autumn breeding season, known as the Rut.

Despite their size, moose have a fast trot and can cover ground with enormous strides, which means you should never approach a moose on purpose. If your family does come upon a moose, stop and assess another way around or wait until he/she decides to move on. This could take a while, however, since moose, despite swiftness of tack, are not at all deft of brain, and decision-making is not always their strong suit. Should a moose become agitated at your presence, its ears will flatten and the hair on its neck and back will rise. Leave quickly and don't stop for photos. Moose can kick with both their front and back feet, and risking serious injury is not worth the Facebook upload. Residents, including kids, will tell you when you are out of line with respect to moose, as children from preschool on are well versed in moose safety via local schools.

Bears

Alaska has three types of bears: brown, black, and polar. Unless your family is keen on traveling to the Arctic Circle and communities like Barrow, polar bears will not be a factor in your bear safety plan. But black bears and their larger brown bear cousins (also known as grizzlies or Kodiak brown bears, depending upon your location in the state) are frequently spotted all over Alaska, even in the most-populated city of Anchorage.

It is important to note that despite television programs portraying Alaska's bears as bloodthirsty creatures bent upon causing destruction, "bearanoia" is not an adequate reason for keeping your family from an Alaska wilderness vacation. While bears can and do come in contact with humankind on a fairly regular basis, especially during summer salmon runs, more often than not people and bruins resolve their encounters peacefully. Of course, the best defense is correct information, since almost all bear-human encounters result from misinformation or improper behavior on the human's part.

Brown bear

I will be completely honest in stating that recreating in Alaska's bear country with my children does make me nervous, even after eight years of living and breathing the wilderness around us. However, after multiple attendances at bear-safety programs geared toward families and after practicing bear-safety techniques, and seeing with my own eyes the positive results of my behavior, I am a more confident mother and recreation enthusiast. You can be, too, with the right information.

The American black bear (*Ursus americanus*) is the smallest in the bear family, and also the most common of the species. Black bears are frequently seen in and around forested areas and, sadly, many Alaska neighborhoods, due to their attraction to trash cans and coolers left on porches, despite warnings from local game officials. Black bears are excellent climbers and can scale a 12-foot fence with little effort, not to mention a tree. They are easily startled and tend to run from humans, but every bear, like every person, is unique and will act differently from its cohorts. Keep in mind that all black bears are not necessarily black in color—they're a colorful bunch and also come in shades of brown, tan, and cinnamon. Beyond size, the best way to distinguish a black bear from a brown bear is through its profile: black bears have a humped nose while brown bears sport a "dished" nose.

Alaska Fact

The enormous and beautiful Kodiak brown bear is a complete subspecies unto itself, thanks to taxonomist C. H. Merriam. These bears, who only live on the island of Kodiak, are thought to be related to the brown bears of the Alaska Peninsula.

The brown bear (*Ursus arctos*) is very large, weighing anywhere from 500 to 1,400 pounds and sporting long, sharp claws effective for digging. Known as grizzlies up north near Denali National Park and as coastal brown bears or Kodiak brown bears near the coastal areas of southcentral and southeast Alaska, this bear is a formidable creature to happen upon.

Both brown and black bears eat a lot during the short summer months. In fact, chowing down is number one on their list of priorities and they don't like to be interrupted, but who can blame them? Winter hibernation means a bear must gain an extra 300 to 400 pounds of body fat (lucky them), so packing on pounds as fast and effectively as possible is crucial before finding a place to sleep, or "den up," usually in November.

Families who recreate in Alaska forests and meadows might view a bear, but it is more common to see signs of a bear. Hair, scat (poop), and trails through brushy areas, particularly along streams and rivers, indicate a bear has been in the area. Use caution, especially during the summer months when salmon runs mean constant use. Humans are merely guests in the bears' habitat, and respect is mandatory.

If you choose to take your kids into bear country, always be aware of your surroundings and environment. Hike in groups, make a lot of noise (we taught our youngest son to sing every Christmas carol he could remember, the louder the better), don't allow kids to run farther ahead than you can reach, and carry bear spray. If you are fishing, follow the guidelines outlined by the Alaska Department of Fish and Game or your fishing guide/outfitter, and follow them to the letter. Never, ever approach a bear, even if it appears to be quite a distance from you. Brown bears can run up to 40 miles per hour and believe me—even the most protective parent can't cover that kind of distance when faced with an angry mama bear.

Remember to keep any smelly items, not just food, in a hard-sided vehicle when not in use. This includes deodorant, sunscreen, bug repellent, soaps, personal care products, and, most of all, fishing gear. Bears have very keen noses and can sniff out interesting scents from two miles away.

Managing Mosquitoes

One reason Alaskans love winter so much is the absence of the mosquito and a billion or so of her closest friends. As spring rolls around

Take One More Step and I'll Pump You Full of Pepper!

Bear spray is also known as "pepper spray" or "big game deterrent." Most agencies advocate deterring bears through preventative methods: not getting oneself into a situation where a bear feels surprised and thus threatened by a human. But should a bear become aggressive toward a human (or group of humans), bear spray is an effective deterrent. Marketed under brand names like CounterAssault, bear spray is a powerful combination of nonlethal chemicals, including capsaicin or cayenne pepper oil. It is most effective at close range (50 feet or less) and must be delivered properly via a high-pressure canister to be of any use at all. These canisters can be purchased at any Alaska outdoor outlet for around $50. If you are planning on any sort of outdoor activity in bear country, this product can be the best investment of your trip, despite cost and the fact that it cannot be transported via air due to the pressurized contents. For a complete description of ingredients and use of bear spray, contact the Alaska Department of Fish and Game (www.adfg.alaska/gov).

> ### PARENT PRO TIP
>
> Kids tend to forget (or at least pretend to forget) about mosquitoes as long as adults around them do, too. A vacation among mosquitoes can be as cheerful or miserable as you choose; do so wisely and you'll have a lot more fun.
>
> —The author, mother of two

and snow begins to melt, mosquitoes magically appear and the females chew upon the tender skin of both humans and beast. Mosquitoes have been around for 100 million years and I can bet as long as humans have walked the earth, people have spent countless hours trying to figure out a way to deter them.

A Game of Keep-Away

Face the fact that you will encounter mosquitoes in Alaska, but here's our best prevention in a four-part prescription.

Repel: Folks in the know recommend insect repellent that contains DEET (a really strong chemical developed by the military, with such a long name they gave it a cool acronym to make it sound better). It repels mosquitoes effectively—that is, more than other products. Yes, it is a chemical and yes, you might be opposed to spreading it all over your children (ages one and up only), but DEET works, albeit in smaller percentages for smaller people. Try the OFF! FamilyCare line of products with a lower concentration of DEET. If you really want to try a nonchemical solution, Burt's Bees offers an alternative that smells better and *might* keep a few of the bugs away. Another natural repellent receiving high marks is Repel Lemon Eucalyptus, which contains a similar concoction to Burt's Bees. All of these products are readily available at local sporting-goods stores, along with a lot of other products that promise to repel bugs. Be sure to wash hands after applying and consider washing kids well at the end of the day.

Preferring humidity (rain, standing water, sweaty people, and the like), mosquitoes thrive in Alaska, where summers are wet and water is all but guaranteed. Parental preparations are a must. Kids will have more fun— and subsequently, so will you—if you've taken a little bit of time to meet these insects head-on before you find yourself miles away from a store and unable to sleep due to the biting and whining around you (from either kids or mosquitoes, take your pick). Do note there is no one product that will guarantee 100 percent protection from mosquitoes; after all, they've managed to live this long without being eradicated.

Dress for success: While some particularly bloodthirsty mosquitoes can and do bite right through your clothing, in general it is exposed skin that is most vulnerable. Dress kids in long pants, long sleeves, and hats. Consider a head net (or larger) if you'll be in marshy, swampy areas. Many types of nets exist for a variety of purposes, including covers for strollers and shields for the entire body. Find these at a local sporting-goods store.

Take cover: Mosquitoes are most abundant in the early morning and early evening hours, although some days they never seem to go away completely, especially during a rainy, warmish spell of weather. Take extra precautions at these times, carrying repellent with you to reapply if necessary.

Sooth the itching: It will happen. There will be itchy red bites (red badges of courage?) on display after some of your adventures. Try soothing them with a little calamine lotion or pick up a tube or two of AfterBite (an alcohol-based miracle remedy that takes a little of the insult out of the injury) on the shelves of any Alaska sporting-goods store.

CHILDREN WITH SPECIAL NEEDS

Alaska can be a good destination for children with disabilities. A large number of older travelers with mobility issues means many adaptive environments throughout the state, from lodging to transportation and attractions, perfect for parents who need the same. Also, children who require less sensory excitement may find quiet activities in smaller communities to be a welcome change of scenery, without too much outside disruption. However, traveling around Alaska as a family with additional needs can present a few challenges, and below we offer some tips for making the most of your experience.

Planning

It goes without saying that advance planning is of paramount importance. That said, Alaska has some unique characteristics that could prove challenging for parents wanting to show the state to their kids with special needs, so remember the following:

- Advance arrangements are a must, for everything from hotel rooms to seats on a train. I advise prompt phone calls or emails to businesses as soon as you know trip dates.
- Be flexible with dates and locations. Consider reversing an itinerary so a hotel room will be available on a specific day, or waiting for a noisy festival to end so children with sensitivity to loud noises will be more comfortable.
- Contact local visitor centers well ahead of your visit and in person once you arrive in a community. Make sure you know the location of pharmacies or medical centers (provided in this book for each city) and have a map.

- Plan for delays. Alaska, as we've mentioned, does have the occasional challenging road, weather, or other delay. Carry food, clothing, medication, movies, books—whatever your child needs to stay comfortable during a delay.
- Relax. A no-brainer, right? We learned while traveling with our oldest son, challenged by autism, that finding a beach with safe boundaries for digging up rocks and building a fort out of sticks was a brilliant decision.

Equipment and Car Rentals

If your child requires adaptive equipment, you know that traveling with it can be cumbersome and expensive. Also, Alaska's rugged outdoor environment may prove challenging for those without appropriate tools. Challenge Alaska (www.challengealaska.org) is an Anchorage-based organization providing rental equipment; check their website for rates and availability. Advance reservations are a must; the more popular equipment rents out fast.

Wheelchair Getaways of Alaska (www.wheelchairgetaways.com, 800-471-2312) offers accessible vans for rent from a variety of locations across Alaska. The company will pick you up at the airport or train station and offers 24-hour roadside assistance.

The bottom line? Know your family's vacation style, keep in mind each child's particular needs and triggers, and plan accordingly.

Parks for All

In 2013, the Anchorage Park Foundation dedicated its newest play space, designed specifically for children with special needs. Called the Parks for All Project at Cuddy Park, the space is located in the Midtown area of Anchorage and features all the favorites, from swings to slides, but with fully accessible attributes and plenty of areas for family relaxation. Visit the Park Foundation's website (www.anchorageparkfoundation.org) for information and directions.

DIVIDE AND CONQUER

"We Alaskans, even though we live
up here in the Territory a lifetime, look
surprisingly like you who live Outside. We
sit down to three meals a day, get about
eight hours of sleep a night . . . and go
in for fun, foolishness and frolic just as
anyone else does."

—Herbert H. Hilscher, *Alaska Now* (1950)

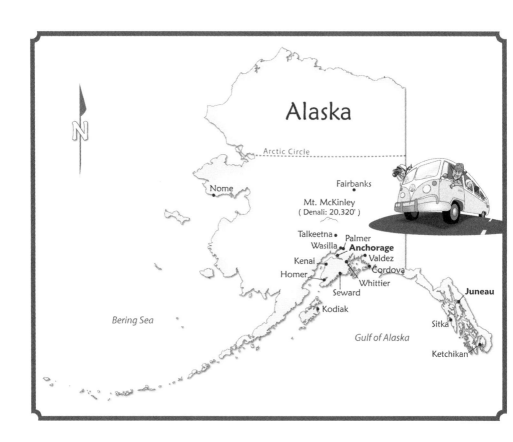

Alaska

Arctic Circle

Nome

Fairbanks

Mt. McKinley
(Denali: 20,320')

Talkeetna
Palmer
Wasilla
Anchorage
Kenai
Valdez
Cordova
Homer
Whittier
Seward

Juneau

Kodiak

Sitka

Bering Sea

Gulf of Alaska

Ketchikan

ALASKA'S LAYOUT

During my first trip to Alaska, well before the age of smartphone apps and GPS, a friend and I decided to rent a camper van and drive around the state for a week. We drove all right. Up the Parks Highway, across the Denali Highway, then around and through and over and away until we had exhausted both ourselves and the 1970s-era vehicle that insisted on breaking down at regular intervals. We saw far fewer Alaska attractions and far more roads because we simply didn't appreciate the state's sheer volume. In short, we didn't do our homework.

In order to preserve precious vacation time and family harmony, I've provided a basic primer of Alaska geography that, I hope, will prevent aimless wandering—unless, of course, that's what you want to do, but we'll talk about that later ("Road-Tripping with the Fam").

Alaska is unofficially divided into geographical regions, each with unique characteristics, historical significance, and activities.

Southcentral Alaska

Known simply as "Southcentral" to locals, this area encompasses the border of Canada to the east, from the Gulf of Alaska to Cook Inlet and west, past Lake Clark National Park and Preserve, to rural communities with names like Naknek and Holy Cross. Anchorage, Alaska's largest city, sits at the end of Cook Inlet, a shipping lane and access point for the Kenai Peninsula, a popular playground for Alaskans due to a plethora of accessible fishing, boating, and hunting opportunities. Stretching north from

Anchorage is the Matanuska-Susitna Valley, Alaska's agricultural region and pseudosuburb to Anchorage, as well as a gateway to Denali National Park to the northwest and the only road connection for the Lower 48 to the northeast.

Geology plays a big role in southcentral Alaska's landscape. Known as the area of "fire and ice," volcanoes and glaciers are in the fore and backgrounds of most Southcentral views, and visitors will have many opportunities to learn about both.

Southcentral is home to a number of Alaska Native groups, including the Dena'ina people, the first residents to settle around upper Cook Inlet somewhere around the last Ice Age of AD 500–1000. Finding the area much to their liking for communication and trade with other Native groups, the Dena'ina enjoyed their location between land and sea, living off the bounty of both.

Prince William Sound, near the Gulf of Alaska, provides hunting and gathering grounds for the Alutiiq people, an Alaska Native group who utilize the sea as a driving force for the rhythm by which all life moves. Relying upon an 8,000-year history in the area, the Alutiiq are skilled kayak and boat craftsmen, and are committed to continuing such traditions with today's youth.

Southeast Alaska

The "Panhandle," snuggled up tight against British Columbia and the Yukon Territory of Canada, is where all northbound cruise ship visitors receive their first glimpse of Alaska. A strip of mountainous land, Southeast is a beautiful introduction, with towering evergreen trees, narrow fjords, and abundant wildlife. Here, boating is akin to driving a car, and just about every resident owns some sort of watercraft. Alaska's capital city, Juneau, is the state's third-largest community and a great place to become acquainted with the southeast region as a whole and its historical part in Alaska's gold rush melodrama. Other communities—like Ketchikan, Sitka, and Skagway—provide a look into relationships between Native Alaska groups of Tlingit, Haida, Eyak, and Tsimshian and historical events affecting each. A deep connection to the coastal waterways of the

Inside Passage drives Southeast Native culture, starting with the complex clan system of governance and tradition.

Southeast Alaska can be crowded, with thousands of cruise ship passengers descending gangways May through October. Temperatures are moderate, but it's the rain most people remember after a trip through this region. Buckets and buckets of liquid sunshine are possible, even probable, but it's worth every minute, even if you have to wring out your socks at the end of the day.

Visiting southeast Alaska is best done by boat; choose from a cruise ship (see Chapter 3, "If You Cruise") or the Alaska Marine Highway System. Coupling ferry routes with ports of call is a memorable experience, but parents should come prepared for nasty weather and a full docket of preplanned activities (and this guide), since the ferry does not provide scheduled excursions like those found on cruise ships. (See Chapter 2, "How to Get Here," for more information about traveling the Alaska Marine Highway with kids.)

Interior Alaska

Encompassing the central region of the state, with vast rivers, valleys, and mountains, is the majestic Interior. Alaska's second-largest city, Fairbanks, is a popular destination for visitors due to its rich gold mining history and myriad opportunities to hike, bike, or take a paddle on one of the area's many rivers and lakes. Along the scenic but less-traveled Denali Highway, enormous Mount McKinley and the Alaska Range dwarf everything else, and Denali National Park along the George Parks Highway beckons visitors with snowy peaks, abundant wildlife, and easy access to rugged outdoor recreation. Temperatures in the Interior are drier than down south but also more extreme, with wintertime digits consistently below zero and summertime temperatures reaching the high 80s (Fahrenheit).

Interior Alaska is home to the Athabascan people, who rely upon a subsistence lifestyle even today, traveling to summertime fish camps along one of five prime salmon-spawning rivers—the Yukon, Tanana, Susitna, Kuskokwim, and Copper river drainages—and are drawn by the cycle of seasons.

The Bush

Bush Alaska is not really a region, per se; it's more a state of being, where subsistence lifestyles and a harsh environment collide with modern technology for the mostly Native Alaskan resident base. For many visitors, the bush is not part of a typical itinerary, although, with the advent of adventure and ecotourism, it's becoming more of a bucket-list item for hardy travelers bent on seeing as much of the world as possible.

This area of Alaska is a stark contrast to other parts of the state, featuring tundra, vast ocean views, and few trees. It's wild, but it's also beautiful.

Who Are "Native Alaskans"?

While traveling around our fair state, child in tow, visitors often ask us whether we are "native Alaskans," meaning, in most cases, if we grew up here. While this innocuous query would indeed be appropriate in other places, in Alaska the terms "Alaska Native" or "Native Alaskan" are reserved for the group to whom they belong: *only* to the state's indigenous people, who make up a culturally rich and diverse 18 percent of Alaska's population. Alaska Native heritage is closely guarded and intensely preserved, and visitors should be prepared for gentle correction should they refer to non-Native Alaskans in this manner.

Alaskans who were born and raised here refer to themselves simply as "residents" and even "homesteaders" or "sourdoughs," depending upon how far back the family tree extends.

The University of Alaska Fairbanks partners with Alaska Native communities around the state to operate the Alaska Native Knowledge Network (www.ankn.uaf.edu), an online portal accessible to anyone, with resources, event listings, publications, and even school curriculum ideas.

Distant from Alaska's road system, rural communities rely on snowmachines, four-wheeled all-terrain vehicles, ferries, and airplanes for transportation, which means cost is an important factor to consider, and the lack of modern conveniences will indeed influence the price of everything from taxi fares to toilet paper. From the Canadian border north and east, to the Aleutian Islands and Alaska Peninsula to the south and west, the bush represents much of the quintessential definition of the phrase "Last Frontier."

Encompassing a large swath of northern Alaska land, bush Alaska is a broad term, without official boundaries. It is home to the Iñupiaq, St. Lawrence Island Yup'ik, and Cup'ik Native groups of the arctic interior and the Unangax and Aleut people of the Aleutian chain to the west.

The term "Cheechako" means "newcomer" or "tenderfoot" and is used to describe anyone freshly arrived in Alaska. First coined in the late 1890s during the gold rush, the word is also used to label those who have yet to spend a full winter up here. It is not a bad word.

Alaska Fact

ANCHORAGE: YOU CAN GET THERE FROM HERE

From the ground, Anchorage looks like any other urban sprawl and not at all like the tourist brochures. It isn't until they step off the ordinary, everyday sidewalks and into a wealth of activities that visitors realize "real" Alaska was indeed right here all along. For families, this means the convenience of urban resources combined with an allure of rural wilderness, and most often, the two meet quite comfortably.

Also known as "Alaska's largest village" for its diverse concentration of Alaska Native corporations and their headquarters of tribal governance,

Anchorage

Population: 298,000 (2012 census)

Founded in: 1915, as a tent city to build the Alaska Railroad along Ship Creek

Known for: Transportation hub and center of Alaskan commerce. Ninety percent of goods sent to Alaska are shipped to the Port of Anchorage.

Interesting fact: Most Alaska legislators keep offices in downtown Anchorage, and every so often someone lobbies to move the state capital from Juneau to Anchorage.

Hot tip: Spend at least three days here, visiting museums and cultural centers and experiencing local festivals (see Chapter 17, "Party On—Special Events with Kid Appeal").

Anchorage is a colorful tapestry of traditions, cultures, and languages. In all, 20 different Native groups speaking 50 different dialects make up 18 percent of Alaska's total population, with many shareholders residing in Anchorage.

Since most travelers begin and end their Alaska journey via Anchorage, it's a natural place to become acquainted with both the state and its attributes before heading out for additional exploration. However, Anchorage is also within striking distance of many day excursions that, with a little planning, can be just as exciting as a multiday trip, thus making it the perfect base camp for a family vacation.

Arriving

BY AIR

Anchorage is most often (and most easily) accessed via the Ted Stevens Anchorage International Airport. Flights during the busy summer season arrive and depart on a 24-hour basis and, fortunately, so do taxi and shuttle services. We like Eagle River Shuttle Service, a door-to-door company that provides comfortable, safe transportation for larger groups, families, or the single traveler (www.alaskashuttle.net, er@alaskashuttle .net, 907-694-8888). Many hotels around Anchorage also offer complimentary shuttle service door-to-door; ask when making reservations about hours, accommodations for children, etc. See our recommendations for Anchorage lodging later in this chapter.

BY BOAT

Both the Alaska Marine Highway System (ferry) and many cruise lines utilize communities within a few hours' drive of Anchorage as a stopover destination, airport transportation hub, or both. If your family arrives in Alaska via cruise ship or ferry, you have a few options for making your way north to Anchorage. Eagle River Shuttle Service offers transportation from Seward and Whittier. Alaska Cruise Transfer and Tours provides motorcoach transfer from Whittier to Anchorage and throws in a bit of a narrated schtick, too (www.whittiershuttle.com, 888-257-8527). Salmon

Berry Tours offers a combination tour/transfer option well suited for families, from either Whittier or Seward (www.salmonberrytours.com, reservations@salmonberrytours.com, 888-878-3572).

BY RAIL
The Alaska Railroad provides service from Whittier (62 miles south of Anchorage) where a deepwater port provides moorage for some cruise ships and the Alaska Marine Highway System ferries. Between mid-May and mid-September hop aboard the railroad for a trip along Turnagain Arm, arriving in downtown Anchorage two hours later. If your cruise ship docks in Seward, the Alaska Railroad provides a four-hour ride 126 miles north to Anchorage in both Adventure- and Goldstar-class cars. Full meals, a snack bar, and a dome car await your family—not to mention outstanding views of southcentral Alaska along the way (www.alaskarailroad .com, 800-544-0552).

Note: The Alaska Railroad also runs north all the way to Fairbanks, stopping at many small communities and Denali National Park on the way, and heads south from Whittier to Seward, on the Kenai Peninsula.

BY CAR/RV
If you've chosen to drive to Alaska, you'll arrive in Anchorage from the north along the Glenn Highway, driving right into the heart of downtown. If your family has embarked upon an RV or camping/driving adventure to Alaska, check out our list in the lodging section of this chapter for suitable campgrounds and RV parks in the greater Anchorage area.

Getting Around
Anchorage is fairly easy to navigate. With two highways and a multitude of major arterials, getting from point A to point B requires little more than a current map of the city and some basic bearings.

The city is situated in a bowl between the Chugach Mountains to the east and silty Cook Inlet to the west. Ship Creek, near downtown, empties into Cook Inlet, and each summer thousands of hopeful fishers flock along its slippery banks to hook a salmon. Downtown is a square

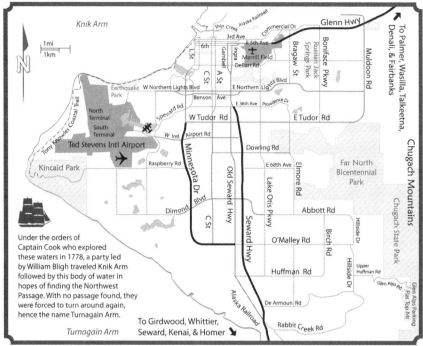

Anchorage Bowl

grid of shops, restaurants, hotels, and offices, and many visitors content themselves with wandering the blocks of the First through Sixth Avenue core. However, Anchorage is much more than downtown, especially with kids. The entire city is actually a borough (we have no counties in Alaska) stretching north toward the Matanuska-Susitna Valley and south to the community of Girdwood, a 1,961-square mile package.

With the Alaska spirit of exploration in mind, Anchorage offers plenty of car rental agencies and most offer models to accommodate the entire crew. For the best deal, rent off the premises of Ted Stevens International Airport, since many agencies offer shuttle service to and from their offices. A few options:

Avis (www.avisalaska.com, 907-243-4300)
Enterprise (www.enterprise.com, 907-248-5526)
Hertz (www.hertz.com, 907-562-4595)

PUBLIC TRANSPORTATION

Anchorage's sole public transportation service is through People Mover bus service (www.peoplemover.org). Serving the Anchorage Bowl and the nearby suburb of Eagle River, People Mover offers 16 different routes that crisscross the city with varying stages of efficiency. Many of the routes begin and/or end at the downtown Anchorage Transit Center on Sixth Avenue, a location frequented by many homeless adults and teens. Heated discussions have erupted in the past few years regarding the safety and security of Transit Center passengers, and our family has experienced some uncomfortable moments while waiting for a bus or accessing the parking garage housed in the same structure. That said, use your better judgment; People Mover buses themselves are fairly well policed and if your family is acquainted with public transportation and is willing to hoof it to and from random bus stops that may or may not be near your preferred attraction or place of lodging, go for it. Fares range from $1/kids ages five to 18 to $1.75/adults. Kids ages four and under ride free. Day passes can be purchased through the People Mover website or by calling (907) 343-6543.

VISITOR INFORMATION

Visit Anchorage, the city's visitor bureau, is located at 524 West Fourth Avenue (www.anchorage.net, 907-276-4118) and is open from 8 a.m. to 7 p.m. June through September, with varying hours the rest of the year. Visit Anchorage provides information about Alaska's largest city and the entire state with the help of both actual people and a comprehensive interactive website. Start your Anchorage journey at the Log Cabin Visitor Center on Fourth Avenue and F Street, where most trips can be plotted and planned fairly easily. It's a small building and busy during the summer months, so if the line is long, walk behind the cabin to the main office behind. Additional information for travelers can also be found at the CVB office at Ted Stevens International Airport near the baggage claim area.

Lodging

Many Anchorage hoteliers have yet to figure out the finer points of accommodating traveling families and as a result do not possess the amenities of some Outside hotels. That said, those who have stepped up to the challenge are fine examples of meeting the needs of frazzled parents, enthusiastic kids, and budget-conscious consumers who want to make every dollar count in an extremely expensive state. Below are several options for families, ranging from expensive and fancy to simple and clean. For the sake of convenience, I've arranged them from most expensive to least expensive by geographic area of town, using a highly subjective, nonscientific price code tool. Remember, everything costs more in Alaska.

$$$ More Expensive
$$ Moderate
$ Budget

DOWNTOWN ANCHORAGE

Copper Whale Inn $$$

440 L St., Anchorage, AK 99501
(866) 258-7999, (907) 258-7999, fax (907) 258-6213
cwhalein@alaska.net

Located on a little bluff overlooking Cook Inlet, Copper Whale Inn is a consistent winner of Best B&B awards every year. Originally built in 1936 as a residence for a local doctor, the inn is now a popular retreat for visitors, business travelers, and locals seeking downtown accommodations after a concert or play. Copper Whale's 14 rooms are comfortable and cozy, offering either a private bath (extra) or shared. Kids are welcome at Copper Whale, and four of the rooms offer a queen-twin combo. Portable cribs and a smaller rollaway are also available. The views are fantastic, downtown access couldn't be better (the Tony Knowles Coastal Trail, an 11-mile paved pathway that hugs the coastline, is right below the inn; bikes can be rented on the property), and innkeeper Glen Hemingson knows a ton of interesting history about both the inn and Anchorage. Breakfast is European-style continental, with fresh fruit, cereal, and wonderful baked goods. No transportation.

Note: The concept of a shared bathroom might seem strange but is very common in smaller communities of Alaska. A "shared bath" simply means a bathroom like the one you use at home, with a lock on the door for privacy. Inn staff keep these spaces spic and span, too.

Thumbs-up for: Proximity to walking/biking trail, playground, restaurants, and downtown Anchorage attractions, plus personal attention by staff. Internet access throughout the property.

Sheraton Anchorage Hotel and Spa $$$
401 East Sixth Ave., Anchorage, AK 99501
(800) 325-3535, (907) 276-8700
info@sheratonanchorage.com

Located near the east end of downtown, the Sheraton has undergone a transformation in the last several years and now provides sleek, chic accommodations. While not close enough for most families to walk to local attractions, other than the Anchorage Museum a few blocks away, the Sheraton is still worth considering for downtown lodging. Junior suites are a great option for larger families, with a pull-out couch, seating area, and adjoining room. Families might also consider purchasing access to The Club for an additional $30/night, a penthouse-style area with continental breakfast, hot snacks in the evening, unlimited beverages and access to television, a work area, and fantastic views. The property has one restaurant on site, Jade Steak and Seafood, offering breakfast, lunch, and dinner and a nice selection of kid-friendly foods. Transportation is available to or from the airport or train depot for a fee. Alaska residents receive 15 percent discount all year long. Internet is available for free in all common areas and in rooms for $10.

Thumbs-up for: Sleek styling and easy parking access. The Club is a nice touch.

Anchorage Grand Hotel $$
505 West Second Ave., Anchorage, AK 99501
(888) 800-0640, (907) 929-8888
www.anchoragegrand.com, info@anchoragegrand.com

A renovated 1950s apartment building, the Anchorage Grand combines space with function in a unique format that appeals to the traveling family. Perched on a slope directly above the Alaska Railroad depot (what kid wouldn't dig that?), the hotel offers 31 suites with kitchenettes, full bathrooms, Wi-Fi, and a continental breakfast. Close to popular Fourth Avenue and the majority of downtown Anchorage attractions, the hotel's proximity means families merely stroll a block or two for concerts in the park, farmer's markets, restaurants, and access to other Anchorage attractions via shuttle. Prices are reasonable for this prime downtown location. No transportation. Internet in the lobby.

Thumbs-up for: Kitchenette, location, access to tourism offices and downtown attractions.

MIDTOWN ANCHORAGE

Embassy Suites $$$
600 East Benson Blvd., Anchorage, AK 99503
(907) 332-7000, fax (907) 332-7001
www.embassysuites1.hilton.com

Large and stylish, Embassy Suites is one of the newer hotels in Anchorage. Part of the Hilton family of resorts and hotels, Embassy Suites offers a range of rooms for every family size. From two-bedroom/two-bath suites to a two-room/one-bath suite, parents and kids will have plenty of space.

Enjoy a complimentary, cooked-to-order breakfast each morning at the in-house restaurant, Pi, and a nightly manager's reception. Kids will love the swimming pool, too. Conveniently located near the Seward Highway, Embassy Suites makes sense for those traveling with a vehicle. In a typical strip-mall sort of neighborhood, there is not much reason to walk around, but a bakery and restaurant are just a block away, as is a local mall. Rooms have high-speed Internet and phones with voicemail. Transportation is available to/from the airport.

Thumbs-up for: Swimming pool, roomy accommodations, and complimentary breakfast.

Residence Inn Anchorage Midtown $$$
1025 35th Ave., Anchorage, AK 99508
(800) 314-0781, (907)-563-9844
www.marriott.com

Another set of suites that caters to families is the Residence Inn, located just east of the Seward Highway in Midtown Anchorage. Situated next to the BP building and filled with employees and business folk traveling to/from Alaska, the hotel is nonetheless a great option for parents who wish to spread out a bit in one of the hotel's 148 suites. Full kitchens provide ample cooking space and bedrooms are available for larger families. Each suite also has a cozy gas-burning fireplace by which to relax at the end of a long day. Continental breakfast is served each morning and receptions with heavy snacks (dinner, really) are served Monday through Thursday. Our family stayed here for two months after the big move to Alaska, and frankly, I didn't want to leave; free food and someone to clean my place every day was almost too good to pass up. Airport/rail transfers with advance reservation. Swimming pool.

Thumbs-up for: Full kitchens, swimming pool, breakfast, and happy hour. Family-conscious staff.

Hampton Inn $$
4301 Credit Union Dr., Anchorage, AK 99502
(907) 550-7000
www.hamptoninn.hilton.com

Ninety-seven rooms, airport transfer, full breakfast (and a nifty Hampton Breakfast on the Go bag for fast morning getaways), close to airport. Not really near any attractions of note, but convenient access. Internet.

NEAR THE AIRPORT

Holiday Inn Express $$
4411 Spenard Rd., Anchorage, AK 99517
(800) 315-2621, (907)-248-8848
www.hiexpress.com

The Holiday Inn Express has 128 rooms, three suites, easy access to airport, complimentary shuttle and breakfast, and is close to both museums and downtown. Located in one of Anchorage's oldest neighborhoods, Spenard, the area is funky, but full of true Alaska charm. Internet.

Hotel Alternatives

Anchorage Alaska Bed and Breakfast Association
(907) 272-5909
www.anchorage-bnb.com

More than just a list of available bed-and-breakfast facilities in Anchorage, the association also provides a comprehensive search tool on its website that makes it easy to find just what you're looking for—or what you're not. Use the "Search by Amenity" tab and check the box "children welcome" to find those hosts who cater to kids.

CAMPING

Anchorage has a number of family-friendly camping options, most of which are located outside the immediate Anchorage bowl. Our favorites retain much of that campground charm you might recall from your own childhood, yet are close enough to town for a meal out or a bit of sightseeing. Do remember that camping in Alaska means sharing the forest with a healthy population of wild critters, among them moose and bear. See Chapter 5, "Alaska's Wildlife," for more information about recreating around Alaska's animal friends.

Eagle River Campground is located 12 miles from Anchorage along the Glenn Highway. This Chugach State Park facility has 57 RV/tent sites, accessible bathrooms, and access to hiking trails. $15/night with a four-night limit. Call (907) 694-7982 for reservations. **Note**: Reservations recommended.

Eklutna Lake Campground can be accessed via the Eklutna Lake exit from mile 26.6 of the Glenn Highway. Part of Chugach State Park, the campground features 50 tent/RV sites, plus an additional overflow camping/parking area to accommodate up to 15 additional sites. Hugely popular with families, the campground has paved roadways just right for biking, and the nearby Eklutna Lake Trail is 12 miles of dirt tread perfect for easy hiking or biking. Accessible bathrooms, parking, and picnic areas make this a great option for multigenerational use. $10/night, 15-night limit. Call (907) 694-7982 for reservations. **Note**: Very crowded during peak months of May–August; reservations are a must for weekend visits.

Bird Creek Campground, located 20 miles southeast of Anchorage along the Seward Highway at Milepost 101.2, was recently renovated. With 28 campsites and a 35-foot RV size limit, it's not a large campground, but its charm and accessibility to a major road/trail system make it a winner for families. Accessible bathrooms, fire rings, and flat campsites all make for a pleasant experience, as does the nearby Indian-Bird-Girdwood Trail, a paved biking and hiking trail perfect for the stroller set. $15/night, seven-night limit. Call (907) 269-8400 for information.

Centennial Park campground/RV park is located in east Anchorage, nestled between Boundary Avenue and Muldoon Road. While not exactly a wilderness experience, Centennial Park is an excellent choice for the family wishing to spend their days sightseeing or exploring in Anchorage, with an easily accessed place to crash at night. The park has 100 tent/trailer sites, six pull-through sites, and two group sites for overnight stays, to the tune of $25/night. Restrooms are fully accessible, and showers are available for $5. All stays are limited to 14 nights, and campsites are first-come, first-served, with an exception made for RV caravans. Operated by the Municipality of Anchorage, Centennial Campground is on the bus line and is a short drive from the popular Alaska Native Heritage Center and a major shopping mall/movie theater. Call (907) 343-6986 May–September and (907) 343-6992 October–April for information and/or group reservations.

Feeding the Family

We love eating in Anchorage. The uniqueness of an Alaska location combined with a rich diversity of culture brings a certain level of excitement to dining out. From fresh seafood to homegrown vegetables, our restaurants are a sensory delight, even for kids. Many restaurants, too, are supporting the Alaska Grown concept, serving food grown or made in Alaska, meaning the ingredients on your plate couldn't be any fresher, a big bonus for health-conscious parents.

Below are some favorite eateries in the greater Anchorage area, all of which appreciate younger diners and their accompanying grown-ups.

DOWNTOWN

Glacier Brewhouse $$–$$$
737 West Fifth Ave., Anchorage, AK 99501
(907) 274-BREW (2739)
www.glacierbrewhouse.com
Hours vary; serving lunch and dinner. Open all year.

Billed as the establishment "where Alaskans meet Alaskans," Glacier Brewhouse is a noisy, lodge-style restaurant that truly does enjoy its pint-size guests. From a dynamic kids' menu featuring everything from french fries to individual pizzas and home-brewed root beer, the Brewhouse is a kid-pleaser from start to finish. Fresh Alaska seafood is always on the main menu, along with craft ales to whet the adults' whistles after a busy day of exploring. Chicken, steaks, pizza, and vegetarian options abound as well. Reservations are a must, as the restaurant is always crowded, especially during the holiday and summer seasons (use the Open Table feature on their website). Try dining during late-afternoon hours, when the atmosphere is calmer and kids have a better chance of sitting near a window or the warm and cozy fireplace.

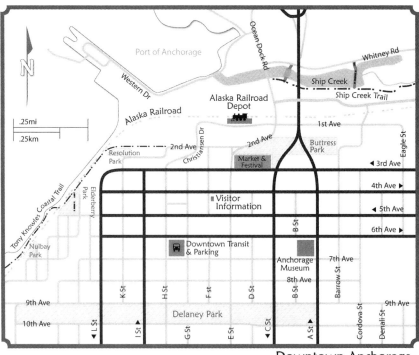

Downtown Anchorage

Snow City Cafe $$

1034 West Fourth Ave., Anchorage, AK 99501
(907) 272-CITY (2489)
www.snowcitycafe.com
Open Monday–Friday 7 a.m.–3 p.m., Saturday–Sunday 7 a.m.–4 p.m.

Perhaps the best breakfast option in Anchorage, and certainly the most popular, Snow City Cafe has been voted such for the past 10 years, serving up fresh food with friendly service to thousands of diners. A noted hangout for families, especially on the weekend, Snow City offers kids their own menu, crayons, and the freedom to be kids. Although wait times can be long, Snow City makes valiant attempts to mitigate them, with a call-ahead policy and plenty of free coffee for parents, books and games for kids, and understanding staff. A recent remodel created even more seating, with booths replacing tables for the ultimate in urban Alaska dining. Menu items include a variety of Eggs Benedict, silver dollar pancakes, and fresh soups made daily, as well as a fabulous coffee bar. A must-do when visiting Anchorage, maybe even more than once. You'll probably see us there, too, savoring the Polar Bear Breakfast.

MIDTOWN ANCHORAGE

Spenard Roadhouse $$–$$$

1049 West Northern Lights Blvd., Anchorage, AK 99503
(907) 770-7623
www.spenardroadhouse.com
Open Monday–Friday 11 a.m.–11 p.m., Saturday–Sunday 9 a.m.–11 p.m.

The Spenard Roadhouse is a shining star among Anchorage's usual dining options. Located along bustling Northern Lights Boulevard in the Midtown area, Spenard Roadhouse has become a hangout for locals looking for traditional food with a contemporary twist, featuring unique ingredients and fresh favorites that appeal to the whole family. My husband's favorite is the Bacon Jam Burger with a heavenly apple-bacon spread slathered on top; our son prefers the children's menu pizza options with a side of crunchy veggies and dip; and I truly enjoy their appetizer menu featuring bacon, bacon, and oh, more bacon. Spenard Roadhouse offers daily specials, too, like TV Dinner Sunday, where Mom's Salisbury steak never tasted so good.

Beartooth Theatre Pub and Grill $$-$$$
1230 West 27th Ave., Anchorage, AK 99503
(907) 276-4200
www.beartooththeatre.net
Grill open Monday–Friday 11 a.m.–11:30 p.m., Saturday–Sunday 10 a.m.–11:30 p.m.
Theatre Pub hours vary with showtimes, call for information.

The place to be when the weather turns sour and even when it's not, Beartooth Grill and adjacent Theatre Pub offer unique dining experiences for both parents and kids. Two options are available: the cafe/theatre pub, where families can nosh on pizza, tacos, and home-brewed root beer and craft ales while watching a movie, and the sit-down grill, where Southwestern favorites make an ordinary day special indeed. The weekly fresh sheet reads like an organic garden list, with Alaska-grown vegetables dominating the menu. Try the burritos and tamales or perhaps some pasta with a fresh sauce. Stop by for brunch on Saturdays and Sundays and enjoy fresh

KIDSPEAK

My favorite restaurant is the Spenard Roadhouse because they have yummy bacon.
—Susannah, age four and a half
(I like her.)

Coffee Time!
Anchorage likes its coffee so much there are drive-through establishments on nearly every street corner and many coffee houses dot the city. One of the most successful of these is Kaladi Brothers (www.kaladi .com, 907-344-4480), a locally owned, locally roasted coffee company whose brand animal is a red goat. With 12 cafés and a thriving wholesale business, Kaladi Brothers is sure to please even the most discriminating coffee drinker. What we like most, however, is their commitment to the Anchorage community, donating time, money, and even their employees to events that will ultimately benefit all.

fruit and a lovely assortment of egg dishes that will make you even happier it's the weekend. Warning: can be extremely crowded on movie nights and/or weekends, so call ahead.

Arctic Roadrunner $
5300 Old Seward Highway, Anchorage, AK 99518
(907) 561-1245
Open Monday–Friday 10:30 a.m.–8 p.m., Saturday 11 a.m.–7 p.m.

Let's just be clear from the start: this is not a health-conscious burger joint. It is solid, unpretentious, and kid-friendly dining along the banks of babbling Campbell Creek. Burgers, fries, and a few chicken/fish sandwich options are cheap and filling, and the place is always bustling with locals. Visit during the summer and enjoy the sandy "beach" seating area, a huge bonus in our book. The biggest drawback is the cash-only policy that has us hunting behind sofa cushions for money or hitting an ATM on the way. The ambiance and fresh food, however, can be worth the hassle.

Moose's Tooth Pub and Pizzeria $$–$$$
3300 Old Seward Highway, Anchorage, AK 99503
(907) 258-2537
www.moosestooth.net
Open Monday–Thursday 10:30 a.m.–11 p.m., Friday 10:30 a.m.–12:30 a.m., Saturday 11 a.m.–12 a.m., Sunday 11 a.m.–11 p.m.

The partner restaurant to the Beartooth, Moose's Tooth has become an institution among residents and visitors alike, and we'd be remiss if we failed to mention their homemade pizzas, craft ales, and boisterous atmosphere. Sitting along the Seward Highway in Midtown Anchorage, Moose's Tooth provides a little something for everybody: sandwiches, salads, soups, and those home-brewed drinks, but pizza is the star. Pies like the Backpacker and Blackened Halibut bring diners here in droves, and kids are not left out of the menu selection

> **PARENT PRO TIP**
>
> We love Moose's Tooth, but it's difficult to find seating. We've started arriving when the restaurant opens at 10:30 a.m.—perfect for our toddlers since plenty of tables are available.
>
> —Lia, Anchorage mother of two

with reliable pepperoni on whole-wheat crust and a fresh root beer. The establishment underwent a major renovation a few years ago, which helped wait times, but this place is packed day in and day out, so plan on bringing the coloring books or travel games while listening for your name.

FAMILY FUN IN ANCHORAGE

It's a rare day when Anchorage's trails, parks, waterways, and public spaces are not bustling with active folks. Anchorage residents pride themselves on an admirable dedication to staying busy, indoors or out.

Bypassing Anchorage for other, more rural areas is a mistake, despite snarky comments from sourdoughs who say one can see real Alaska from here. A dynamic, colorful city, Anchorage offers families plenty of meaningful opportunities and activities. Below are some of the best bets.

Museums and Cultural Experiences

Anchorage Museum at Rasmuson Center
625 C St., Anchorage, AK 99501
(907) 929-9200
www.anchoragemuseum.org
Open daily 9 a.m.–6 p.m. (May 1–September 30); Tuesday–Saturday 10 a.m.–6 p.m., Sunday noon–6 p.m. (October 1–April 30)
Admission: $12/adults; $9/seniors, students, military; $7/kids 3–12; Free for ages two and under ($2 suggested donation)

The Anchorage Museum, the largest of its kind in Alaska, has been in its original downtown location since 1968. A recent massive renovation expanded both space and content, and the museum now blends art, history, and science within a tasteful, easy-to-navigate facility of 180,000 square feet. A planetarium, four floors of exhibit space, and a designated children's area known as the Imaginarium Discovery Center are a wonderful introduction to Alaska. Don't miss the Smithsonian Arctic Studies

Center and the Alaska History Gallery for an intricate look at Alaska from different cultural perspectives. Special "Family Days" offer free admission and encourage new visitors through activities and events.

Alaska Museum of Science and Nature
201 North Bragaw St., Anchorage, AK 99508
(907) 274-2400
www.alaskamuseum.org
Open Monday–Saturday 10 a.m.–5 p.m.
Admission: $5/adults, $4/seniors and military, $3/kids 3–12

A favorite among all members of our family, the Alaska Museum of Science and Nature has endeared itself to visitors through a practical, hands-on approach to the natural world. From dinosaur skeletons to ancient man to an ice age, the museum strives to challenge the critical thinker in all of us. Not at all fancy but absolutely stellar in its exhibit quality and scientific data, the museum encourages touching, listening, and seeing how our world has evolved to the present day. Allow time for kids to dig in "the Pits," a series of small, mock archeological sites that hide all sorts of treasures. Weekly programs for preschool children and self-guided scavenger hunts are awesome fun for kids while you explore. Don't worry: the museum is a mere 12,000 square feet, so you'll always know where they are.

Visitors are greeted by an arch of whalebone at the Alaska Native Heritage Center in Anchorage.

Alaska Native Heritage Center

880 Heritage Center Dr., Anchorage, AK 99504
(800) 305-6608
www.alaskanative.net
Open daily 9 a.m.–5 p.m. (May–Labor Day). Open for special events only the rest of the year.
Admission: $24.95/adults; $21.15/seniors, military; $16.95/kids 7–16; Free for kids six and under. Purchase a "Culture Pass" and combine your visit with a trip to the Anchorage Museum for $29.95, a savings of 30 percent. A free shuttle is available from downtown Anchorage.

A 26-acre testament to the indigenous people of Alaska, the Native Heritage Center merges the unique cultural characteristics of Alaska Native groups into one facility, providing an outstanding opportunity for children and parents to explore and investigate. Featuring both indoor and outdoor exhibits and experiences, the Alaska Native Heritage Center is worth the steep admission price for a day of immersion into a culture many have forgotten. Visit the Hall of Cultures where each Native group is explained in detail, learn an Alaska Native dance, play a Native game, then head outdoors to six authentic Native dwellings around little Lake Tiulana, where kids can learn what it was like to live during a simpler time through artifacts and explanations from elders and youth stationed inside.

Alaska Aviation Museum

4721 Aircraft Dr., Anchorage, AK 99502
(907) 248-5325
www.alaskaairmuseum.org
Open daily 9 a.m.–5 p.m. (May 11–September 15); Wednesday–Saturday 9 a.m.–5 p.m., Sunday noon–5 p.m. (September 16–May 10)
Admission: $10/adults, $8/seniors, $6/kids 5–12 . Free for veterans and children four and under.

Four hangars and a chunk of tarmac featuring every kind of aircraft known to the 49th state—that's the Aviation Museum. So close to Ted Stevens Anchorage International Airport that one could easily confuse the parked 737 Combi (passenger-cargo) as ready for duty, the museum is chock-full of interesting information and mechanized air wizardry. Alaska would be nowhere fast without the use of the airplane, and the Aviation Museum explains the role of aircraft for commercial, personal, and security interests in a comprehensive, hands-on way. Don't forget to stop in and take a turn in the new space shuttle simulator or let the kids punch buttons and pull levers in the cockpit of a Boeing 727.

Downtown Fun

Exploring downtown Anchorage is fun with kids. Part frontier town, part urban chic, downtown is a conglomeration of old meets new meets funky, which makes for interesting sightseeing. The easiest way to become acquainted with downtown is hoofing it, checking out a stream of sights and sounds and colors and textures along the way. A great way to find upcoming events and activities in downtown Anchorage is through the Anchorage Downtown Partnership (www.anchoragedowntown.org), a dynamic group of downtown merchants committed to keeping residents and guests hopping.

Alaska Public Lands Information Center
605 W. Fourth Ave., Suite 105, Anchorage, AK 99501
(907) 664-3661
www.alaskacenters.gov
Free admission
Open all year; summer hours are daily 9 a.m.–5 p.m., winter hours are
Monday–Friday 10 a.m.–5 p.m.

Take a walking tour showcasing the life and adventures of Captain Cook or learn about Alaska animals on Alaska Zoo Day, both offered throughout the summer. Center staff are interpretive rangers from various federal and state agencies and can provide kids with some super hands-on activities, including the popular Animal Scavenger Hunt. A store makes available all sorts of Alaska-themed books, audio books, maps, gifts, and even state parks passes.

Note: Since the Public Lands Information Center is located within the old federal building, visitors must pass through security and adults must possess a valid ID.

Anchorage City Trolley
Departs from Fourth Ave. Log Cabin Visitor Center
(907) 277-4545
www.bearsquare.net
Admission: $15/person, regardless of age

This "old-timey" trolley, as my son calls it, is a fun and interesting way to capture the essence of the greater downtown area of Anchorage. It's a little touristy but still a fine hour and a half in Alaska's largest city. Narrated by a driver who is amusing, the tour takes passengers through downtown proper, the Alaska Railroad yards, and Ship Creek (Anchorage's birthplace) before swinging southwest toward the Turnagain area, where the great earthquake of 1965 caused the entire neighborhood to slide into Cook Inlet. At Earthquake Park, visitors will see some of the remnants left behind after that horrible day. The trolley also passes through Lake Hood, the busiest seaplane port in the world, before heading back downtown.

Note: Seats consist of wooden benches (it's a trolley, after all), with no seat belts or restraint systems.

Bear and Raven Theatre
Fourth Ave. and E St., Anchorage, AK 99501
(907) 277-4545
www.bearsquare.net
Admission: $12.50/adults, $10.50/kids

I was surprised the first time we visited the Bear and Raven Theatre; after all, how long could my five-year-old sit through another wildlife movie? The treasure of Bear and Raven is not necessarily in its films, although they too are a lot of fun: 30-minute documentaries that throw in a lot of music, fun narration, and even some fake fog. No, the real kick is in the lobby, where kids can step into a hot-air balloon basket and take a virtual ride over Valdez, Alaska, via a floor cam, or reel in a halibut wearing fishing garb. Mom and Dad can even take photos of their young mushers dressed in traditional fur parkas. Two shows are available: *The Amazing Trail*, documenting the famous Iditarod Trail Sled Dog Race, and *Those Amazing Bears*, set at McNeil River in southwest Alaska.

Anchorage is one of the few places where people can do some world-class salmon fishing right downtown. Many businesspeople bring their gear to the office for a little break-time or after-work fishing at nearby Ship Creek. Now that's cool.

Alaska Fact

Outdoor Recreation

Anchorage families love their outdoor time. After all, in mere minutes parents can have their offspring dressed, geared up, and on a trail, at a playground, or in a park. Year-round recreation is the mantra of many Anchorage moms and dads, translating into kids who like nothing better than hiking, biking, berry picking, fishing, or simply stomping in a mud puddle.

One of the simplest ways to experience Anchorage's outdoors is through its local parks and playgrounds, which offer a great opportunity to run squirrelly kids and spend a little time interacting with local families. The Municipality of Anchorage (www.muni.org/parks) boasts 223 parks, 82 playgrounds, and 250 miles of trails and greenbelts linking neighborhoods together in a wonderful tapestry of urban wilderness. The Anchorage Park Foundation (www.anchorageparkfoundation.org) also launched a new smartphone app that provides directions, reviews, and layout for the city's parks and playgrounds.

Many local trails are paved, making navigation with a stroller much easier. These trails are quite popular, however, especially on a pleasant day, so do watch for bikers, runners, skaters, and dogs. The longest, Tony

Beware of Mudflats!

While walking along trails of Southcentral Alaska, the urge may be strong to venture out upon what looks like a sandy beach. These "beaches" are actually mudflats, a coastal wetland created through deposits from rivers and/or lakes. What you see at low tide is bay mud that, if walked upon, is sticky, gooey, and extremely dangerous! Anchorage residents remember not too long ago when a woman walked out on local mudflats and became stranded in the thick muck. Her friends called for help, but despite efforts by local EMS officials, she drowned with high tide. Lesson? Stay away, even if the area looks safe, and heed signs and warnings. All of them. Always.

Knowles Coastal Trail, leads from downtown on Elderberry Street (just below the Copper Whale Inn) and runs southwest along Cook Inlet for 11 miles to Kincaid Park. Walk along the trail from either end or hook up somewhere in the middle via local park access.

OTHER FAMILY-FRIENDLY TRAILS IN ANCHORAGE

Campbell Tract/Campbell Creek Science Center

Located off Elmore Road in southeast Anchorage, the Campbell Tract features level, easily marked, and accessible trails for every ability. Managed by the Bureau of Land Management and supported by a dynamic Friends of Campbell Creek Science Center organization, the area is as wild as wild can be, yet it sits within the city limits. Stop in the Science Center (www .blm.gov/ak/st/en/prog/sciencecenter.html) for a map and discussion with knowledgeable naturalist staff who know the area inside and out. Our favorite trails are the Moose Track to Coyote, a two-mile hike from the parking lot to the Center and around the active Campbell Airstrip (stay on the marked trail). Look for moose, brown and black bears, eagles, and ptarmigan.

Connecting with Local Parents

Need a little adult conversation while the kids frolic in the great Alaska outdoors? Skedaddle Kids is a fabulous option for visiting parents. Skedaddle Kids (www.akskedaddle.com) is a weekly playgroup that meets at various parks around the greater Anchorage area. Rain, shine, snow, or sleet, these hardy kiddos of all ages meet up to play while parents enjoy a little grown-up chatting time. Visitors will glean valuable information, too, about events and activities going on around town.

Eagle River Nature Center

Located 20 miles southeast of Anchorage, Eagle River Nature Center (www.ernc.org) offers family-friendly hiking and programs at its small nature facility. Catering especially to kids, ERNC provides many drop-in programs throughout the year, most notably the Junior Naturalist and Knee-High Naturalist experiences. Hikes range from the short Rodak Loop (three quarters of a mile) to the longer Dew Mound trail (six miles). Don't miss the beaver pond overlook and an old hollow tree as you explore the property.

Anchorage Coastal Wildlife Refuge—Potter Marsh

Stretching 16 miles between Point Woronzof (along the Coastal Trail) to Potter Creek at the south end of the city, the refuge—and especially Potter Marsh (www.adfg.alaska.gov/index.cfm?adfg=anchoragecoastal .main) just off the Seward Highway—is a wonderful spot to view wildlife and the scenery surrounding the tidal flats. Watch for a multitude of birds, as this spot is the hottest destination for birders in Anchorage and salmon enter Potter Creek each summer to spawn. A raised boardwalk offers aboveground travel and excellent interpretive signs provide interesting tidbits of information. Bring binoculars if you have them, although there are a few telescopes available.

Arctic Valley

Looking for high-alpine adventure? Head to Arctic Valley (www.skiarctic .net), one of the most popular locations in Anchorage for hiking, berry picking, and, in the winter, backcountry skiing. Part military installation (the road and part of the property belongs to Joint Base Elmendorf-Richardson), part Chugach State Park, Arctic Valley boasts miles of alpine meadow hiking and world-class views. Be prepared to pay the $5 parking fee for Chugach State Park (dnr.alaska.gov/parks/units/chugach/). Trails are narrow and occasionally steep, so bring a carrier for small children, but the views are completely worth any extra effort.

Other Adventures

Alaska Zoo
4731 O'Malley Rd., Anchorage, AK 99507
(907) 346-2133
www.alaskazoo.org
Admission: $12/adults; $9/seniors, military; $6/kids 3–17
Free shuttle from downtown Anchorage visitor center

The only zoo in Alaska, the property has provided a home for injured, orphaned, or captive-born arctic and subarctic animals since the 1960s. Located along the hillside of south Anchorage, the Alaska Zoo is a delightful experience for all ages, with forested trails, family-friendly programs, and year-round opportunities to learn about animals that inhabit the far north. Summer brings weekly concerts to the grassy lawn of the zoo and winter sees a giant explosion of holiday twinkling with ZooLights. Kids can participate in seasonal day camps. Weekly programs called Wildlife Wednesdays provide teens and adults insight into a chosen animal.

The facility is stroller- and sled-friendly, depending upon the season, and a small snack bar exists on the property. Allow two hours to adequately explore the zoo.

Lifetime Adventures Bicycle Rentals
Fifth Ave. and L St., Anchorage, AK 99501
(800) 952-8624
www.lifetimeadventures.net/anchorageCoastalTrail

Summertime rentals start at $10 for two hours. Tandems, trailers, and tagalongs available, along with helmets, gloves, and a map of Anchorage. Exploring Anchorage by bike is a wonderful way to see both the city and its attractions without feeling like part of the crowd. Lifetime Adventures, on the property of Copper Whale Inn, rents bikes and appropriate accessories for the whole family. A nice family ride begins downhill from the inn, accessing the Coastal Trail and heading southwest toward Westchester Lagoon (and its new playground), Earthquake Park, and Point Woronzof, where jets take off overhead from Anchorage International Airport. Do watch for moose.

Lifetime Adventures also rents kayaks and bikes at Eklutna Lake, 40 minutes northeast of Anchorage by car.

Alaska Botanical Garden

4601 Campbell Airstrip Rd., Anchorage, AK
(907) 770-3692
www.alaskabg.org
Admission: $5/person, free for kids under two

Cross my heart, kids will like the Alaska Botanical Garden! Not just one garden but five, plus two excellent trails, the Alaska Botanical Garden is 110 acres of family-friendly walking and light hiking. Fully fenced (but not immune to the occasional moose), the garden features every northern-type flower, tree, and shrub its small cadre of staff and bevy of volunteers can find. The trails are lovingly maintained and delightfully mysterious, and the Lowenfels Family Nature Trail is one mile of Alaska wild discovery. Open all year, the Alaska Botanical Garden is a little wilderness gem in Anchorage that shouldn't be missed. Visit its website for a host of events and activities geared toward kids. We love to wander the gardens in the evening during the summer months and snowshoe or ski during our long winters.

FISHING

The best options for fishing can be found along placid Campbell Creek or at one of the stocked lakes around the city. Anchorage—and Alaska in general—is a victim of the concept known as "combat fishing," whereby fishermen and -women line up elbow-to-hip-wader in a river or stream and do everything they can to not hook each other in the ear as they pursue a salmon. Kids can fish for trout in lakes and salmon in the streams and rivers. Rods and reels can be rented in downtown Anchorage at 6th Avenue Outfitters (907-677-0246) during the summer months.

Kids under 14 years of age do not need a fishing license in Alaska. However, it behooves savvy parents to purchase licenses for themselves, because one never knows how long a child will last on a shoreline waiting for a fish to bite (usually around 10 minutes in our family). Additionally, a host of potentially confusing, detailed rules exist as to where, when, and how a fish can be caught in Alaska, so pick up a copy of current sport fishing rules, available at just about any local store, sports shop, or information center. The Alaska Department of Fish and Game regulates sport fishing in Alaska, and their website (www

.adfg.alaska.gov/index.cfm?adfg=fishingSportFishingInfo.main) is a helpful catchall of important information, including a list of special kids-only fishing days.

> ### KIDSPEAK
>
> Jewel Lake has *huge* arctic char. It needs to be frozen, though.
>
> —Duke, age two, speaking about ice fishing in Anchorage

Make sure children are outfitted with a life jacket and appropriate footwear/outdoor gear. Alaska's water is always cold, and it takes less than a minute, even in the summer, for hypothermia to develop.

Tours

Short on time, or just want someone else to handle all the details of sightseeing? Consider hiring a tour company that can handle every detail, from driving to finding elusive wildlife. Particularly nice for multigenerational groups, tour companies offer accessibility and diversity, a nice combination when different members of one family want different experiences from their Alaska vacation.

Anchorage has quite a few tour operators who can be contacted via Visit Anchorage (www.anchorage.net) and range from large (serving 50 or more guests at one time) to smaller (serving fewer than 15). One of our favorites is Salmon Berry Tours, located on Fourth Avenue in downtown Anchorage (www.salmonberrytours.com, 888-878-3572). Specializing in day or overnight tours and special family-friendly options, Salmon Berry prides itself on seeking out experiences that delight the younger visitor.

Tours are small (no more than 20 guests) and can be tailor-made to fit a family's budget, schedule, and demographic. Owner Candice McDonald makes sure guides carry snacks and drinks on each trip, and she even provides car seats for the smallest clients.

Alaska Fact Alaska's average temperature is a chilly 35.5°F. Brrrrr.

Day Trips from Anchorage

If you have a few days to explore beyond Anchorage, consider a longer excursion to what could be considered the 'burbs. These suburbs, though, are less about dense housing and more about rural living, and commuters brave icy roads in the winter and crowded passing lanes in the summer to reap benefits of living outside the formal boundaries of Anchorage. As a result, visitors can find many activities appealing to a wide range of interests.

GIRDWOOD

Situated 40 miles south of downtown Anchorage is the site of a gold-mining operation turned ski-bum town turned world-class resort. Originally called Glacier City, Girdwood (named for miner James Girdwood, a Scottish-Irish miner who staked the first claims) used to sit along the shores of Turnagain Arm. After the devastating 1964 earthquake that caused much of the little town to disappear under the muck, residents moved inland about three miles to the current site. Visit the Girdwood Chamber of Commerce website (www.girdwoodchamber.com) for some interesting history and facts about this little town.

Now a bedroom community for Anchorage, Girdwood is home to Alyeska Resort (www.alyeskaresort.com), a thriving year-round destination property that prides itself on steep and deep skiing or hiking coupled with an elegant resort atmosphere. Busy with both Outside visitors and local residents, Alyeska boasts Nordic and alpine skiing, snowshoeing, hiking, mountain biking, and a decided European atmosphere not often seen in the 49th state.

Hiking the North Face trail at Alyeska Resort.

Allow an hour to get from Anchorage to Girdwood, with time for stops at designated pullouts along the scenic Seward Highway. Historic Turnagain Arm is so named thanks to Captain James Cook and a navigational error that necessitated a turnaround at the end of the passage. The roadway is narrow but beautiful, with skyscraper cliffs leading to alpine meadows. The waters of Turnagain Arm are dark and cold but also possess a healthy population of beluga whales—white, cheerful-looking mammals who ride the incoming tides in search of small fish and other marine treats. Two particularly good spots to see the whales are Beluga Point and Bird Creek pullouts, where telescopes, safe parking, and interpretive signs explain the inner workings of the Turnagain Arm area.

Those with gold fever can stop by the small community of Indian and indulge in a bit of panning at the **Indian Valley Mine** at mile 104. For $1 per person, guests can wander through the fascinating collections of authentic (and very old) mining and homesteading equipment gathered by the owners. Buy your very own bag of pay dirt ($10 a bag) to pan for gold. My son, however, prefers to play with the odd selection of toy trucks and cars and even odder collection of live ducks, geese, and chickens.

Once in Girdwood, stop by the **Chugach National Forest** office for trail maps and other information about the area. The office is only open during regular business hours, however, so don't be surprised if you show up on a weekend and are greeted by locked doors.

Crow Creek Mine is located 2.7 miles up Crow Creek Road in Girdwood. Family-owned for over 40 years, the mine and outbuildings date back to 1806 and are interesting to wander. Pan for gold or take a guided tour of the area, watching for anxious color-seekers to "strike it rich" (www .crowcreekmine.com, 907-229-3105).

Girdwood possesses a vibrant "community cares" attitude, so much so that the town pitched in to build a playground a few years ago. Swings, sandboxes, a castle, music area, and other enticing attributes beckon children from birth on up, and we cannot visit Girdwood without at least one play session. Bigger kids get their chance for fun at an adjacent skate park.

Trek the well-marked and maintained trails of Girdwood, like popular **Winner Creek Trail**, beginning at Alyeska Resort and leading to the fast-moving creek, a distance of five miles round-trip. A new, almost-adjacent trail was recently developed by the Girdwood Nordic Ski Club for winter recreation purposes, and the wide, winding five-kilometer trail is perfectly appropriate for a family hike. Access is found at the end of Arlberg Road on the resort's property.

For the truly adventurous, try hiking up the **North Face** ski run in the summertime and earn a free tram ride down, courtesy of Alyeska Resort. With 20 switchbacks to the top, it's a tough scramble. This hike is not for the faint of heart, but every time I visit I see kids leading the way.

Note: Be sure to outfit kids properly for a hike of this magnitude; hiking boots are a must, as are breathable layers, a warm hat, and rain gear since weather on the mountain can change in an instant. The tram ride is a highlight for any age. Round-trip tram tickets are $20/adults, $17/students 13–18, $12/kids 6–12. Find a complete map of all Girdwood trails on the Alyeska Resort website.

Biking is a great way to see Girdwood, with bicycle rentals available at either Alyeska Resort or Girdwood Ski and Cyclery (www.girdwood -ski-and-cyclery.com, 907-783-BIKE). Easy riding leads through boreal forests, around the lush Moose Meadows, and on out toward the Seward Highway, where hardy riders can link up to the famous (or infamous) Bird to Gird trail that heads north toward the small town of Indian, a ride of around 20 miles. But for we mere mortal moms and dads, the five miles to the highway and back are usually enough.

The state tree of Alaska is the Sitka spruce (*Picea stichenensis*), found everywhere in southeast, and most areas of southcentral Alaska.

Alaska Fact

Girdwood eateries are few in number but high in quality. Below are a few favorite spots to dine:

Chair Five Restaurant $$
171 Linblad Ave., Girdwood, AK 99587
(907) 783-2500
www.chairfive.com
Open daily 11a.m.–1 a.m.

Grilled cheese, pizza, burgers, and a fabulous kids' coloring contest make this my Girdwood numero uno for families. I love the halibut tacos with a zippy cajun spice, and our son adores the grilled cheese and fries. No personal checks.

The Bake Shop $$
Olympic Circle, Girdwood, AK 99587
(907) 783-2831
www.thebakeshop.com
Open Sunday–Friday 7 a.m.–7 p.m., Saturday 7 a.m.–8 p.m.

Casual dining in this cozy restaurant is perfect before or after an active day exploring Girdwood. Soups, cinnamon rolls, and pizza are the top-selling items here and folks flock in for a homestyle breakfast on the weekends. A big drawback for visiting families is the no-credit-card policy, but give it a whirl anyway; the food is worth it.

Jack Sprat $$–$$$
165 Olympic Mountain Loop, Girdwood, AK 99587
(907) 783-JACK
www.jacksprat.net
Open Monday–Friday 5–10 p.m., Saturday–Sunday 10 a.m.–2:30 p.m. (brunch),
4–10 p.m. (dinner)

We love Jack Sprat for its European flavors and commitment to organic foods. A kids' menu includes gluten-free items and simple, healthy choices that most children enjoy.

Aurora Bar and Grill $$$
Alyeska Resort
1000 Arlberg Ave., Girdwood, AK 99587
(800) 880-3880
www.alyeskaresort.com
Open daily 11 a.m.–9 p.m.

Located on the third floor of Hotel Alyeska, the Aurora Bar and Grill features many of the usual pub favorites but in a lovely alpine setting, complete with fireplace, view of the ski hills, and a menu that reflects Alaska cuisine. The kids' menu features items like cheeseburgers, chicken strips, and pasta with meatballs, all on a wonderful page full of busywork activities.

North on the Glenn Highway

More than a mere route to points north, the Glenn Highway provides visitors a number of easily accessed day trip options. The community of **Eagle River** (www.cer.org), 17 miles north of Anchorage, sits along swift-flowing Eagle River and the scenic Eagle River Valley, where hiking, mountain biking, and fishing can make for an interesting and active day. Take the kids to Eagle River Nature Center (www.ernc.org) for a day hike or family program any time of year or go it on your own along one of the many Chugach State Park trails along Eagle River Road.

At Milepost 26.5 of the Glenn Highway is the exit to **Eklutna**, an Alaska Native community and home to the inspiring Eklutna Village Historical Park. Combining Russian Orthodox theology with a rich Alaska Native culture, the park is a collection of "spirit houses" designed by the Athabascan–Russian Orthodox believers to help the deceased on their way to the next life. While young children may not be interested in much beyond the brightly adorned little houses atop gravesites, older kids may take away an appreciation for unique cultural traditions. $5 donation. Open May–September.

On the other side of the Glenn Highway is access to both **Thunderbird Falls** and busy **Eklutna Lake**. The falls can be reached via a one-mile trail to the waterfall, a kid-pleasing hike with an obvious reward at the end. Follow the directional signs to the trailhead from the Glenn Highway/ Eklutna exit or take the Thunderbird Falls exit at Mile 25.

WARNING: This is an extremely buggy hike in the summer months, so dress kids in long pants and long sleeves and load up on the bug spray. Parking fee of $5 per day.

Eklutna Lake is ten miles along the lake road from the Glenn Highway. Part of the Chugach State Park system (along with Thunderbird Falls), Eklutna Lake is a great place for hiking, biking, picnicking, or paddling a canoe or kayak. Rent bikes from Lifetime Adventures (www.lifetimeadventures.net) and ride along the 13-mile roadbed toward Eklutna Glacier, or stroll lakeside paths that lead to a muddy but lovely shoreline suitable for rock-throwing or wading. A small store a few miles before the park entrance offers great milkshakes and snacks during the summer months. Parking fee of $5 per day at the park.

Eklutna Lake and Ship Creek provide 90 percent of Anchorage's water supply. **Alaska Fact**

Palmer-Wasilla

Farther north along the Glenn Highway (www.glennhighway.org) are the communities of Palmer and Wasilla, close on the map and as diverse as can be in makeup and atmosphere. Approximately 35 miles from Anchorage, Palmer and Wasilla are part of the Matanuska-Susitna Valley (also known as Mat-Su or simply The Valley), where colonists settled in the 1930s on land parceled out for their use by then-President Roosevelt. The Mat-Su is an agriculturally rich landscape, in part due to massive glaciers that formed this valley thousands of years ago, and is surrounded today by three mountain ranges: the Alaska Range, the Talkeetna, and the Chugach Mountains. As a result, views are stunning and options for recreating run the gamut from simple to elaborate, including the famous **Alaska State Fair** (www.alaskastatefair.org), held each August in Palmer. This is where giant vegetables make their debut, with cabbages or pumpkins weighing in at a whopping 1,500 pounds and beets rivaling the girth of a volleyball.

The **Mat-Su Convention and Visitor Center** (777 E. Visitors Ct., Palmer, AK 99645, www.alaskavisit.com, 907-747-5000) is conveniently located right in between the split of the Parks and Glenn Highways. Step into the log cabin just in front of the Mat-Su Community Hospital and enjoy the hospitality of volunteers, many of whom have lived in this area of Alaska their entire lives.

Palmer is easily reached via the Glenn Highway, due east where the George Parks Highway begins taking over near Wasilla. The home for most of the colonists, Palmer has a charming feel to its tiny streets, especially in the **Palmer Museum and Visitor Center** (www.palmermuseum .org, 723 S. Valley Way, Palmer, AK 99645, 907-746-7668). Stop in and explore the history of Palmer, taking note of the beautifully preserved artifacts from local farming families. You can find information about activities and events in the valley here, too.

Just beyond downtown Palmer is **The Musk Ox Farm** (Mile 50 Glenn Highway, Palmer, AK 99645, www.muskoxfarm.org, 907-745-4151), where the world's shaggiest creatures live a knock-kneed existence in relative peace and quiet. A grand opening party every year on Mother's Day weekend brings visitors out in droves to see the annual crop of soft-as-silk calves and marvel at the amount of hair these animals have. Called *qiviut*, it's the warmest natural fiber known to man. Take a tour, browse the gift shop, or simply wander the expansive picnic grounds in the shadow of Pioneer Peak. Open May–late August, 10 a.m.–6 p.m. Admission is $9/ adults, $5/kids 5–17, free for kids four and under.

More animals abound at the **Williams Reindeer Farm** in Palmer (5561 S. Bodenburg Loop, Palmer, AK 99645, www.reindeerfarm.com,

907-745-4000), where 150 reindeer, 35 elk, two bull moose, and a very personable bison reside along with the Williams family. Open daily May–September, with special events and tours going on the rest of the year, this place is tons of farm-y fun with kids. Get up close and personal with a reindeer after listening to an interesting talk about these fascinating animals or take a hayride and see the entire expanse of property in the shadow of Pioneer Peak. Admission varies by season and activity. Call for current rates.

PARENT PRO TIP

The Reindeer Farm is a fabulous place, any time of year. Where else can kids see a bison, moose, and a herd of reindeer that might make Santa's own team jealous?

—Lindsey, Anchorage mother of two

High atop the southeast section of the Talkeetna Mountains is an alpine mecca called **Hatcher Pass**. Reached via Fishhook Road in Palmer or through the Parks Highway from Willow (on the other side of the pass), Hatcher Pass offers year-round access to gold panning, hiking, Nordic skiing, and sledding. Perched along these mountains, **Independence Mine State Historical Park** (dnr.alaska.gov/parks/units/indmine) offers insight into the world of gold mining at its restored townsite and museum. Stop in at **Hatcher Pass Lodge** (www.hatcherpasslodge.com, 907-745-1200) on the way back to town for an order of fondue or homemade soup while ogling the breathtaking views from your seat at 3,000 feet.

Hatcher Pass Bed and Breakfast (www.hatcherpassbb.com, 907-745-6788) is also an excellent option for families. Stay in a log cabin along scenic Fishhook Road and revel in the forested atmosphere. The breakfast part is accomplished by your own hands, but the inn's owners provide you all the ingredients to cook at your leisure. Great for larger families or those wanting a more secluded experience.

Matanuska Lakes State Recreation Area offers fishing, canoeing, hiking, and biking, with tent camping available for $10 a night. Trails connect to other Mat-Su pathways, and canoeing here is great for families (http://dnr.alaska.gov/parks/aspunits/matsu/keplerbradlksra.htm).

Wasilla is located northwest of Palmer, along the George Parks Highway, and has the distinction of being the home of former Wasilla mayor, Alaska governor, and vice presidential candidate Sarah Palin. Previously a hunting and trapping community and vital link in the Alaska Railroad chain, Wasilla is now considered a bedroom community of Anchorage.

Most visitors merely pass through Wasilla; its random collection of shops, strip malls, and lack of continuity make for a somewhat confusing tourism experience, but we do enjoy a visit to the **Museum of Alaska Transportation and Industry** (www.museumofalaska.org, 907-376-1211). A six-acre collection of every implement, machine, automobile, plane, or train used in Alaska over the state's vibrant history is here. Your kids (and you, too) will be amazed at the depth and breadth of transportation, from old and clunky to bright and shiny, in the 49th state. Innovative machinery was absolutely necessary to make it possible to get to and from remote places, and the tireless efforts of many volunteers make this museum an absolutely fantastic stop. Open daily 10 a.m.–5 p.m. (May–September). Admission $8/adults, $5/kids 3–17, or $18/family. Military and senior discounts available.

> **KIDSPEAK**
>
> I loved the transportation museum! I got to walk through a real train and climb in the caboose!
>
> —Owen, seven

Dream a Dream Dog Farm (www.vernhalter.com, 907-495-1197, 866-4AK-MUSH) is located in the town of Willow, about 90 minutes from Anchorage along the Parks Highway. Owned by Iditarod musher Vern Halter, it is an excellent place to learn more about Alaska's state sport. Halter has a kennel full of friendly sled dogs, complete with summertime litters of puppies, and he provides a lesson in dog care, mushing, and a history of the Iditarod. Open daily all year, with tours starting at $69/per person, and kids 11 and under are half-price.

The **Greater Wasilla Chamber of Commerce and Convention and Visitors Bureau** (415 E. Railroad Ave., Wasilla, AK, 99654, 907-376-1299) is a good place to find additional activities in this town of around 8,000.

Eating in the valley is fairly simple; most chain restaurants are spread out along the Parks Highway in Wasilla, so kid-friendly feeding time should not be an issue. In Palmer, do try **Turkey Red** (www.turkeyredak .com, 550 S. Alaska St., Suite 100, Palmer, AK 99645, 907-746-5544) for fresh Alaska cuisine with a decidedly urban twist. Breakfast, lunch, and dinner available and all sorts of specials from their bakery are available anytime. Beer and wine served.

Another kid-friendly option is found across the highway from the Alaska State Fairground property in Palmer. **Colony Kitchen** (1890 Glenn Highway, Palmer, AK 99645, 907-746-4600) is the home of the Noisy Goose Cafe, where local residents come for three squares of homestyle cookin'. Soups and half-pound burgers are hearty, and the homemade pie is excellent. Open daily 6 a.m.–10 p.m.

During the selection process of appropriate colonists for President Roosevelt's New Deal project of the 1930s, people were chosen from Minnesota, Wisconsin, and Michigan, since these states were assumed to be similar to Alaska climate-wise, but also because so many residents were already on social service programs due to the Great Depression.

Alaska Fact

THE KENAI PENINSULA

"When describing travel in just about any part of Alaska,
it is hard not to get carried away with superlatives and
this is also true when one talks about the town of Seward."
—Tay Thomas, *Only in Alaska* (1969)

Alaska's most accessible playground, the Kenai Peninsula is located due south of Anchorage and includes Seward, Soldotna, Kenai, Homer, and beautiful Kenai Fjords National Park. The Kenai is miles of untamed wilderness and outdoor recreation. Accessible by air, road, or rail, the Kenai Peninsula is a wonderful area for independent travel. We love it, our kids love it, and even better, visiting friends and relatives love it.

The Kenai Peninsula is home to the Russian and Kenai Rivers, and anglers from all over the world toss out lines in the hopes of hooking the big one each summer. Also boasting some of the best halibut fishing in the world, the peninsula hosts a thriving charter industry in Seward and along the Sterling Highway to Homer (I'll discuss that in greater detail later on in this section).

The Kenai Peninsula sits between two bodies of open water: Cook Inlet to the west and Prince William Sound to the east (Resurrection Bay protects Seward from the Gulf of Alaska). For thousands of years, the Chugach Eskimos used the narrow passage as their transportation route between the sound and the peninsula, settling on the southern tip of the peninsula before being uprooted by other groups. The Chugach now lay claim to many islands in the Prince William Sound area.

The Kenai Peninsula officially begins in the former community of Portage, 47 miles from Anchorage at the end of Turnagain Arm, a tiny town wiped out during the large earthquake of 1964. Today, Portage is the junction between the Portage Highway to Whittier and the Seward Highway to Seward. It's also a stop along both the Glacier Discovery and Coastal Classic routes of the Alaska Railroad.

While you can see some of the following sights during a day trip from Anchorage, I highly encourage families to spend at least one night in the company of eagles, otters, and happy fishermen.

Consider visiting the **Alaska Wildlife Conservation Center** (www .alaskawildlife.org, 907-783-2025) at Milepost 47 while you're in the neighborhood. This large facility of meadow and forested acreage is home to experimental herds of wood bison and plains bison as well as injured, orphaned, or ill animals who can no longer survive in Alaska's wild. Moose, brown and black bears, caribou, lynx, elk, and a cheeky porcupine named Snickers will entrance animal lovers of all ages and provide insight about their existence in the 49th state. Open all year, AWCC is fully accessible, with the option for driving through the property along dirt roads or by walking around the same, stopping at each enclosure to converse with the animals. A gift shop, restrooms, and a small education hut complete the experience. $10/adults; $7.50/military; $7.50/kids 4–12; free for kids under four. Maximum charge per vehicle is $30. Hours vary with seasons, but in the summer months AWCC is open 8 a.m.–8 p.m.

> **PARENT PRO TIP**
>
> We like to visit AWCC in spring and early summer to see bottle-fed moose calves. Ask at the park entrance when feedings are scheduled and plan your walking or driving route accordingly.
>
> —Jamie, Anchorage mother of one

A favorite Portage Valley activity with our brood is a stop at the **Begich, Boggs Visitor Center** (907-783-2326) at the end of the six-mile Portage Highway (a left turn at the Portage Junction). Built in 1986 and rededicated in 2001, the center is operated by the U.S. Forest Service and sits on the shores of Portage Lake, smack on the leavings of fast-receding Portage Glacier. Browse the interactive displays about ice worms, see an exhibit showcasing the history of greater Portage Valley, and view *Voices from the Ice* in the center's theater. Admission to the center is $5 for adults, with kids 15 and under free.

> **KIDSPEAK**
>
> I like visiting places that take me to another world…but not too many worlds.
>
> —Eryn, age seven

Also take time to walk the lake's rocky shoreline, capturing a glimpse of the occasional chunk of ice floating by. There is no easy lake access right from the parking lot, but a short walk south will lead you to a beach with space for stick gathering and rock throwing.

Note: The lake is extremely cold, even in the summer, so I discourage actual wading, although I do advocate sticking one's finger or toe in said lake water, just for the experience.

We also enjoy a hike or bike along the **Trail of Blue Ice**, a five-mile path that shadows the Portage Highway. This mostly flat gravel path is perfect for kids. Glaciers, trees, babbling streams that keep spawning salmon busy—it's all here along this fully accessible out-and-back trail. The Williwaw Fish-Viewing platform around mile four is an excellent place to spot salmon, and Moose Flats Day-Use area is fun for a picnic lunch. Bring bug repellent, however.

One of the highlights of the area is viewing **Portage Glacier** up-close via the M/V *Ptarmigan*. Once so accessible people could paddle their own canoes up to its icy face, Portage Glacier is now around the corner and out of visual range. A cruise aboard the *Ptarmigan*, operated by Gray Line Tours of Alaska, is a one-hour narrated journey right to the glacier. A worthwhile trip if you don't think you'll be able to see other glaciers (either on a cruise ship or day cruise). Tickets are an affordable $34/adults, $17/ kids 12 and under. Purchase tickets online at www.graylinealaska.com or call 800-544-2206.

Note: The Alaska TourSaver coupon book (www.toursaver.com) has a two-for-one adult ticket for the one-hour cruise.

Alaska Fact **The state of Alaska has three million lakes and 29 volcanoes.**

Within sight of the Begich, Boggs Visitor Center is the last stretch of the Portage Highway and a final pullout before vehicles and trains enter the tunnel separating the city of Whittier from the rest of the state. We explain the significance of Whittier, its history, and a few activities below.

Whittier

Whittier is located on the northeast shore of the Kenai Peninsula, at the head of Passage Canal. Although only 60 miles from Anchorage, Whittier remains remote and elusive, thanks to high, craggy mountains preventing any sort of viable highway through the rocky expanse. The Chugach Indians would simply climb up and over these peaks, but in 1943 the surveyors of World War II built an engineering marvel: **Anton Anderson Tunnel,** the only highway/railroad structure of its kind, which persists as a passageway for people and materials between Whittier and Anchorage.

Whittier's location affords amazing views of glaciers, wildlife, and green forests. Most activities are centered around water: glacier and wildlife cruises, fishing, kayaking, and the like. Visit the **Greater Whittier Chamber of Commerce** website (www.whittieralaskachamber.org) for a complete listing of activities that might appeal to your family, including a tunnel access schedule and accompanying regulations pertaining to same.

An interesting characteristic of Whittier is its approach to housing. With little infrastructure beyond the highly industrial docks and boat harbor, and due to steep mountains at their back door, most residents live in the 196-unit Begich Towers (www.begichtowers.com), a tall condominium building that also houses the local school, medical clinic, post office, police department, and grocery store. During the harsh winter months, children attending the local school walk underground, beneath a parking lot, to school.

Princess Cruises and the Alaska Marine Highway System ferries dock in Whittier to exchange passengers, so most visitors are in the community only a short time. If you have a few hours, however, here are some ideas for kid-friendly activities:

Phillips Cruises and Tours (www.phillipscruises.com, 800-544-0529) offers unforgettable access to Alaska's famous glaciers and abundant wildlife through its trips from Whittier.

The 26 Glacier Tour takes passengers 145 miles in around five hours, showing off the glaciers by name and number, as the name suggests. A Chugach National Forest ranger is on board all ships to provide narration and help kids through the fun Junior Ranger program. Lunch consisting of chicken strips or cod fillets is offered, too. $139/adults, $79/kids 2–11.

The shorter **Glacier Quest** tour is completed in just under four hours and takes passengers to two glaciers in Blackstone Bay and Shotgun Cove—perfect for families with smaller children or those with time constraints. Forest ranger narration and kids' Junior Ranger program is on board this tour, as well. $89/adults, $59/kids 2–11.

A new addition to the community, the **Prince William Sound Museum** (www.pwsmuseum.org)—housed in the Anchor Inn Hotel—pays tribute

Portage Valley Weather Alert!

As a 14-mile isthmus connecting mainland Alaska to the Kenai Peninsula and the former residence of enormous Portage Glacier, the Portage Valley is a deep, wide passage, with dramatic weather patterns. Even if the sun shines in Anchorage, Girdwood, or along the Seward Highway, things might not be so tranquil along the Portage Highway, where whipping winds and/or cloud cover can make an unprepared visitor quite miserable. Bring warm clothes, mittens, hats, and rain gear at any time of year—you'll be glad you did!

to the valuable contributions of Whittier, past and present. It's quite fascinating to see the military port take shape in photos and witness the absolute dependence upon the railroad for delivery of goods. A new exhibit will feature explanations of the U.S. Coast Guard's role here, all the way back to an 1898 rescue of the U.S. whaling fleet. Definitely worth a stop while waiting for your boat or even if you're simply curious about the history and texture of this interesting port city. Open daily 10 a.m.–6 p.m. $3/adults, $1.50/kids 12 and under.

Alaska Fact "It's wetter in Whittier." Or, if you prefer, "It's prettier in Whittier." Okay, maybe that's more of a mantra, but both phrases apply to this unique community.

RESTAURANTS

Whittier has a number of small establishments that serve coffee, hot chocolate, and such (and other things for adults), but our favorite is the Lazy Otter Cafe (www.lazyotter.com, 800-587-6887), located on the boardwalk of Whittier's waterfront. Offering sandwiches, wraps, soups, and boxed lunches, the Otter is committed to quality food, fast. They also have fabulous ice cream and milkshakes. Find them near the ferry dock, to the east, and look for a big green roof.

Seward

A scenic 126 miles from Anchorage, Seward is best known for its gateway status, from the first rush to Southcentral Alaska in the early 1900s up until the great earthquake of 1964. Until fires and a mighty tsunami crushed the town's maritime infrastructure and forever changed the way people enter and leave Alaska, Seward was a thriving port city, with hundreds of individuals and goods arriving daily. Retaining its small-town charm, Seward is a major force on the Alaska tourist circuit, and is the endpoint for cruise ships sailing north along the Inside Passage and the destination for the Alaska Railroad's Coastal Classic train from Anchorage.

From a natural history perspective, Seward is also a great place to capture the power of nature as you investigate glaciers, mountain trails, and rocky coves. From sea birds to bears, Seward is an excellent place to show children the cooperative and competitive circle of life.

GETTING THERE

Driving

The easiest (and cheapest) way to get to Seward is by car. Also quite practical when traveling with kids, a road trip south along the Seward Highway is lovely and affords many opportunities for stretching legs or satisfying curiosity.

Turnagain Pass at Milepost 70 is the highest point on the Seward Highway and offers views of the surrounding peaks and emerald-green meadows. At the top of the pass a rest stop with clean pit toilets provides a good spot for a break, and the paved walkways are fun to wander. We like to stop and have a snack here if the weather is nice, but mosquitoes are often a factor

> **KIDSPEAK**
>
> I like to ride on the ocean side to spot belugas, but I need binoculars.
>
> —Duke, age two

Seward

Population: 2,693 (2012 census)

Founded in: 1905 by the Ballaine brothers in August of 1903, but early settlers made the area their home in the late 1800s, and Russian explorers poked around Resurrection Bay in the 1700s.

Known for: A vital marine terminal for coal transport, fishing, and tourism.

Interesting fact: The Iditarod National Historic Trail begins in Seward and stretches 2,300 miles north toward Nome.

Hot tip: Find out when the cruise ships will be in town by contacting the Seward Chamber of Commerce, then plan your visit accordingly.

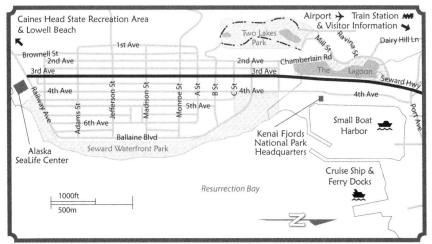

Downtown Seward

in how long we remain outside the vehicle. Also popular for winter activities like Nordic skiing, snowshoeing, or snowmachining.

Note: This is the beginning of a 20-mile or so dead zone for cell phones; Alaskans know this and complete all calls before heading farther south.

The little community of **Hope** (www.hopealaska.info) is a perfectly preserved village of past mining, and yet many Alaska visitors drive right on by, wanting to expedite travels down the road. The Hope cutoff at Milepost 56.7 of the Seward Highway beckons with its views of rapid Six-Mile Creek (really a river) and Turnagain Arm in the distance, so if you have a few hours to spare, Hope is worth the 16.5-mile side trip. Home to 200 or so year-round residents and a handful of recreational cabin owners, Hope offers quaint exposure to gold-mining days and the quiet hospitality of Alaskans. Visit the Discovery Cafe for a soft drink served in a jelly jar and some fabulous clam chowder, then stop by the Sunrise Historical and Mining Museum or the library, where interesting items related to mining, fishing, and homesteading are on display. If you have time to take a hike, try the Gull Rock trail from Porcupine Campground, a 10-mile round-trip hike that is easily done in smaller sections with kids. It's always fun to gaze across Turnagain Arm toward the Seward Highway and look back at a road just traveled.

Summit Lake Lodge (www.summitlakelodge.com) at Milepost 45.5 is another solid rest stop. It's right along the Seward Highway, against tranquil Summit Lake, perfect for a little bit of wading or fishing. Summit Lake Lodge is the site of a seasonal restaurant (open Memorial Day through Labor Day), rooms, and small coffee stand/gift shop. If you have time, swing around the northeast side of the lodge and lake to the U.S. Forest Service Tenderfoot campground and a newly renovated picnic area.

Seward Highway meets up with the Sterling Highway at Milepost 37 and at this junction lies **Tern Lake**, a popular place for photos with towering mountains in the background. Sometimes swans can be spotted sailing around the still water with arctic terns, and the occasional moose will browse willow thickets of the shoreline. Look high in the treetops for bald eagles, too.

Kenai Lake will take up much of the view around Milepost 23. This 24-mile lake holds greenish-blue water caused by glacial silt, so lovely that even the most car-weary kid will sit up and take notice.

Seward is located at Milepost 0, creating a fun game of backwards counting that sure beats "99 Bottles of Beer on the Wall." Drive right to Milepost 0 at the head of Resurrection Bay and begin your Seward adventure.

Train

A very popular mode of transportation to Seward is the **Alaska Railroad**'s Coastal Classic train (www.alaskarailroad.com, 800-544-0552). The four-and-a-half-hour journey starts early for southbound departures, around 6:45 a.m., but the crack-of-dawn wake-up call is worth every minute of lost sleep.

> **KIDSPEAK**
>
> That train is loud. Yep.
> —Charlotte, age two

Offering two classes of train travel—Goldstar (first-class style) and Adventure (for the rest of us)—the Alaska Railroad treats all passengers

The Alaska Railroad Coastal Classic makes its way through a mountain pass on the way to Seward.

to fine dining, access to dome cars, and great service by staff and high school students trained by a local vocational program to act as tour guides.

The Coastal Classic runs daily mid-May through mid-September. Passengers depart from the downtown Anchorage depot at 6:45 a.m. and arrive in Seward anywhere between 11:30 a.m. and noon, depending upon delays of the mechanical or wildlife kind (remember, this is Alaska). Most hotels offer shuttle service from the small Seward depot, as will cruise lines (the dock is a short but difficult distance from the depot for those with small kids and luggage). Hertz (www.rentacaralaska.com, 800-654-3131) operates a small rental-car agency near the depot.

The train departs Seward each day at 6 p.m. and arrives in Anchorage at 10:15 p.m. the same evening.

VISITOR INFORMATION

The Seward Chamber of Commerce and Convention and Visitors Bureau (www.seward.com, 907-224-8051) is located on the west side of the Seward Highway, just as you enter town. Stop in for their newest visitor guide and current information about attractions and events going on around the community.

MEDICAL CARE

Seward has one hospital and medical center, **Providence Seward Medical Center**, located at 417 First Ave. (www.alaska.providence.org/locations/psmcc, 907-224-5205).

LODGING

Seward's blessing and curse is its popularity with both Alaska residents and Outside visitors, thanks to a close proximity to Anchorage. Summertime sees droves of Alaskans for great fishing, camping, hiking, and the frenetic buzz generated by the Mount Marathon race each Fourth of July. Add to the mix a flotilla of cruise ships, and this city of almost 3,000 swells to gazillions from May through September. Fortunately, however, the community also has options, ranging from tent camping to comfortable hotels.

HOTELS/MOTELS

Seward Windsong Lodge $$$
Mile 0.5 Exit Glacier Rd./Herman Leirer Rd., Seward, AK 99664
(877) 777-4079
www.sewardwindsong.com

Along the Resurrection River, Seward Windsong Lodge is owned and operated by an Alaska Native Corporation that takes great pride in providing guests with excellent service. The property's 180 guest rooms are spread out among several buildings, and come standard with a small flat-screen television, wireless Internet, hair dryers, and coffee makers. A standard room features two queen beds and an outdoor entrance; some rooms have outdoor decks. Suite rooms feature two queen beds and an extra-long twin. Accessible rooms are available, but make reservations well in advance. The property also provides a free shuttle into town and offers guided hikes at nearby Exit Glacier. The lodge is part of the Kenai Fjords Tour company; ask about day trips at the front desk when you check in, or visit the links on the lodge's website. The Resurrection Roadhouse restaurant is on site.

Thumbs-up for: Forested location, great service, easy arrangements for activities.

Holiday Inn Express—Seward Harbor $$$
1412 Fourth Ave., Seward, AK 99664
(800) 315-2621
www.hiexpress.com/hotels

If location matters, this place is handy. Located on the Seward Harbor, the hotel features both standard rooms and suites, some with a glimpse of Mount Marathon and surrounding peaks and others with views of the Small Boat Harbor. Amenities include the only hotel pool in Seward and a breakfast bar. Wireless Internet is also available. The property is close to popular activities like glacier and wildlife cruising, fishing, or visiting the Kenai Fjords National Park headquarters, all located in a cluster of shops right out the door. Downtown is a short walk via the town's paved trail and so is the Alaska Railroad depot.

Thumbs-up for: Small swimming pool, continental breakfast served daily, proximity to Small Boat Harbor.

Breeze Inn $$
303 North Harbor Dr., Seward, AK 99664
(888) 224-5237
www.breezeinn.com

Also close to the Small Boat Harbor, Breeze Inn underwent a remodel in 2008 to add 22 Executive rooms that offer sweeping views of the surrounding landscape. With 100 rooms, the Breeze Inn provides access to activities, dining in their on-property restaurant, and rates more affordable than other, higher-end hotels nearby. Sixty of the rooms offer two double beds, and accessible lodging is also available. A solid option for families wishing to have a nice place to crash at the end of a busy day.

Thumbs-up for: Reasonable rates, even in the summer months, and access to the boat harbor's activities.

Harborview Inn $$
804 Third Ave., Seward, AK 99664
(888) 324-3217
info@sewardhotel.com, www.sewardhotel.com

Clean and charmingly decorated, the Harborview Inn is a value's value. Located in the heart of downtown, the property is a great choice for larger families. With large suites and even an apartment (a few blocks away), families will find plenty of elbow room. The suites and apartment have dishwashers and kitchens, perfect for saving a few dollars in the food budget. All of the 30 standard rooms and the suites offer wireless Internet, and the inn also offers a free shuttle service from the cruise ship dock or railroad depot.

Thumbs-up for: Larger accommodations and location, location, location.

Cabins

Serenity By the Sea Cabins $$$
14000 Shady Lane, Seward, AK 99664
(877) 239-3637
info@serenitybytheseacabins.com, www.serenitybytheseacabins.com

This cluster of three cabins is located around the corner from downtown Seward on Lowell Point, a distance of about two miles. Access to town is easy, however, with water taxi, bike, or your own vehicle, and there is something to be said for staying farther away from the hustle and bustle of Seward during the summer months. Each cabin offers sleeping arrangements for four to six people, a kitchen, and a gas grill. Reservations are accepted from the end of May through the end of August.

Thumbs-up for: Easy access to beaches, fishing, and hiking.

Seward Alaska Cabins $$
Exit Glacier/Herman Leirer Rd., Seward, AK 99664
(907) 224-6040
www.sewardalaskacabins.com

With a full-service restaurant next door, these little cabins are located two miles from Seward, right after the turn onto Exit Glacier Road. Four cabins, each housing four to six adults, feature cable TV, microwaves, a small refrigerator, and a coffee maker. Close enough to town to make it easy to access if you have transportation, but far enough away you'll escape the noise.

Thumbs-up for: Restaurant next door, quaint decor and style, away from downtown. Also quite reasonable in price.

Camping

Miller's Landing
Miller's Lowell Point
P.O. Box 81, Seward, AK 99664
(907) 224-5739
millerslanding@alaska.com

Located two miles from downtown, Miller's Landing offers either beach-side or forest camping with views of Resurrection Bay and access to hiking, boating, and fishing. Both RV and tent sites are available, and the best feature on-the-beach hookups and access to a mile of rocky shoreline. Restrooms, showers, RV hookups, a small store (with free coffee), and the option of a water taxi service to and from downtown Seward make Miller's Landing a fun spot. Take a hike along one of the nearby trails or watch a raft of otters float past; it's all here. $26/night tent, $36/night RV, based upon four-person occupancy ($5/additional person). Reservations recommended.

Thumbs-up for: Water taxi, lots of beach space, access to recreation.

Seward Municipal Campgrounds
City of Seward Parks and Recreation Department
702 Aspen Lane, Seward, AK 99664
(907) 224-4055
www.cityofseward.net/parksrec

The City of Seward maintains six municipal campgrounds within the city limits, 99 sites of which are designated as utility sites with water and electricity. Tents are always allowed, as are small recreational vehicles within the space confines. At just $10/tent, $15 for dry RV sites, the city campgrounds can be a real bargain, too. The utility sites are $30/night, competitive with other privately owned campgrounds. With the exception of the Forest Acres campground (tent only), campgrounds are located along the waterline of downtown Seward and close to community activities. The Seward Bike Path is right at your feet, as is the wonderful Seward Community Playground. A major drawback, however, can be the noise—tough for parents with small children. But if you're of the mind-set not to care, the community campgrounds can be a wonderful option for their accessibility. No reservations except for caravans of 10 or more RVs.

Thumbs-up for: Economy and proximity to downtown activities.

Exit Glacier Campground
Kenai Fjords National Park
Mile 8.5 Herman Leier Rd. (Exit Glacier Rd.), Seward, AK 99664

If your family tent camps on a fairly regular basis and can be self-sufficient for any length of time, consider the Exit Glacier Campground. The area's 12 sites are tent-only and offer nothing in the way of amenities or services, not even picnic tables. There is, however, a bear locker for all food and smelly items, and it must be used to keep frequently spotted bruins from invading your gear. Located a short distance from the Exit Glacier Visitor Center, the area offers some great hiking nearby and a healthy dose of relaxation time. No reservations. Tent sites are free. Cabins start at $119/night.

Thumbs-up for: A truly remote location, away from any hustle and bustle of Seward.

Other Lodging

Seward Military Resort
2305 Dimond Blvd., Seward, AK 99664
(800) 770-1858
www.sewardresort.com

With the nation's highest number of veterans per capita, Alaska supports its active-duty and retired military in a variety of ways. The Seward Military Resort is a collection of hotel rooms, townhouses, and camping options a short drive from downtown. Forty tent and RV sites and six yurts make up the camping area in a quiet, forested area well maintained by the military's Family Services Center. Accessible to all active-duty, retired military, or DOD civilians, the resort can arrange activities, fishing charters, or day trips, and even hosts special events on a regular basis. Rooms and camping sites vary in price and are based upon rank/grade, so call ahead for specifics.

Thumbs-up for: Activities, tours, well-maintained grounds and buildings.

STORES/GROCERIES

Seward has one official grocery store, Carrs/Safeway, located on the west side of the Seward Highway as you enter town (1907 Seward Highway, 907-224-6900). Groceries, pharmacy, bakery, deli, and a coffee shop. Open daily, 5 a.m.–midnight. Carrs/Safeway is also a great place to pick up an Alaska TourSaver coupon book, available in the customer service area of all stores throughout the state.

Pick a Picnic Instead!

Sometimes when traveling for extended periods with my crew, I tend to become a little weary of dining out. Between eating food I didn't cook and wrangling an overtired and active child, some nights I simply tell my husband to point the car to the nearest deli. No deli? Many Alaska restaurants offer takeout for busy seasonal workers, so take their hint and grab a meal to go and head to one of Seward's parks or docks for breakfast, lunch, or dinner alfresco. Good spots include the Seward Community Playground along the bike path or near the Small Boat Harbor, where kids can see fishing and tour boats come and go. Another option is a drive up Exit Glacier Road; hang out in the parking lot of the Visitor Center for a tailgate party. My kids always love swigging their chocolate milk from the curb, then dashing into the little forested area to investigate rocks and bugs while my husband and I recline on camp chairs in utter bliss. Whatever your choice, take advantage of an opportunity *not* to say, "Sit down and be patient!"

FEEDING THE FAMILY

For such a small city, Seward has plenty of good eatin' establishments catering to a variety of appetites and tastes. Seafood dominates the market, as it should, but one can also find a nice variety of filling, kid-pleasing dining options as well.

Restaurants

Resurrection Roadhouse $$-$$$

Mile 0.5 Exit Glacier Rd./Herman Leirer Rd., Seward, AK 99664
(877) 777-4079
www.sewardwindsong.com/resurrection-roadhouse.html
Open daily 6 a.m.–10 p.m. (May–September)

Resurrection Roadhouse features classic Alaska specialties and a lively menu. Part of the campus of Seward Windsong Lodge, this seasonal restaurant provides a great kids' menu, too, complete with a coloring page of interesting Alaska facts. Big burgers, chicken, fish and chips, pasta, and some awesome sweet potato fries are hot items. Also serves breakfast and lunch.

Apollo Restaurant $$-$$$

229 Fourth Ave., Seward, AK 99664
(907) 224-3092
www.apollorestaurantak.com
Open year-round, call for hours

A sort of Greek-Italian place, Apollo is conveniently located in downtown Seward and serves up international flair to this fishing village. With its huge menu and friendly service, the restaurant's somewhat dated (but always clean) interior is forgotten as diners dig into selections like lasagna, pizza, and enormous calzones, not to mention gyros and an awesome eggplant sandwich. Kids can choose ravioli, spaghetti, or just split a plate of noodles; staff here are pretty accommodating.

Exit Glacier Salmon Bake $$

Exit Glacier/Herman Leirer Rd., Seward, AK 99664
(907) 224-2204
www.sewardalaskacabins.com
Open May–September, call for hours

Located just after the Exit Glacier turnoff from the Seward Highway, the Exit Glacier Salmon Bake restaurant is a delightful family dining experience. Salmon and halibut are the stars here for sure, but burgers, salads, sandwiches, and a nice baby-back rib dinner can be had for a reasonable price. A fine children's menu features all the favs like corndogs and grilled-cheese sandwiches. A full line-up of Alaska beers also makes this a fun stop for mom and dad, who might enjoy a cold one after a busy day of fishing or hiking.

The Smokehouse/The Shack $-$$
411 Port Ave., Seward, AK 99664
(907) 224-7427
Open all year, but hours vary

This eclectic array of old Alaska Railroad cars housing a small overnight establishment and two take-away restaurants can be off-putting to some. After all, it's a little funky, a little worn, but folks who visit swear by the place. It's all about comfort food here; try the smoked burger, pork sandwich, or chicken burrito, favorites among our family of hearty eaters.

FAMILY FUN IN SEWARD

With so much hustle and bustle in Seward, it's no wonder most guests spend their entire visit in the downtown area. Day cruises, walking tours, museums—the possibilities are many, but in our opinion, no trip to Seward with kids would be complete without venturing away from the city's boundaries for some in-depth exploration of this fascinating side of the Kenai Peninsula. The following pages offer some of our favorite destinations within easy driving distance from downtown Seward, in addition to the most popular attractions you should see anyway.

Museums and Cultural Experiences

Seward Museum/Resurrection Bay Historical Society
336 Third Ave., Seward, AK 99664
(907) 224-3902
Open daily 10 a.m.–5 p.m. (May–September)
Admission: $2/adults, $.50/kids five and over; free for kids under five.

Seward has but one actual museum and it's not exactly designed for kids. However, older children (age nine and up) might be impressed by two films describing the history of Seward and the famous Iditarod trail, both shown daily. The small museum also features a number of interesting ivory carvings and Native Alaskan baskets. If you're around near the end of August, the museum's annual Open House honors the founding of Seward in 1903. Volunteers provide walking tours and special showings of exhibits during that time.

Alaska SeaLife Center

310 Railway Ave., Seward, AK 99664
(907) 224-6300
www.alaskasealife.org, visitaslc@alaskasealife.org
Admission: $20/adults, $15/students 12–15 (or with ID), $10/kids 4–11
Open daily 9 a.m.–6 p.m.

Alaska's only public aquarium and ocean wildlife rescue center, the SeaLife Center uses a "window on the sea" approach to exhibits and education.

Located at the end of the Seward Highway at Milepost 0, the SeaLife Center is easy to find—popular both with cruisers and as a field-trip destination for local schools and day camps.

Note: Visit toward the end of the day, when cruisers have

> **KIDSPEAK**
>
> I like the boat at the SeaLife Center. And the seals.
> —Abby, age seven

Try an Up-Close Encounter!

If you have extra time and a few extra dollars, your older kids will enjoy a SeaLife Center behind-the-scenes tour. Three experiences are offered: Puffin, Octopus, and Marine Mammal (age requirements vary, so ask when you make reservations). Kids even get to feed some of these marine wonder-creatures! Call (888) 378-2525 for information and reservations. Prices range from $10 to $79, depending upon the tour, in addition to regular admission.

returned to their ships and day campers to their parents, creating a calmer atmosphere by which to experience the animals, birds, and aquatic life.

Don't miss the salmon tanks housing Alaska's five salmon species, or the aviary, where a flirty Tufted Puffin named Fabio awaits your presence. Kids like Woody the sea lion, too, but my favorite is the giant Pacific octopus, who always manages to squeeze himself or herself (they change up who gets the tank) into a corner for a little nap. A touch tank is available nearby for a little hands-on activity, too.

Kenai Fjords National Park Information Center

1212 Fourth Ave. (Small Boat Harbor), Seward, AK 99664
(907) 224-7500, (907) 422-0500
www.nps.gov/kefj
Open May–September 8:30 a.m.–7 p.m. Hours vary the rest of the year, so visit the park website for specific times.

Kenai Fjords National Park sits at the edge of the North Pacific Ocean and is one of the few Alaska national parks where visitors can access its natural wonders in a variety of ways. Glaciers are the crowning glory of this beautiful wilderness, with the Harding Icefield capping the 36-plus glacial rivers of ice that have uniquely shaped the landscape. Kenai Fjords National Park also requires careful attention, as its wildlife and environment can be harsh, no matter the season.

Stop by the **Park Information Center** for maps, reading material, videos, and interpretive displays about the flora and fauna of this beautiful area. Kayakers will want to stop in here before they put their boats in the water; changing iceberg patterns and weather can stymie even the most experienced paddlers. Plus, it's fun to chat with the rangers about itineraries and ideas; many of them spend their off hours exploring, too.

Seavey's Ididaride Sled Dog Tours

Mile 1.1 Old Exit Glacier Rd., Seward, AK 99664
(907) 224-8607
www.idiaride.com, info@idiaride.com
Summer tours open mid-May through mid-September
Admission: Tickets for 1.5-hour tour, $69/adult, $34.50/kids 2–11
Tour times: 8:30 a.m., 10 a.m., 11:45 a.m., 1:45 p.m., 3:30 p.m., 6 p.m.

Owned and operated by one of the first families of dog mushing, Ididaride is a fun all-ages tour just outside of Seward. Take a cart ride behind a team of sled dogs, cuddle pups, and try on heavy arctic clothing necessary for mushing at −40°F. Ididaride offers other tours, too; their all-day Explore Seward tour explains area history and how dog mushing factored into the success of Alaska. Lunch is included in this tour that is best suited for older children with a real interest in dog mushing and Alaska history. Bring suitable clothing on all tours; you'll be outside for the majority of activities.

> **PARENT PRO TIP**
>
> Bring a snack and some quiet activities for younger children; they may need something with which to stay occupied during the presentation. That said, our family loved visiting the Seavey kennels!
>
> —Christy, Homer mother of two

Seasickness and Kids

Not everyone has the internal constitution of Captain Cook. While most day cruise companies use modern, double-hulled catamarans that minimize rocking and rolling upon the ocean blue, some people, regardless of the conditions, find themselves queasy. We are fans of Dramamine tablets that, when taken in the proper dosage well before a trip, can cut way down on seasickness. Follow the instruction label carefully, and check with your pediatrician to be sure your kiddos meet the age/weight criteria before administering. Other remedies include soda crackers (available on many tours), ginger ale or ginger candy, or purchase of sea bands, little wrist bands with focus on a pressure point that supposedly cuts down on at-sea nausea. Eat lightly, keep hydrated, and try to stay outside, too. If you've never taken a boat ride with your kids and are at all questioning the staying power of their lunch, start with a short, around-the-bay cruise and see how they do—and ask your tour provider if they offer a "no seasickness guarantee," just in case.

Glacier and Wildlife Cruises

Seward is well known for its day cruises. Along with Whittier, Seward has access to cruises ranging from three to nine hours, with a variety of opportunities to see wildlife and those beautiful glaciers.

Day cruising with kids can either be a fabulous occasion to educate and inspire your offspring or a long experience to be endured. Knowing the facts of a particular tour, your route, and even a bit of the operator's experience with children goes a long way toward a pleasant cruise. Day tours are suitable for children preschool age and up. Infants small enough to remain in their car seats or in a pack do well, but crawlers and early walkers will almost certainly become frustrated by the lack of space. Listed below are tour companies in Seward with solid reputations for kid-friendliness.

Kenai Fjords Tours
1304 Fourth Ave., Seward, AK 99664
(877) 777-4051
www.kenaifjords.com,
info@kenaifjords.com
Prices range from $90/adults, $47/kids for the shorter cruises to $144/adults, $70/kids for longer cruises. Inquire for your specific tour.

With eight cruises available to day-tripping visitors, Kenai Fjords Tours excursions range from the 2.5-hour Spring Resurrection Bay Tour late February through early March to the spectacular Northwestern Fjord Tour that delves deep into Kenai Fjords National Park. Most guests with children choose the six- or eight-hour national park cruises. With the help of on-board wilderness guides, kids can look for humpback whales, orcas,

Getting silly at Seward's small boat harbor.

and sea lions while cruising toward the park and Alaska Maritime National Wildlife Refuge. Three trips are offered each day, departing at 8 a.m., 10 a.m., and 11:30 a.m. Lunch is served on all, with a buffet dinner available on the 10 a.m. departure at Fox Island, owned by CIRI Tourism (parent company to Kenai Fjords Tours).

Another popular trip is the 4.5-hour Resurrection Bay Tour with a short stop at Fox Island and salmon or prime rib buffet. It's a nice combo of sea and land, and the food is spectacular. The advantage of this trip is its short duration, but since the boat will stay in the sheltered area of Resurrection Bay, one might not see the variety of wildlife found farther out. Ask about their combination fishing/Fox Island trip, too.

Major Marine Tours

1302-B Fourth Ave., Seward, AK 99664
(907) 224-8030, (800) 764-7300
Admission: $69/adults, $39/kids 2–11 for half-day cruises to $159/adults, $79.50/kids for longer tours

Major Marine has a unique spread of tours, including a Signature Cruise lineup featuring the six-hour Kenai Fjords cruise and a shorter half-day tour of Resurrection Bay for either four or five hours. Families unsure of their children's staying power on a boat might want to choose this company. Unlike Kenai Fjords Tours, however, Major Marine charges extra for meals, at $19/adults, $9/kids 2–11. Trips generally depart Seward throughout the day, an advantage for families wishing to indulge in other sightseeing adventures before boarding the boat.

Major Marine cruises also provides park rangers on board every tour, and kids can earn the National Park Service–wide Junior Ranger badge at the end of the cruise.

OUTDOOR RECREATION

Hiking

Caines Head State Recreation Area is located on Lowell Point (near Miller's Landing campground and cabins), a mere two miles from Seward. Caines Head has a great black sand beach to sink one's toes to the depths and nice hiking with views of Resurrection Bay. Try the historic North Beach hike from Lowell Point, a distance of 4.5 miles that can only be traversed at low tide, a highlight for kids. Look for the old army dock that survived the 1964 earthquake and have lunch at the picnic shelter before heading back. Best for kids age seven and up, or all ages if you stay near the beach area by the entrance.

Fishing Is King

Fish are the reason hordes of grown-ups descend upon the Kenai Peninsula every summer. With a slightly maniacal gleam in their eye, people from all walks of life and every corner of the world spend hundreds and sometimes thousands of dollars in the attempt to hook their limit of Alaska's most golden natural resource—fish. Be they chunky, funky halibut from the bottom of the bay or one of the five species of salmon making their way upstream to spawn (known as the run), fishing is big biz on the Kenai Peninsula.

There are two ways to catch fish in Alaska. The first and most fascinating to watch is commonly referred to as combat fishing, whereby anglers stand shoulder-to-shoulder and sometimes even closer than that, trying to entice an angry salmon to bite. It's absolutely crazy, in my opinion, and unless your family are practiced fishers, it's also very difficult.

The second method involves chartering a boat and motoring out into the saltwater of Resurrection Bay or beyond, depending upon tides,

Exit Glacier, part of Kenai Fjords National Park (www.nps.gov/kefj), is perhaps the most-hiked stretch of forest in Seward. Easily accessible with lots to see, Exit Glacier gives kids a sense of accomplishment as they round the last corners of a switchback and spy the enormous, glaring field of ice before them. Reach Exit Glacier and the visitor center along Exit Glacier Road two miles north of Seward. Follow the road 8.6 miles to the visitor center, stop inside for a map, and choose your family-friendly trail. The visitor center also has information on the Art for Parks backpack program, whereby kids can draw Exit Glacier and turn it in for a prize, or the popular Junior Naturalist program. The Nature Center Trail, a one-mile accessible loop, is perfect for toddlers and preschoolers; turn left at the trailside kiosk to continue along the Toe of the Glacier and Glacier's Edge trails. Take water and snacks, dress for chilly winds coming off the glacier itself, and be constantly bear-aware at all times. The higher trails are suitable for kids ages five and up, as there is no stroller access for higher trails; bring a front pack or backpack instead.

weather, and the intestinal fortitude of passengers. Many of these charters operate under the simple half-day or full-day rule, meaning that, at the least, your kids will be subject to four hours of rocking and rolling with other fishermen and -women who may not share your values of "time well spent." These folks want fish and charters want their money, so boats won't come back to the harbor until the limit is reached for every paying passenger.

Best bets for kids? Visit the Alaska Department of Fish and Game's website (www.adfg.alaska.gov/index.cfm?adfg=fishing.main) for a complete listing of where, when, and what kinds of fish are suitable for smaller anglers. Our son loves to find a stocked lake and cast his little fishin' pole for rainbow trout, and many opportunities exist for kids in Alaska. ADF&G also hosts a Rod Loaner program, whereby kids can borrow a rod and reel for a day or two, perfect for the visiting family. We'll talk more about Alaska's fish later in this chapter, in the section on Homer.

Kayaking

Sunny Cove Sea Kayaking offers a variety of day trips for young kayakers and their parents, with a minimum age of eight. Choose from three locations—Kenai Fjords National Park, Lowell Point, or nearby Fox Island, each of which provides wonderful opportunities for viewing wildlife, checking out rocky shorelines, and plenty of paddle time. Trips start around $70/per person. If you have big kids, ask about overnight paddles that venture farther out into the wild and wonderful Kenai Fjords National Park, or combine hiking and kayaking adventures (www.sunnycove.com, 800-770-9119, 907-224-4426).

Biking

The greater Seward area offers a multitude of mountain bike trails suitable for most solid riders. If you have tweens and teens, take them on a guided trip through the forest with **Seward Bike Tours** (www.sewardbiketours .com). From trips up the Resurrection River to exploring the forested areas near town, adventures are the stuff of cool cellphone photos to friends.

Many Anchorage rental shops will outfit riders for multiple days and might offer an even better deal if you simply want to explore on your own. Riding the paved, flat trail along Seward's waterfront is the perfect way for a family to explore the community without worrying about searching for a parking lot in the often-crowded harbor areas. Do make sure the rental company provides you with a lock, however.

Other Fun

Seward boasts some fabulous options for free playtime. Try the newish **Seward Community Playground,** next to the Seward Campground. Right on the water with a spectacular view of Resurrection Bay and soaring mountains, it can't be beat for ambiance. Constructed by residents, the playground also has a skate park for older kids who need to shred or pipe-line or whatever it is they call it these days.

Seward Elementary School (Diamond Blvd. and Sea Lion Ave.) is located directly behind the Seward Military Resort, just outside the main downtown area. A favorite destination for our son, the school playground (during nonschool hours, of course) fea-tures interesting equipment and wide, grassy fields. Make sure everyone has used the bathroom before you visit, however, as no facilities are available. We always bring water and a few snacks, too.

> **KIDSPEAK**
>
> Seward has the best playground there! I get to go on slides, play on swings, and go into a fire truck and the train and school bus, too.
>
> —Susannah, age four and a half

Sterling Highway: Soldotna, Kenai, and Homer

After a visit to Seward, many families simply call it good and head back to Anchorage, thinking they've seen all there is on the Kenai Peninsula. However, remember the junction at Tern Lake a few miles back along the Seward Highway?

The Sterling Highway is the only road linking the communities of Soldotna, Kenai, Homer, and others to the big city of Anchorage, and as a result many folks consider this area of the Kenai Peninsula to be perfect. They're not alone, either. Cabins and camping property dot the entire length of the Sterling Highway, and people spend days and days fishing, hiking, clamming, and relaxing.

From the Tern Lake Junction, the Sterling Highway stretches 142 miles to the town of Homer.

GETTING THERE

Flying

It is possible to fly to Kenai/Soldotna and Homer, but why would you? It costs a bundle and unless time is of the essence, you'll get more out of your peninsula experience by driving. However, if you do fly, PenAir (www.penair.com), Grant Aviation (www.flygrant.com), and Era Alaska (www.flyera.com) all have service from Anchorage.

Driving

With so many areas to explore, allow at least five hours to drive from Anchorage to Homer and at least three or four to drive from Seward. Sterling Highway is a narrow, mostly two-lane road that becomes choked with cars, RVs, and people hoping to catch a glimpse of a feeding bear, fishing tourist, or browsing moose, much to the dismay of the tractor-trailer behind them hoping to make it to his delivery on time.

Cooper Landing is the first town you'll pass through after the Tern Lake Junction. Beginning at Milepost 48, Cooper Landing is situated along the shores of beautiful Kenai Lake and the rushing Kenai River. It's a salmon-fishing town all right, with a handful of cabins and year-round residents who work hard to keep their little roadside community

K'beq Footprints Cultural Site

If you have time, stop by this wonderful example of Alaska Native culture at Milepost 52.6, directly across from the Russian River campground. Operated by the Dena'ina Athabascan Kenaitze Indian tribe, the K'beq Footprints (www.kenaitze.org/Kbeq, 907-283-3633) site is open daily May through September, usually in the afternoons. Here, walk a nature trail, meet Alaska Native storytellers, and learn about connections to land, water, and the people who have lived here for centuries.

The small community of **Sterling** at Mile 81 is not much more than a pass-through, but it does have homesteading history and a few of the pull-out interpretive signs are interesting to read.

Soldotna, at Mile 94, is a junction to the town of Kenai (via the Kenai Spur Highway, around 11 miles) and the last place to fuel up, stock up, and feed the kids before making the last push to Homer. It's a busy place, and fishing is definitely the activity of choice, but there are a few family fun spots to take a break or even stay overnight if you just can't drive anymore.

thriving. Stop at the Sunrise Inn (www.alaskasunriseinn.com) for an enormous breakfast with local flavor, then drive a short distance south to Quartz Creek Campground/Picnic area (www.usfs.gov), where the sandy shores of Kenai Lake make for the perfect rest stop. If you have time, visit the quaint **Cooper Landing Museum** (www.cooperlandingmuseum.com), where two historic buildings full of Kenai Peninsula history await your inspection. Youngsters will enjoy the full bear skeleton assembled by local schoolkids, and all will appreciate the homesteader's cabin.

If viewing the river from a boat sounds exciting, try **Alaska Wildland Adventures** (www.alaskawildland.com, 800-334-8730). A two-hour float of the upper Kenai River is full of opportunities to see wildlife, fish, and scenery. Plan to spend around $54 plus tax per person, kids 5–11 $34 plus tax. Alaska Wildland also offers other multiday trips from their very intimate (and very exclusive) lodges, but their service and knowledge is worth investigating. Best for kids five and up.

Around Mile 52, you'll enter the realm of every fisher's dream. The **Russian River** is home to thousands of salmon and at least as many folks jostling to catch them. Stop in at Bing's Landing or the turnout where a small ferry transports people across the river to prime fishing spots. You might even spot a bear splashing up and down the river, but be wary! Park in designated areas and watch for cars; this place is a madhouse in the summertime.

MEDICAL CARE

Central Peninsula Hospital is located in Soldotna (250 Hospital Place, www.cpgh.org, 907-262-4404).

LODGING

Try the **Aspen Hotel** (www.aspenhotelsak.com, 907-260-7736), located along the Sterling Highway right above the Kenai River and in the middle of all the action. With a free breakfast, Wi-Fi, and indoor swimming pool, it's a great place to hang out while other family members are fishing (trust us).

Centennial Park and Campground (www.ci.soldotna.ak.us/centennial) is a nice option for families who are RV or tent camping. This first-come, first-served campground near Kalifornsky Beach Road has beautiful access to the river via a raised boardwalk and 176 wooded campsites.

FEEDING THE FAMILY

Moose Is Loose Bakery $
44278 Sterling Highway, Soldotna, AK
(907) 260-3036

For coffee and some of the yummiest baked goods for miles, stop in at this bakery along the main drag (Sterling Highway) of Soldotna, in a little strip mall. Homemade goodies and coffee will inspire even the most tired traveler to keep on going.

Don't Forget Kenai!

The Community of Kenai juts into Cook Inlet along the Kenai Spur Highway, about 11 miles from Soldotna. As with many other peninsula communities, Russian influence is strong here and visitors will see the first of many "onion-top" churches denoting the Russian Orthodox faith. But Kenai actually began as a Native Alaskan village, where the Dena'ina people settled on the *kena*, or flat meadow lands, quietly living life with few interruptions. Russian fur and fishing traders found this area to their liking as well and in the mid-1800s set up their own system for trade and commerce. They brought more than fur and fish, however; a smallpox epidemic in 1838–1839 wiped out half the local Native population and forever shaped the beliefs of Dena'ina Native people toward the white man.

The discovery of oil in the 20th century brought a new prosperity to Kenai and a road to Anchorage. Today the city of Kenai boasts just over 7,000 residents over a 29-square-mile swath of land. It is known for its fishing connections and rich cultural traditions and is worth checking out if you have a few hours to spare. The view, especially, is worth a stop, since

St. Elias Brewery $$-$$$
434 Sharkathmi Ave., Soldotna, AK
(907) 260-7837
www.steliasbrewingco.com

St. Elias Brewery is a great place to stop for lunch or dinner. With a box of coloring books and a vibrant menu suitable for the whole family (not to mention craft ales) the brewery serves up a little oasis of sanity after a busy day. Try their homemade rustic pizza, it's delish!

Stores/Groceries

Fred Meyer
43843 Sterling Highway, Soldotna, AK 99669
(907) 260-2200

The one-stop shopping center for food, fuel, and supplies. The store also has a deli, liquor store, and coffee shop.

Note: This is the cheapest gas on the Kenai Peninsula, so fill up here.

four active volcanoes (Mounts Redoubt, Spurr, Iliamna, and Augustine) all reside across the waters from Kenai along the Alaska Peninsula and occasionally belch ash and steam from their tops.

Visit **Holy Assumption Russian Orthodox Church** for a look into the past. This lovely little church near Mission and Overland Streets is one of the oldest churches in Alaska, with a bell tower and typical high, square roof of such places of worship. It's free to visit the outer grounds of the church, but unless clergy are present, guests are generally not admitted inside.

The whole family will enjoy a stop at the **Diamond M Ranch Resort** (48500 Diamond M Ranch Rd., www.diamondmranch.com, stay@diamondmranch.com, 866-283-9424), a small but charming RV park and hotel with true kid appeal. From the antique cars to the small herd of horses, cows, and llamas, Diamond M is, frankly, one of the best reasons to take a time-out in the Soldotna/Kenai area. The resort offers scheduled activities on a daily basis, run by the family who is lucky enough to own this family-friendly resort. They'll also help you find fishing charters.

FAMILY FUN IN SOLDOTNA

The **Soldotna Chamber of Commerce** is located along the Sterling Highway. Stop by for maps, brochures, and maybe even some fishing advice. This is, after all, the city where the world-record king salmon was caught, at a whopping 97 pounds, 4 ounces in 1985. Find the chamber offices at 44790 Sterling Highway (www.soldotnachamber.com, 907-262-9814).

Near the entrance to Centennial Park is the **Soldotna Historical Museum and Historic Homestead Village.** Show kids the lifestyle of a typical Alaska homesteader, with tools, clothing, and a furnished log home. It's free, too, and a great stop along the way to further Kenai Peninsula adventures. Open 10 a.m–4 p.m. Tuesday–Saturday, 12–4 p.m. Sunday. Suitable for all ages.

The **Kenai National Wildlife Refuge Visitor Center** (www.kenai .fws.gov, 907-262-7021), located on Ski Hill Road in Soldotna, is the best place to learn more about this section of the peninsula. A short, one-mile nature trail is an excellent option for kids wanting to stretch their legs (as is a longer two-mile trail for those wanting more), as are the exhibits and free programs. Open 8 a.m.–5 p.m. Monday through Friday, 9 a.m.–5 p.m. Saturday–Sunday from May through August. Open 8 a.m.–4:30 p.m. Monday through Friday from October through May. Suitable for all ages, but school-agers will enjoy more than younger children.

The **Soldotna Community Playground**, similar to Seward's beautiful structure, is always a nice stop. Find it at Soldotna Creek Park, taking a left on States Avenue when traveling along the Sterling Highway from Anchorage. Picnicking is great here, too. For all ages.

> ### KIDSPEAK
>
> One of our first RV trips was to Ninilchik, and it was cool to stay right on the beach to fish and dig clams.
>
> —Matt, age 18

Clam Gulch lives up to its name. At Milepost 118, its fame comes from the beautiful (and delicious) Pacific razor clams you can dig up with a license, tide book (found at any store in Southcentral Alaska), clam shovel, and a bit of patience. Follow highway signs to Clam

Gulch proper, dropping down a steep dirt road to the beach below (RVers, heed all warnings along the highway stating the risks of attempting a gravel road). Walk the beach, watch clam enthusiasts, or collect shells; from here on out the beaches are tons of fun for children. Pay attention to tides and cliffs, however, since both are unpredictable.

The small village of **Ninilchik** sits at Milepost 118 and can be identified by the small bright-white Russian Orthodox church overlooking the village. Visit the church grounds before driving below to the actual village; it's a lovely view and a pristine site for photos. Ninilchik is the starting point for some 50 miles of ocean fishing, through both private boaters and charter companies. A small but thriving community, Ninilchik's old village can be accessed through a right turn from the Sterling Highway at Milepost 118 (watch for the sign as you cross the Ninilchik River); the rest of the town sits above the village and features a number of small stores, coffee shops, the local school, and a tiny library. Ninilchik does, however, host the Kenai Peninsula State Fair each August, a fun event that has all the favorites (funnel cakes, a rodeo, and some rides) without the flair of a big-city event.

> **KIDSPEAK**
>
> I like to play in the open water while fishing, I fish…play in the water…fish. I like catching fish, too, because cutting them open is so interesting.
>
> —Eryn, age seven

Anchor Point is the last town before reaching Homer and the end of the Sterling Highway. Located along the highway at Milepost 156, Anchor Point is considered by many to be the most pristine fly-fishing area in all southcentral Alaska with the Anchor River flowing through town on its way to Cook Inlet. It's fun to take a photo at the end of Beach Road, the westernmost point in the North American Highway system, reached via Old Sterling Highway. Smile!

Homer

Homer, on the southwest side of the Kenai Peninsula, is the terminus for the Sterling Highway and quite possibly our family's favorite Alaska getaway. The area's first residents were the Dena'ina and Alutiiq people, who used the ice-free Kachemak Bay for fishing, clamming, and transportation. When homesteaders began arriving in the 1800s and after World War II made the newfound coal deposits a boon to the community, Homer established itself on the territory's map. In fact, many original homesteads are still owned and occupied by longtime Homer families, signaling a reluctance to give way to more modern dwellings. Surrounded by mountains and water, the area is tranquil yet busy, with an Alaska Marine Highway terminal, fleets of fishing boats, and curious tourists. It's eclectic, liberal, and a really fun place to bring kids.

VISITOR INFORMATION

The Homer Chamber of Commerce (201 Sterling Highway, www .homeralaska.org, info@homeralaska.org, 907-235-7740) is located along the Sterling Highway at the entrance to town. The chamber offers a wide range of information about lodging and activities, as well as current tide tables and fishing regulations. It is a must stop before embarking upon further Homer adventures.

MEDICAL CARE

The South Peninsula Hospital is located at 4300 Bartlett St. (www .sphosp.com, 866-235-0369, 907-235-8101).

Homer

Population: 5,400 (2012 census)

Founded in: 1889 as a coal distribution center, but wasn't named Homer until 1896, when Homer Pennock tried to establish the Alaska Gold Mining Company.

Known for: Halibut charters, early homesteading, and the famous Homer Spit.

Interesting fact: Storyteller and former Homer resident Tom Bodette rose to fame through his folksy tales of life at "the end of the road."

Homer is also a jumping-off point for many rural southeast Alaska communities with a small boat harbor and Alaska Marine Highway System ferry dock.

LODGING

Lodging options in Homer range from funky to fantastic and everything in between. Choices lie in accommodations on the Spit or off the Spit and depend upon your family's tolerance for crowds and noise (usually found on the Spit). Summer travelers should book well in advance, especially when traveling with children, as the most popular places fill up fast.

Hotels/Motels

Best Western Bidarka Inn $$
575 Sterling Highway, Homer, AK 99603
(866) 685-5000
www.bidarkainn.com

Nothing fancy, here, but the Best Western name for quality stands true in Homer. Bidarka Inn has 74 rooms, with free wireless, a microwave and refrigerator, a seasonal restaurant, and year-round bar and grill. A free shuttle can transport to/from the Homer Airport and some activities; inquire when making reservations. Children 17 and under stay free with a paying adult and the hotel has a free continental breakfast every morning.

Note: This is *not* a smoke-free establishment, so ask about air quality management before booking if this is a concern.

Thumbs-up for: Free stay for kids, shuttle service, restaurant on-site.

Lands End Resort $$$
4786 Homer Spit Rd., Homer, AK 99603
(800) 478-0400
www.lands-end-resort.com

Located directly on the Homer Spit at the very end of the Sterling Highway, with an unobstructed view of Kachemak Bay and surrounding mountains. Lands End is the only hotel-type lodging available on the Spit and makes the most of its location with higher prices than other properties. It is a little dated but clean and comfortable, and kids will be able to fully enjoy beachcombing or fishing from the shore.

Six different room layouts are available, including suites, so larger families will appreciate the space. Lands End also rents high-end luxury condos next door. The property also features a restaurant, bar, and espresso/gift shop.

Thumbs-up for: Beachside access, great views of Kachemak Bay and boats.

Driftwood Inn $–$$$
135 West Bunnell Ave., Homer, AK 99603
(907) 235-8019
www.thedriftwoodinn.com, driftwoodinn@alaska.com

The Driftwood is located in Old Town Homer and is a favorite. This historic little inn offers clean rooms at affordable prices with the decided bonus of easy access to nearly every kid-friendly amenity one would want in a beach town. Rooms are tiny, I warn you, but you'll be too busy playing on the beach, eating, or enjoying the Driftwood's own playground to spend much time indoors, anyway. Ask about early- or late-season specials, too.

Thumbs-up for: Little playground, proximity to Bishop's Beach and Old Town Homer.

Cabins/Cottages

Homer boasts a wealth of opportunities for families wanting their own space combined with a little Alaskana. **The Homer Cabins and Cottages Cooperative** (www.cabinsinhomer.com, 888-364-0191) offers a complete listing of available places to rent for a day, a week, or longer. Some offer every luxury of home, others not so much, but you'll have to decide what your family requires.

Homer Seaside Cottages $$–$$$
128 East Bunnell Ave., Homer, AK 99603
(907) 399-7688
www.homerseasidecottages.com, lodging@homerseasidecottages.com

These cottages provide our family with a getaway at least once or twice a year. With a cluster of three cabins of varying size in Old Town Homer (just down the street from the Driftwood Inn), the Seaside Cottages offer prime access to all the aforementioned goodies of the Driftwood Inn, with a full kitchen and run-around room. Well stocked with essentials, the cottages are perfect for larger families or groups of friends who want their own space but need a central location for meals or playtime. A separate, larger home, "Alaska By the Sea," sits five miles east and is perfect for those wanting to truly get away.

Note: Dogs are welcome in the Garden Shed cottage only.

Thumbs-up for: Spacious; walking distance to bakery, beach, and Islands and Ocean Visitor Center; clean, charming decor.

Accommodation Alternatives

The **Homer Bed and Breakfast Association** (www.homerbedandbreakfast .com, 877-296-1114) is a coalition of property owners who offer a wide variety of B&B opportunities for guests. Properties' amenities for families are ever-changing, so it's best to contact them directly for a current listing.

Camping/RV

Camping is to Homer what music was to Woodstock, or something like that. At any rate, there are many folks who feel a trip to Homer wouldn't be complete without a night or two spent on the beach, listening to lapping waves and watching sea otters frolic in the surf. Below are a few options for those who wish to experience Homer the old-fashioned way.

Homer Spit Campground
4535 Homer Spit Rd., Homer, AK 99603
(907) 235-8206
stay@homerspitcampground.com
$29–$35/night, depending upon site
Open May through September or October, depending upon weather.

This campground has 22 tent and 111 RV sites located at the end of the Homer Spit, in full view of the glorious mountains and Kachemak Bay. Restrooms, showers, and laundry facilities complete the package.

Note: Can be noisy at night due to the general hubbub of Homer Spit activities and a fair amount of young adults staying up way, way too late (see how old I'm getting?).

Heritage RV Park
3550 Homer Spit Rd., Homer, AK 99603
(800) 380-7787
www.alaskaheritagervpark.com, HeritageRVPark@alaska.net
$78/night
Open mid-May through mid-September

107 RV-only sites in a clean, orderly, and well-managed park near the fishing lagoon and bike path. A half-mile of private beach makes for family memories of beachcombing and evening chats around the fire pit. Power, water, dump station, and pull-through sites. Nice gift shop and activities desk. **Note:** Ask for a beach site. Views are great, but reserve early!

Karen Hornaday Park
Fairview Ave. and Hornaday St., Homer, AK 99603
$6/night for tents; $10/night RV

Away from the beach, Karen Hornaday Park is located in the foothills of Homer, about a mile from downtown. It's quiet, with a nice view of town and the surrounding neighborhoods. A bonus is the nearby playground featuring creatively designed play structures to be enjoyed by both little tykes and older kids. Adults must wait their turn to use the hand-operated back hoe in the sand pit. It's for the kids, after all.

Note: Black bears occasionally wander through the wooded area, so heed bear safety rules and keep a clean camp.

STORES/GROCERIES

Homer is a culinary delight, in my opinion. From locally harvested fish, clams, and oysters to locally grown produce, Homer seeks to satisfy everyone. A great place to discover the treasures of this seaside town is at the **Homer Farmer's Market** (www.homerfarmersmarket.org), open each Wednesday and Saturday, May through September. Sample homemade soup and bread or stock up on fresh veggies for your stay, all while listening to local musicians perform on a makeshift stage.

Note: The market is also a great place to buy gifts for those back home, hear some local tunes, and savor the flavor of this beachside community. We dig it a lot.

Safeway
90 Sterling Highway, Homer, AK 99603
(907) 226-1000

Find groceries, camping necessities, and deli and pharmacy items here. They also have a coffee shop and attached liquor store, and one can secure a fishing license as well.

FEEDING THE FAMILY

Two Sisters Bakery $$-$$$
233 E. Bunnell Ave., Homer, AK 99603
(907) 235-2280
www.twosistersbakery.net
Open Monday–Friday 7 a.m.–6 p.m., Saturday–Sunday 7 a.m.–4 p.m. Dinner
served Wednesday–Saturday 6–9 p.m. Winter hours vary, so call ahead.

It's hip, Two Sisters is, with wholesome food and an atmosphere of cheer
to keep customers returning. Two Sisters is a stone's throw from popular
Bishop's Beach, and families enjoy a stop for hot chocolate, fresh baked
goods, and excellent service. Not just about sweets, either, the establishment also offers counter-style breakfast, lunch, and dinner on Wednesdays
through Sundays. A small play area off the rear porch entertains kids, and
customers can watch the food being baked in brick ovens from the bar
seating. Wine served at dinner.

Cosmic Kitchen $$-$$$
510 E. Pioneer Ave., Homer, AK 99603
(907) 235-6355
www.cosmickitchenalaska.com
Open Monday–Friday 9 a.m.–6 p.m., Saturday 9 a.m.–3 p.m.

Located on Homer's main drag, Cosmic Kitchen serves a nice variety of
menu choices. Burgers, hand-cut fries, sandwiches, soups, and a great
breakfast lineup satisfy even the hungriest sightseer. A fresh salsa bar
nicely compliments the breakfast burrito, by the way. Beer and wine.
Seating is indoor or outside on the deck.

Fresh Sourdough Express Bakery and Restaurant $-$$$
1316 Ocean Dr., Homer, AK 99605
(907) 235-7571
www.freshsourdoughexpress.com

One of the most popular spots for breakfast, lunch, dinner, or a quick
snack in between, Sourdough Express is on the way to Homer Spit, in
a small hollow that would easily be missed if it weren't for the hordes of
people gathering on the front porch waiting for a table. Started more than
25 years ago by a couple who wanted to create a sustainable restaurant
using fresh, local foods, everything here is homegrown and homemade,

from the chocolate syrup in your mocha to the raspberry jam served with huge biscuits. Seafood is local, too. Kids will enjoy a menu just for them, and the sandbox out front.

Captain Patties Fish House $$-$$$
4241 Homer Spit Rd., Homer, AK 99603
(907) 235-5135

Who comes to Homer and doesn't try fish at least once? Captain Patties is fish and nothing but fish, although they do have other stuff. Fried or grilled, their fish is great and the service is pretty fine, too. French fries are moist and mealy and portions are adequate. With kids, eat lunch at Captain Patties, since dinner menu prices go way, way up.

Note: Chefs will cook your own catch of the day if you bring it to them cleaned.

Alaska Fact   **Homer's town motto is "Where the land ends and the sea begins."**

FAMILY FUN IN HOMER
It took us awhile to make the most of our visits to Homer, though the community clearly welcomes children with open arms. Try the following with your crew.

Museums and Cultural Experiences

Pratt Museum
3779 Bartlett St., Homer, AK 99603
(907) 235-8635
www.prattmuseum.org
Open daily 10 a.m.–6 p.m. (May through September); Tuesday through Saturday noon–5 p.m. (rest of the year)
Admission: $8/adults, $6/seniors, $4/kids 6-18, $25/family of four, free for kids under six

The only natural history museum on the Kenai Peninsula, Pratt Museum features both indoor and outdoor attractions, including the historic Harrington homestead cabin, where kids can see firsthand how folks lived without television, electric lights, and DVR. Also committed to Native culture and marine ecology, the museum provides a true understanding about who has inhabited the peninsula, when, and where. Do check out the fascinating (and sobering) exhibit about the *Exxon Valdez* oil spill of 1989; older kids in particular can grasp the impact of the event on all Alaskans. Suitable for children five and older; younger kids may become restless. Ideal for school-agers and tweens/teens.

Culture/Education

Islands and Ocean Visitor Center
95 Sterling Highway, Homer, AK 99603
(907) 235-6961
www.islandsandocean.org
info@islandsandocean.org
Open daily 9 a.m.–5 p.m. (Memorial Day through Labor Day); Tuesday through Saturday 9 a.m.–5 p.m. (September through May)
Admission: Free

This beautiful building overlooking Kachemak Bay Research Reserve and Beluga Slough is a must-see and is full of interesting, hands-on opportunities for kids. Better still, it's free! (Although donations are greatly appreciated.) The facility is accessible indoors and out, with restrooms, a gift shop, and many free programs throughout the year, thanks to staff from the offices of state and federal fish and wildlife agencies. Start by admiring the bronze sea lion near the entrance, then move into the interpretive exhibits, including a night/day perspective from nearby Gull Island. Embark on a short walk outside and spot sandhill cranes, moose, eagles, and a plethora of shorebirds. Volunteers can assist you with maps and other information about local flora and fauna, too. Fun for older preschoolers on up.

Center for Alaskan Coastal Studies
708 Smokey Bay Way, Homer, AK 99603
(907) 235-6667
www.akcoastalstudies.org, info@akcoastalstudies.org

Since 1982, the Center has guided thousands of visitors toward a more intimate relationship with nature through experiential learning. While the main office is in downtown Homer, the real gems are located at

Carl E. Wynn Nature Center off Skyline Drive (up on the bluffs) and across Kachemak Bay at Peterson Bay Field Station, where everyone can garner an appreciation for the unique plants, animals, and environments of the Kenai Peninsula. During the summer months, the center also opens a small yurt on the Homer Spit, where daily activities and programs are held for those who may be on a tight schedule or perhaps cannot navigate the landscape of Wynn Nature Center or Peterson Bay. Appropriate for the whole family, infants to grandparents.

OUTDOOR RECREATION

Hiking

Kachemak Bay State Park (dnr.alaska.gov/parks/units/kbay/kbay.htm) lies across the bay from Homer. Alaska's first state park and its only wilderness park, the area features miles and miles of hiking and camping opportunities, if you're willing to take an extra step to get there. With no road system, the park is accessed via floatplane or boat, easily arranged for a fee from Homer. Look for views of glaciers, wildlife, and sparkling water from the trail, but be aware that the solitude and scenery also come at a price: you are in a wilderness area with no services, so you must carry anything you need. That said, trails like China Poot, Halibut Cove Lagoon, and Grewingk Glacier are stunning reminders of the reason you came to Alaska in the first place.

Note: Dress kids in hiking boots and layered clothing and bring plenty of snacks and water. Practice bear safety at all times. Find information about transportation to and from the park from the Homer Chamber of Commerce (www.homeralaska.org).

Carl E. Wynn Nature Center (www.akcoastalstudies.org, 907-235-5266) has five miles of marked trails, ranging from boreal forest to mountain meadow and featuring spectacular views of Homer, Kachemak Bay, and mountains beyond. A little log cabin acts as visitor center and provides

Homer offers miles of beach for walks and play.

maps, as well as information on plants and animals of the area.

Note: Mosquitoes can be fierce during the summer, so bring plenty of bug repellent and/or a net for stroller-bound babies. Admission fees of $7/adult, $5/kids under 18 help keep the center maintained and beautiful for visitors. Suitable for all ages.

Bishop's Beach is located in Old Town Homer. Popular with locals, this beach is level and accessible, and we never miss an opportunity to play here. Hike anywhere from 10 minutes to two hours, exploring tide pools, interesting rocks, and the marsh from nearby Beluga Slough. The best time to visit Bishop's Beach is during low tide, when all sorts of interesting things appear and walking is easier near the waterline.

Note: Do keep track of time, since tides that go out also come back in, and you wouldn't want to be stuck without a way to return to your car. Reach Bishop's Beach by taking Sterling Highway to Main Street, turning toward the ocean, then taking a left on Bunnell Avenue. Take a right on Beluga Avenue (Two Sisters Bakery is just ahead) and park in the small lot. Portable toilets and a small picnic shelter are available.

Peterson Bay Field Station (www.akcoastalstudies.org, 907-235-6667) is operated by the folks at the Center for Alaskan Coastal Studies, located across Kachemak Bay and accessible only by boat. Built as a living laboratory, Peterson Bay features extreme low tides and thus a plethora of marine plant and animal life waiting to be explored with the help of knowledgable staff. Daily guided hikes and natural history tours are offered Memorial Day through Labor Day with prior arrangement. Wildlife, marine mammals, and crustaceans are possible sights to see during a day spent playing at the bay. Tours range from $80/kids to $120/adults and include

Savoring Seldovia with Kids

Across Kachemak Bay, nestled in a cozy little cove, lies the community of Seldovia. Inaccessible by car (remember, the highway ends in Homer), part of Seldovia's charm lies in getting there. Whether by Alaska Marine Highway ferry (75 minutes, www.ferryalaska.com), private charter boat, or small plane (expensive), traveling to Seldovia translates into adventure for kids.

With a mere 300 full-time residents, Seldovia is a laid-back collection of artists, fishermen, and folks who don't want to live the fast life, but that doesn't mean people are lacking in the fun department. A day trip to Seldovia means great hiking, biking, and exploring the ocean's treasures.

Start by visiting the **Seldovia Chamber of Commerce** website (www.seldoviachamber.org) for detailed descriptions of transportation options from Homer; we usually take the ferry and spend a few hours, then return in time for a late dinner. Our activities include a fabulous two-mile hike along the Otterbahn trail near the Seldovia school that travels into an old-growth spruce forest, along a meadow, and ends up on a rocky, secluded transportation to the field station. Best for kids preschool and up, including teenagers, who will appreciate staff who challenge and engage with great science activities.

FISHING

Charters

Halibut fishing is a bit different than salmon fishing, because halibut, unlike their active salmon counterparts, are bottom fish, flat and funny-looking. To catch a halibut requires heavy weights, a large pole, and deep water. Usually, halibut charters operate under a half-day (four or five hours) or full-day (up to eight hours) schedule, which means your children will be on a boat, in potentially rough water, for a long, long time if you choose to embark upon a fishing trip. Generally, kids age 10 and up can handle a halibut charter, but be forewarned that boats tend to leave very early in the morning and offer nothing in the way of food or

beach where we've spent hours viewing otters, whales, and sea birds. Take a picnic, water, and your bear-aware behavior.

Back in town, eat at the **Tidepool Cafe** before exploring the old section of the village, where homes are built over the water and you'll feel as if you've been transported back in time. A great way to see town is via bicycle; rent one in Anchorage or bring your own and ride miles and miles of packed dirt roads (see chapter 9, "Family Fun in Anchorage," for more information on bike rentals).

Small children will find the small playground next to the boat harbor a winner; then swing into Parrot's for an ice-cream treat before catching the ferry back to Homer. Make sure you watch for rafts of otters, humpback whales, and puffins, too.

> **KIDSPEAK**
>
> I like the boat ride to Seldovia, and hiking that Otter (Otterbahn) trail.
>
> —Owen, age seven

beverages for clients; you're on your own for making sure kids are warm, well fed, and comfortable.

Note: Follow our recommendations for seasickness prevention mentioned earlier in this section.

A halibut trip can be a fun bonding experience for those traveling with older kids. It's pretty neat to have your fish caught, cleaned, processed, and frozen for transport back home, and nothing says "Alaska vacation memories" quite like pulling a self-caught fillet out of the freezer come January.

Charter companies have their own rules when it comes to kids; some are patient and willing to help children catch their limit (after all, you are the customer), but others are strictly grown-up oriented. How do you know? Ask, ask, ask. Do they have life jackets for children? What is their policy about kids on their boats? How about a canceled charter—will you get your money back? How many passengers do they allow? Can you bring toys?

Alaska Fact

Halibut can weigh as much as 400 pounds, earning them the nickname "barn door," which also refers to their flat shape. Really, though, the tastiest halibut are the "chickens," or smaller fish weighing between 25 and 50 pounds. Small ones are sweeter!

Bank Fishing

The Homer Spit is ideal for saltwater fishing sans boat. Kids flock to the Nick Dudiak Fishing Lagoon, managed by the City of Homer, to reel in salmon. The lagoon has an accessible ramp, picnic tables, a fish-cleaning table, and small restroom facility. This area can be incredibly crowded during the summer, but it's always fun. Find the Fishing Lagoon on the left side of the road as you drive out the Homer Spit.

The end of the Homer Spit, near Lands End Resort and the Alaska Marine Highway System ferry docks, can also provide exciting fishing opportunities for kids. Flounder, cod, and the occasional salmon can be caught, depending upon the day.

FLIGHTSEEING/WILDLIFE VIEWING

For some, a visit to Alaska is not complete until they've seen as many wild animals as possible. Of these, bears usually rate number one on the checklist. While it is possible to spy a brown or black bear along a salmon stream or (more likely) wandering through a neighborhood in search of an unsecured garbage can, the best way to experience a bear in a natural habitat is through a guided viewing excursion.

> **KIDSPEAK**
>
> The best part about a fishing trip is bonking all the halibut.
> —Dan, age nine

While expensive, bear viewing is nonetheless a popular attraction. While we will address wildlife viewing in greater detail in "Continue the Fun," I will give a shout-out to the flightseeing companies based in Homer who do day trips to view wildlife.

Note: Flightseeing is accomplished in a small plane that can seat up to five passengers. These planes are not equipped with any frills or fluff for families, and passengers must sit still for the duration of the flight. Wildlife viewing, too, is full of rules and children under 10 may have difficulty. It is crucial to gather information from a flightseeing company before booking. That said, older kids and teenagers generally consider flightseeing to be a highlight of an Alaska vacation.

One popular Homer-based flightseeing company is **Homer Air** (www .homerair.com, info@homerair.com, 907-235-8591). Homer Air can get your family up in the air for a bear viewing, camping, hiking, or fishing adventure to some of the most beautiful and remote areas of Alaska. Lake Clark, Katmai National Park, and other less well-known beaches are just a few of the destinations offering a unique view of southcentral Alaska.

Homer Air also offers guided kayak trips and hikes. Flightseeing trips range from a 30-minute buzz around the greater Kachemak Bay area, including some of the gorgeous glaciers visible from Homer or a longer trip out toward the Harding Ice Field. Prices begin at $80/person for the 30-minute tour and increase from there, with longer trips costing more than $350/person for a Ring of Fire tour around the Alaska Range.

KIDSPEAK

I like flying the best because it feels like you're in the clouds and really high up in space, sort of like a sandwich with the ground below and us in the middle.

—Eryn, age seven

If you think this is your one and only visit to Alaska, do consider a flightseeing trip. If you will be traveling on to Denali National Park or returning to Alaska some day, choose wisely. We'll describe more flightseeing opportunities in the Denali National Park section and our southeast Alaska sections.

KODIAK BIG BEARS AND BIGGER SCENERY

Many travelers skip Kodiak during their Alaska adventure simply because they don't know enough about it. Heck, most Alaskans don't even know a lot about this archipelago of islands located 158 miles from Homer, across the Gulf of Alaska. Kodiak island itself is 177 miles long, and at 5,000 square miles is roughly the size of Connecticut. Most of Kodiak's Island Borough residents live in Kodiak proper; at 6,000 full-time residents, it holds its own against other rural Alaska towns, but many smaller communities are accessible only by boat or airplane.

> **In 1912, Kodiak was nearly buried by the eruption of Mount Novarupta, which spewed two feet of ash upon town and brought three days of darkness to the entire island.**
>
> **Alaska Fact**

Kodiak's history and culture revolve around its island location and the people who have made their living from the land and surrounding ocean. The Alutiiq people have etched a living from the ebullient marine and land-based bounty, continuing those traditions today, but it was the settlement by Russian fur traders in the 1700s that shifted the tide for Kodiak's place in Alaska commerce, first as the capital of Russian America, then as a major sea otter pelt distributor for many years. Today, Kodiak's prime means of support is through a vibrant fishing industry, and visitors are able to reap the benefits, enjoying halibut, salmon, and crab straight from the water. Kodiak is a wonderful place to explore with children, full of interesting World War II artifacts and Native Alaska culture, not to mention miles and miles of beach and trails to explore.

Getting Here

Kodiak is an easy hop from Anchorage aboard **Alaska Airlines** (www .alaskaair.com, 800-252-7522) or from Homer via **Era Alaska** (www.flyera .com, 800-866-8394, 907-266-8394) or **Grant Aviation** (www.flygrant.com, 888-359-4726).

Many Alaskans take advantage of the **Alaska Marine Highway System's** (www.ferryalaska.com, 800-642-0066, 907-465-3941) regular service to Kodiak from Homer. At nine hours, it's not exactly speedy service, and the water can be rough, but it's decidedly more affordable, and certainly an experience to talk about back home. Watch for whales, puffins, seals, and all manner of fishing boats while traveling.

Heads-up: Weather in Kodiak is unpredictable, damp, and slightly frustrating if you're on a tight schedule. As we've mentioned in previous sections, pack your patience along with your rain gear. Prepare for weather delays by supplying kids with books, toys, and/or movies if you get stuck in the airport.

The **Kodiak Island Convention and Visitors Bureau** (www.kodiak .org, 907-486-4782) is located at 100 Marine Way, in downtown Kodiak. Pick up maps and brochures, or plan a guided tour.

Moving about Kodiak

Since the island is rather large, and with many adventures located beyond the scope of town, it is handy to have access to wheels when visiting Kodiak. **Avis Car Rentals** (www.avis.com, 907-487-2264) is located at the Kodiak airport as is **Budget Rent-A-Car** (www.budget.com, 907-487-2220).

Taxi service is available through **Kodiak City Cab** (907-486-5555) or **Kodiak Island Taxi** (907-486-2515).

Lodging

HOTELS

Best Western Kodiak Inn $$-$$$
Rezanof Dr., Kodiak, AK
(907) 486-5712
www.kodiakinn.com, info@kodiakinn.com

Most folks stay at this Best Western near the downtown area. With an on-site restaurant and convenient amenities, including cribs and rollaways, a complimentary breakfast, and hot tub. Kids under 17 stay free in parents' room.

Russian Heritage Inn $-$$
Yukon St., Kodiak, AK
(907) 486-5657
www.russianheritageinn.com

The Russian Heritage Inn, while dated and a bit thin on upgrades, provides 25 rooms with suites, full kitchens, or kitchenettes. It's the access to cooking facilities that might appeal to families, however, and the property managers are very accommodating and responsive to guest needs. It's affordable, too, with prices depending upon room size and time of year.

Cliff House B&B $$-$$$
1223 W. Kouskov St., Kodiak, AK
(907) 486-5079
http://www.kodiak-alaska-dinner-cruises.com/kodiak-bed-breakfast.html, mygarden@alaska.net

The Cliff House B&B, owned and operated by Marty and Marian Owen, is a great place to spread out with a larger family or group. Located above Kodiak's boat harbor, the Cliff House receives rave reviews for hospitality and decor. Kitchen facilities are always fully stocked, even if you only stay in one room. Marty and Marian also own Galley Gourmet Dinner Cruises, and can arrange harbor tours and other Kodiak adventures.

CAMPING
Fort Abercrombie (dnr.alaska.gov/parks/aspunits/kodiak/fortabercrombieshp .htm) is a fantastic location for camping, with miles of trails, awesome

scenery, and a lake in the middle of the park. With only 13 campsites, though, you must get your hustle on to secure a spot for the night.

Shopping

Kodiak Safeway
2685 Mill Bay Rd., Kodiak, AK 99615
(907) 481-1500

Groceries, bakery, pharmacy, coffee shop, and deli.

Feeding the Family
When it's eating time after a busy day of hiking, boating, or inspecting museums, dine at Kodiak's favorite establishments.

Henry's Great Alaska Restaurant $$-$$$
512 Marine Way, Kodiak, AK 99615
(907) 486-8844
www.henrysalaska.com
Open Monday–Saturday 11:25 for lunch, 4:30 p.m. for dinner; Sunday 12 p.m. lunch, 4:30 p.m. dinner

The only place in Alaska where you can get a true crawfish pie, Henry's is a friendly, honest place that serves up good food on a consistent basis. Children have their own menu of favorites, and adults can find craft ales and a pretty extensive cocktail list.

Noodles $$
1247 Mill Bay Rd., Kodiak, AK 99615
(907) 486-2900
Open for lunch and dinner Monday–Saturday. Call for hours.

Sometimes it's nice to have Thai food, and Noodles lives up to its name with plenty of options for bowls, platters, and curry combinations served with the wonderful, slithery Thai noodles, or rice if you prefer. Fresh rolls are really fresh, too. Plus, I like to say "noodles" to my kids, because they laugh, no matter how old they're getting.

Java Flats $$
11206 Rezanof Dr., Kodiak, AK 99615
(907) 486-2622
www.javaflats.com

Located 13 beautiful miles from downtown Kodiak, and worth every minute of transit time, Java Flats is a unique little coffee shop and bakery that just happens to serve gourmet soups, sandwiches, and loose-leaf teas. Situated on Bells Flats, where bears roam freely and people breathe deeply of the salty mountain air, Java Flats is destined to become a family favorite. Read the backstory of this little place on their website, too; it's rather endearing.

Family Fun in Kodiak

Let's get going! Kodiak has plenty to keep kids hopping, indoors and out, so hit the streets and beaches for a little island exploring. Remember to bring the rain gear, hats, and mittens for any outdoor adventures; Kodiak's wild weather can pop up at any time, and you'll want to be prepared.

HIKING AND WALKING

Start right in downtown Kodiak and walk the paved 3.5-mile trail to Fort Abercrombie. Strollers are great for this trail, but do keep an eye out for joggers and bikers. **The Kodiak Visitors Bureau** (www.kodiak.org) has a very nice listing of walks, hikes, and scenic drives.

Fort Abercrombie State Historical Park (dnr.alaska.gov/parks/units/kodiak/ftaber.htm) is 221 acres of forestland, trails, and beaches. During the summer, rangers offer interpretive walks and tidepooling activities. Nearby Lake Gertrude is great for canoeing or kayaking, too. When World War II ended, the military left its gun emplacements behind, and your family can check out the interesting artifacts dug deep into the hillsides. Stop by the **Kodiak Military History Museum** at the entrance to the park. Allow at least a few hours to explore this wonderful park.

Buskin River State Recreation Site (dnr.alaska.gov/parks/units/kodiak/buskin.htm) is another area with connections to World War II. Located a short drive from the Kodiak airport, the area offers picnicking, camping, and hiking along old roadbeds and river areas. See if you can find the old structures left behind at the end of the war, part of Fort Greely, meant to protect the United States against Japanese invasion. The area is actually owned by the U.S. Coast Guard but leased to the state of Alaska, so be respectful of artifacts found—and always be bear aware, too.

Fossil Beach lies along Pasagshak Road, about 45 miles from downtown Kodiak. Here, find Surfer Beach, where extreme surfers can be found taking advantage of the big waves (and often freezing cold water), and Fossil Beach, a super place to look for shells and fossils. Also interesting is the Kodiak Launch Complex, an Alaska Aerospace Development site hoping to send rockets into space as part of a missile defense system. Pack snacks, warm clothing, and boots, and enjoy the beautiful drive; it's completely worth the time.

MUSEUMS AND CULTURAL CENTERS

Kodiak Wildife Refuge Visitor Center
402 Center Ave., Kodiak, AK 99615
(907) 487-2626
www.fws.gov/refuge/Kodiak/visit/visitor_activities.html
Open daily 9 a.m.–5 p.m. (Memorial Day–Labor Day); winter hours, Tuesday–Saturday 10 a.m.–5 p.m.
Admission: Free

Be sure to stop by the visitor center and see the wonderful exhibits showcasing the wildlife and ecosystems of the Kodiak area, including a complete skeleton of a gray whale and a family of fishing bears. Summer hours bring regular interpretive programs and guided hikes, and visitors can also catch a short movie about the refuge, available on demand. Suitable for the entire family, with elementary and older kids a target audience.

Baranov Museum
101 Marine Way, Kodiak, AK 99615
(907) 486-5920
www.baranovmuseum.org
Open Monday–Saturday 10 a.m.–4 p.m. (summer); Tuesday–Saturday 10 a.m.–3 p.m. (winter)
Admission: $5/adults, free for kids 12 and under

The Baranov Museum got its start in a quonset hut downtown and now occupies the old Russian American building, also known as the Erskine House. This is a history museum, for sure, so little kids might find the weapons, kayaks, and artwork to be a bit boring, but the facility is excellent for older children who are beginning to learn United States history and geography. Lots of military and early American artifacts can be found here, as well as fishing implements and flotsam and jetsam collected over the years.

Alutiiq Museum
215 Mission Rd., Kodiak, AK 99615
(907) 486-7004
www.alutiiqmuseum.org
Open Monday, Wednesday, Friday 9 a.m.–5 p.m., Saturday–Sunday 9 a.m.–3 p.m. (June–August); Tuesday–Friday 9 a.m.–5 p.m., Sunday 12–4 p.m. (September–May)
Admission: $5/adults, free for kids 16 and under

Providing insight into 7,500 years of Native Alaskan culture, heritage, and tradition, this museum ranks high on the list of Alaska must-sees. A real winner with families, the museum features "Wamwik"—A Place to Play just for younger visitors, offering dress-up clothing, traditional toys, games, and puzzles.

Kodiak Fisheries Research Center
710 Mill Bay Rd., Kodiak, AK 99615
(907) 486-9300
www.kodiakak.us
Open Monday–Saturday 8 a.m.–4:30 p.m. (Memorial Day–Labor Day); Monday–Friday 8 a.m.–4:30 p.m. (Labor Day–Memorial Day)
Admission: Free

Stop by the interpretive center and catch some info about marine life, commercial fishing, and fisheries research throughout the Kodiak Archipelago. The best part is a huge cylindrical aquarium and touch tank to do your own tide-pooling.

The Alaska Seafood Marketing Institute (www.alaskaseafood.org) offers a ton of kid-friendly ways to prepare our yummiest bounty from the sea. Even my son likes their recipes, and he's hard to please!

Alaska Fact

12 DENALI NATIONAL PARK

"Today is your day. Your mountain is waiting so . . . get on your way!"

—Dr. Seuss, *Oh, the Places You'll Go!*

Exploring the six million acres of Denali National Park and Preserve is definitely a different experience from other national parks you may have visited. Situated between Anchorage and Fairbanks, Denali National Park, complete with Mount McKinley, is the epitome of unfettered wilderness. Despite thousands of visitors who scramble about its trails, ogle its abundant wildlife, or fly over its icy glaciers, Denali National Park is, and hopefully always will be, the perfect place to get your wild Alaska fix.

Denali was first established in 1917 as Mount McKinley National Park, thanks to the efforts of Don Sheldon, a naturalist, hunter, and conservationist. Things sailed along merrily for some time, with campers, hunters, and tourists showing up in their Model As and knickers, hoping to see The High One, Mount McKinley. Fast-forward to 1972, when the National Park Service, sensing that the interest of visitors was beginning to outweigh the natural integrity of the park, closed the road to private vehicles and switched to shuttle buses. Then, in 1980, the park grew outward when Congress more than tripled the park's size and renamed the swath of land Denali National Park and Preserve to ensure that the subsistence lifestyles of the native Athabascans could continue and to promote important subarctic research in the area.

Today, Denali National Park is a top attraction for visitors to Alaska, and with good reason. The combination of safe transportation, outdoor recreation, and highly visible wildlife means thousands of people can easily access the Alaska experience.

Exploring Denali National Park with children is a fantastic opportunity, provided parents recognize the inherent remote nature of the park. Careful pre-trip organization, an open mind, and a sense of adventure are the top three attributes to pack for an experience in Denali.

Alaska Fact   **The true geographic center of Alaska is about 60 miles northwest of Mount McKinley.**

Making Plans

Few services exist outside the bustling tourist community of Nenana Canyon (or Glitter Gulch, as residents call it), and everything, from bus tickets to campsites, should be reserved ahead of time. More than 400,000 people visit the park annually, and most of them stay and play in the greater Denali National Park area, which means lots of jockeying for bus seats and hotel rooms.

The National Park Service has a fantastic Denali National Park website (www.nps.gov/dena) that provides detailed information about the park and ancillary services offered within. Use this website and the tools provided to find information about reservations for tour and shuttle buses (I'll run through options for bus riding in "Family Fun Inside Denali National Park" later on in this chapter), campsites, and entrance fees.

Denali National Park operates under contract with Doyon/ARAMARK, a joint venture between an Alaska Native company and the well-known National Parks concessionaire. Any reservations for campgrounds will be made through this avenue, as early as December 1 for the following year's visit (www.reservedenali.com, 866-761-6629).

Park entrance fees are collected at the Denali National Park Visitor Center or Wilderness Access Center, depending upon your activity. Unlike other national parks you may have visited, Denali has no formal entrance station, so visitors must stop here to pay, pick up any previously reserved tickets or permits, and make new reservations as walk-ins.

Denali National Park is open year-round, but all winter visitor operations take place out of the **Murie Science and Learning Center** at greatly reduced hours and with a skeleton staff. Any plans for an October through April visit to the park must be meticulously made, allowing for vicious weather along the way and lack of available lodging/food within the Nenana Canyon/Glitter Gulch area. That said, many people think off-season visits to Denali National Park are the best ever; no crowds, stunning views of Mount McKinley resplendent in her snowy jacket, and opportunities for unique outdoor recreation. Visit the Denali National Park website (www.nps.gov/dena/planyourvisit/hours.htm) for specific details about fall, winter, and early spring travel to and within the park.

Getting to the Park

Driving is the easiest and (usually) cheapest way to get to Denali National Park. A straight shot from Anchorage along the Glenn and Parks Highways, it's 240 miles to the park entrance. Allow at least four hours to travel Alaska's busy summer highways and take plenty of breaks, especially near the town of Talkeetna (see the breakout section "Talkeetna: Alaska's Mountain Village" in this chapter).

Alaska Railroad Need-to-Know Family Travel Facts

Travel on the Alaska Railroad is much slower than by car, so be aware of the double time to arrive at the Denali National Park boundary and be prepared with snacks, drinks, and activities for kids. Consider upgrading from Adventure Class to Goldstar Service, whereby your family will be seated in a dome car for the duration of your trip and receive complimentary beverages throughout the journey. Staff are much more attentive to kids, too.

The **Alaska Railroad** (www.alaskarailroad.com, 800-544-0552, 907-265-2494) offers daily rail service north to Talkeetna and Denali National Park and south from Fairbanks aboard its Denali Star train mid-May through mid-September. The Alaska TourSaver coupon book (www .toursaver.com) offers a 2-for-1 special for the Denali Star train, and

Talkeetna: Alaska's Mountain Village

It's funky, it's fantastic—that's what people say about Talkeetna, a little village approximately 120 miles north from Anchorage, just off the Parks Highway. Full of rugged charm and an amicable attitude toward the tourists flocking to the wee village, Talkeetna embraces a simpler life. If you're driving to Denali National Park, Talkeetna is the perfect place to stop midway and get your mountain groove on.

Reached via a 14-mile spur road from the Parks Highway at Mile 98.7, Talkeetna is base camp not only for all climbers wishing to scale Mount McKinley (they are required to check in at the National Park Service's Talkeetna Ranger Station) but for visitors as well. Jet-boat tours, rafting, flightseeing, walking tours, a museum—it's all right here nestled along the banks of the Susitna and Talkeetna Rivers.

Bike around town or along the spur road, renting from **Talkeetna Bike Rentals** (www.talkeetnabikerentals.com, 907-354-1222). Tagalong bikes and trailers are available for little ones. Stop in at the **Talkeetna Historical Society Museum** (www.talkeetnahistoricalsociety.org, 907-733-2487) and see just how long people have been trying to climb Mount McKinley and why. Admission is $3/adults, free for kids under 12.

Looking for high-flying adventure? **K2 Aviation** (www.flyk2denali.com, 800-764-2291) will whisk your family up the flanks of Mount McKinley, and even land on a glacier for a snowball fight during their flightseeing tours. Kids are welcome on nearly all flightseeing trips, and K2's attention to small visitors is evident by a playground at its Talkeetna office. Rates begin around $200/person for a one-hour flightseeing tour.

Speaking of high-flying, **Denali Zipline Tours** (www.denaliziplinetours .com, 855-733-3988, 907-733-3988) is a fun way to take in the scenery, courtesy of nine zips, three suspension bridges, and one rappel, the last

Alaskans often receive special deals throughout the year, including 20 percent off tickets any time, any place. Visit the Alaska Railroad website frequently for seasonal offers, resident or not. Kids 2–11 travel for roughly half the price of adults. During the busy summer months, trains are always full, so reserve seats well in advance.

featuring a 700-foot zip over the top of a lake. Suitable for kids age 10 and up and weighing at least 90 pounds. Transportation provided from their Main Street office.

If it's rip-roaring river boating your family craves, look no further than **Mahay's JetBoat Adventures** (www.mahaysriverboat.com, 800-736-2210, 907-733-2223) and its famous Three Rivers Tour, traveling the Susitna, Talkeetna, and Chulitna Rivers in a fun, fast-moving, three-hour tour. All trips also stop at an authentic Athabascan village site and trapper's cabin so guests can experience life during a simpler time.

Talkeetna is also home to the fantastic **Wildland Community Playground** near the Alaska Railroad station. Built by residents and loved by children of all ages, the playground is made up of Talkeetna-themed and kid-inspired features. Load up a picnic (we like Nagley's store), apply bug spray, and let the kids run wild for a while.

When your kids are hungry, feed their grown-up-sized appetites at the **Talkeetna Roadhouse** (www.talkeetnaroadhouse.com, 907-733-1351), the place to find two things: Breakfast and Not Breakfast. Simple, huh? That's right, guests will receive outstanding sourdough hotcakes, cinnamon rolls, and scrambled eggs for Breakfast and a selection of soup, bread, and pastries for Not Breakfast. No problem. The Roadhouse, in operation since the early 1900s, also offers a few rooms for travelers who wish to spend the night in Alaskan authenticity. If you have the opportunity, do it. Open all year; summer hours are 6 a.m.–8 p.m.

Note: The Roadhouse seats customers family-style to encourage conversation, so don't worry about the kids' manners or your clean shirt; it's all good here. Just listen and learn! Tell owner Trisha Costello I sent you.

Two large tour companies, **Grayline of Alaska** (Holland America, www.hollandamerica.com, 888-425-1737) and **Princess Cruises and Tours** (www.princesslodges.com/rail.htm, 866-335-6379), offer more expensive rail packages aboard their individual cars attached to a regular Alaska Railroad train. With enormous windows and fancier appointments for dining and relaxing, these are options for families who want an all-inclusive Denali National Park experience. Occasionally, both companies will offer special package deals to encourage Alaskans to try out their products at very reduced prices.

Note: Lodging options using such tour companies are limited to company-owned properties next to the Denali National Park boundaries.

Flying to Denali National Park is expensive and cumbersome unless you happen to be friends with a small-plane pilot. However, the National Park Service does offer guidelines on its website for private pilots wanting to fly to the Denali National Park boundary (www.nps.gov/dena/planyourvisit/directions).

What to Bring

Denali National Park is located a long way from any major center of commerce, save for the tourism-driven Nenana Canyon/Glitter Gulch area. While small towns are scattered along the Parks Highway (Highway 3), most of their stores sell items of a souvenir nature and not for family travel survival. Thus, parents should pack with this in mind, including:

- Diapers/wipes
- Kid-appealing snacks, juice, fresh produce, baby food, or formula
- First-aid items/over-the-counter medications for children
- Coloring books, crayons, and other kid amusements (available in gifts shops, but at grossly inflated prices)

Shopping

Canyon Market and Cafe
Mile 328.4, George Parks Highway
Park entrance/Glitter Gulch
(907) 683-SHOP
Open daily 6 a.m.–1:30 a.m. during the summer months

Most expansive grocery store near park entrance. Deli, doughnuts, ice cream, small eating area. Fresh produce available on most days.

Lynx Creek Store
Mile 238.4, George Parks Highway, AK 99743
Park entrance area/Glitter Gulch
(907) 683-2548
Open daily 7 a.m.–11 p.m. during the summer months

Do not expect a full-service grocery; only the basics are available.

Mountain View Liquor & Grocery
Mile 248.9, George Parks Highway (10 miles north of park entrance in the town of Healy), AK 99743
(907) 683-2247
Open daily 8 a.m.–midnight during the summer. Winter hours vary; call ahead.

Offering a wider variety of grocery items, ice, and visitor services.

Medical Services

Interior Community Health Center
Usibelli Spur Rd., Healy, AK (10 miles north of Denali National Park entrance)
(907) 455-4567
www.myhealthclinic.org

Canyon Clinic
Mile 238.8 Parks Highway (in Glitter Gulch, adjacent to Denali Princess property), AK 99743
(907) 683-4433

Lodging

The greater Denali National Park area boasts quite a variety of options for overnight accommodations. Ranging from basic campgrounds to luxury resort-type facilities, the swatch of real estate dedicated to lodging is also diverse in price and availability, so careful consideration to your budget is a must. The park itself only offers a limited number of campgrounds—any hotel, lodge, or related properties are operated by private vendors. Below is a list of overnight options that might appeal to families.

CAMPGROUNDS IN DENALI NATIONAL PARK

There are several campsites within Denali National Park (www .reservedenali.com, 800-622-7275).

Riley Creek is the largest campground operated by Denali NP, with 147 sites accommodating tents and RVs up to 40 feet in length. Closest to the actual park entrance, Riley Creek is an obvious choice for families who want to embrace the wilderness without leaving too many services behind. Ranger programs, bear lockers (to store food and stinky items), a small mercantile store, free shuttle, and other amenities make this campground a winner. Fees range from $14 for a walk-in tent site to $28 for larger RVs. All sites except walk-in tent areas can be reserved. Fees are waived in the winter. No electrical or water hookups, but potable water and toilets are available throughout the area.

> **PARENT PRO TIP**
>
> We loved staying at Riley Creek Campground; each night rangers gave fireside chats—we caught one on ravens that really held my kids' attention.
>
> —Jennifer, Anchorage
> mother of three

Thumbs-up for: Accessibility to services, super system of walking/ biking trails.

Savage River Campground is located at Mile 13 of the Park Road, near the terminus of private vehicle travel (at Mile 15, all private vehicles must either park or turn around, unless special arrangements have been made. The campground features 33 sites and is open to both tent and RV camping, with RVs not exceeding 40 feet in length. Rates range from $22 for tents and RVs less than 30 feet to $28 for RVs 30–40 feet. Ranger programs, guided hikes, and potable water are easily accessible. No showers or electrical or water hookup. This is the smallest of Denali National Park's campgrounds, but it offers wonderful, wide views of Mount McKinley when the mountain decides to be "out."

Thumbs-up for: Proximity to Mountain Vista Day Use Area trails and Savage River, excellent views. Quieter than Riley Creek.

Teklanika River Campground can be reached via the Park Road, at Mile 29. It is one of the few campgrounds within the park itself that allows for private vehicle passage on the Park Road. This 53-site campground is the park's second largest and offers both RV and tent camping. Tek, as it's known, is a great place to experience true Alaska wilderness and thus requires a minimum three-night stay to justify the effort required to get there. Hiking trails, forested views, and access to the park via a Tek Pass are just a few benefits; truly, if you wish to expose your kids to Denali National Park from the ground, this is a great way to do it.

> **PARENT PRO TIP**
>
> I'd recommend Riley Creek Campground for families with kids. We were surprised at how nice the facilities were, but do try and select a site on the loop closest to the creek itself; we found great paths to explore there.
>
> —Steve, Anchorage father of two

Note: Your vehicle must stay parked at the designated campsite for the duration of your stay. A Tek Pass allows for free shuttle transportation within the park only and not to travel to the entrance and back at your whimsy. All sites are $16 per night, with a one-time reservation fee of $4.

Thumbs-up for: Truly remote experience coupled with National Park Service support.

CAMPING OUTSIDE THE PARK

McKinley RV and Campground
Mile 248.5, Parks Highway, Healy, AK
(800) 478-2562
www.mckinleyrv.com

This 87-site facility offers Wi-Fi and a free shuttle to and from the park entrance. Tents and RVs are welcome, starting at $20 per night. A small grocery store is on site, as are fuel and an ATM. Add laundry, shower facilities, and a deli, and you have a pretty fine family stop. Local activities can also be booked through the front desk, including a salmon bake, dogsled ride, and river rafting.

Thumbs-up for: Access to ancillary adventures, fuel for the car, and fuel for people.

Denali Outdoor Center
Mile 1/2, Otto Lake Rd., Healy, AK
(907) 683-1925
www.denalioutdoorcenter.com

Full-service property offering a wide range of Denali activities, cabins, and a campground. Campsites suit RVs up to 30 feet and tents. No electric or water hookups, but potable water is available. Camping is $8/adults, $4/kids. Showers, laundry, and canoe and bike rentals available. DOC staff can also arrange river rafting trips, mountain biking, and kayaking adventures from their compound just south of Healy.

Thumbs-up for: Affordability, upkeep, and great access to DOC's many activities.

Denali Grizzly Bear Campground
Mile 231.1 George Parks Highway, AK 99743
(866) 583-2696
www.denaligrizzlybear.com, info@denaligrizzlybear.com

What could be more fun than sleeping in a tent cabin, protected from the elements and featuring that unique canvas-tent smell? Grizzly Bear's campground offers these, along with standard campsites for both RV and tent campers. With the benefit of the adjoining resort, camping families can enjoy a little store, tour desk, and trails down to the river and around the resort. The property sits near the Denali Park Road, too, so park-related adventures are only minutes away. Campsites range from $25 to $38/night; tent cabins are $32 or $38/night, depending upon the size of your party.

Thumbs-up for: Access to a little store, the river, and cabins.

CABINS

Denali River Cabins and Cedars Lodge $$$
Mile 231.1, George Parks Highway, AK 99743
(800) 230-7275
www.denalirivercabins.com, rivercabins@doyontourism.com

Native-owned Doyon Corporation manages this property located just outside the Glitter Gulch area. Cabins are clean and spacious and add a bit of rustic charm to your stay. Choose from either a riverfront or off-river cabin. Kids 11 and younger stay free. Maximum four guests in one room. Add $20/person for more than two adult guests. Non-smoking.

Thumbs-up for: Clean, well-maintained cabins and choices for river or forested location.

McKinley Creekside Cabins $$–$$$
Mile 224, George Parks Highway, AK 99743
(888) 533-6254
www.mckinleycabins.com, cabins@mckinleycabins.com

Located in the Carlo Creek area of the George Parks Highway, about 13 miles south of the park, McKinley Creekside Cabins are clean, kid-friendly, and quiet, save for the rush of little Carlo Creek right outside your doorstep. A wide range of cabin options are available, including a newly renovated three-bedroom house, open all year. Cabins range from creekside deluxe to standard, but all provide a coffee maker, shower, private bath, and Wi-Fi. A lovely little café is also on-site, offering meals and to-go lunches for busy days. Kids will enjoy the walking trails, toys, and a chance to toss endless rocks in Carlo Creek. No smoking indoors.

Thumbs-up for: Distance from the Glitter Gulch area. Love the creekside location and on-site restaurant.

Denali Grizzly Bear Resort $–$$$
Mile 231.1 George Parks Highway, AK 99743
(866) 583-2696
www.denaligrizzlybear.com, info@denaligrizzlybear.com

The other half of the Grizzly Bear Campground, resort cabins range from rustic, no-frills lodging to those with private baths and stunning views from private decks. All cabins are heated and fully furnished, and will give you the impression of a true backcountry experience.

Thumbs-up for: Access to store and nearby trails, large cabins to fit bigger groups.

HOTELS AND RESORTS

Denali Princess Wilderness Lodge $$$
Mile 238.5 George Parks Highway, AK 99743
(907) 683-2282
www.princesslodges.com/denali-lodge.cfm

Featuring 656 rooms that cater mostly to the cruise ship crowd, Denali Princess is one of the largest properties in the greater Nenana Canyon area. For families seeking a quieter Denali experience, Princess is probably not a first choice. But if a bit of hustle and bustle, combined with myriad scheduled activities, appeals to your crew, Princess is a solid choice. Two restaurants, a dinner theater, walking paths, and shuttle service to and from the Denali National Park entrance complete the package. Cribs available upon request.

Thumbs-up for: Activities on a safe, clean, and attractive property. Tons of kids.

McKinley Chalet Resort $$$
Mile 238.5, George Parks Highway, AK 99743
(800) 276-7234
www.denaliparkresorts.com

Part of the Aramark family of resorts, McKinley Chalet sits right next to the Princess property, and indeed, the two look so much alike visitors often confuse them as one giant facility. Similar in structure and content, McKinley Chalet Resort also offers guided tours, a dinner theater, shuttle service, and tons of wandering space. Rooms are cookie-cutter but spacious and include some larger suites for family groups. Like structure in your family vacation? Find it here. Cribs are available upon request.

Thumbs-up for: Activities, structure that are part of an all-inclusive vacation. Many families.

Grande Denali Lodge $$$
Mile 238, George Parks Highway, AK 99743
(866) 683-8500
www.denalialaska.com/grande-denali-lodge/reservations/

Perched on the side of Sugarloaf Mountain with a view of the Nenana Canyon area and Denali National Park itself, Grande Denali Lodge offers large rooms that seem to fit the average family. Two wings, the Denali Lodge and Kodiak Lodge, offer rooms with two queens or one king bed, private baths, and cable television. A few cribs are available upon reservation. Guided tours, dog mushing experiences, river rafting, flightseeing, and other adventures can be arranged through the tour desk. Alaska TourSaver coupon book (www.toursaver.com) offers two nights for the price of one, with restrictions.

Thumbs-up for: Incredible view.

Feeding the Family

Tired after a long day of hiking, bus riding, or river rafting? Glitter Gulch teems with dining options appealing to both the cruise ship crowd and casual campers. As we mentioned earlier in this chapter, true grocery stores are few and far between, so if you're looking for picnic items, they better already be in your own basket. Below are some of the most popular restaurants. Restaurants accept credit cards unless otherwise noted.

RESTAURANTS

Base Camp Bar and Grill $$–$$$
Denali Princess Wilderness Lodge, Mile 238.5 George Parks Highway
www.princesslodges.com
Open daily 2:30 p.m.–11 p.m. (mid-May–mid-September)

A nice change of pace from standard camping-out fare, the Base Camp offers good pub food with a slightly fancy sort of atmosphere, but they are kind to kids and offer coloring sheets and crayons. Prices are higher since this is on resort property.

Denali Park Salmon Bake $$–$$$
Mile 238.5 George Parks Highway
(907) 683-2733
www.denaliparksalmonbake.com
Open daily at 7 a.m. for breakfast; lunch and dinner served until late at night
(mid-May–mid-September)

The Bake is full of authentic Alaska cuisine with more attention paid to customers and food than to decor. People like it that way and arrive with kids in tow to sample salmon, halibut tacos, burgers, and fish and chips. They also serve breakfast each morning beginning at 7 a.m., a good way to get kids their pancakes and sausage before heading out for a day of playing in the park. Don't have a vehicle? Don't worry, because the Denali Park Salmon Bake will even come pick you up from Riley Creek Campground and other nearby locations. Beer, wine, and cocktails also served for the grown-ups.

McKinley Creekside Cafe $$-$$$
Mile 224 George Parks Highway
(888) 533-6254
www.mckinleycabins.com
Open year-round 6 a.m.–10 p.m., with a break during September and early May

Who'd have thought a little property on the banks of Carlo Creek, way out in the middle of nowhere, could serve such delicious Eggs Benedict, monster cinnamon rolls, and sandwiches to go for day trippers? This is the place to stop if you're traveling north from Talkeetna. Eat on the deck and listen to rushing water, or cozy up inside and view the towering mountains. Kids will enjoy playing outside while waiting for food, but do keep an eye on them near the water. *Psst*: If kids are really good, buy them an Incredible Cookie.

49th State Brewing/Prospectors Pizza and Ale House $$-$$$
Mile 238.9 George Parks Highway
(907) 683-PIES
www.49statebrewing.com
Open daily 11 a.m.–1:30 a.m. (early May–early September)

Within walking distance of most Glitter Gulch hotels and offering a free shuttle from just about anywhere else, 49th State Brewing and the Prospectors Pizza joint is hopping with Alaskana. Not only is their pizza the bomb, but the old-time Alaska photos, artifacts, and maps showing off past and future adventurers are tons of fun to browse while waiting. Pizza, soup, salads, chicken, steak, sausage—the list goes on and on. Dessert is something special, too, with the 49th State Root Beer float a favorite of my guys, followed closely by the wild blueberry pie, baked fresh every morning.

Exploring chilly Savage River in Denali National Park.

Family Fun Inside Denali National Park

Now that everyone is fed and lodged, let's find some fun! Of the six million acres devoted to Denali National Park, the average human has access to whatever sections he/she can hike, raft, bike, flightsee, and/or camp. Outside the national park boundaries, more action awaits, be it through helicopter rides, all-terrain-vehicle tours, or fishing nearby lakes and streams. Here, in the most incredibly diverse area of interior Alaska, visitors truly can have it all.

GETTING ORGANIZED

Upon arrival at the entrance to Denali National Park or at any business within spitting distance, pick up a copy of *Alpenglow*, the park's seasonal newspaper. *Alpenglow* is a great resource, with information, interesting stories, and resources for travel within the park. You can even download a PDF version from the National Park Service website and read it before you arrive (www.nps.gov/dena/parknews/newspaper.htm).

TRANSPORTATION: THE SHUTTLE SHUFFLE

After cruising the park for a few days, most visitors see the value of a shuttle bus system. Both economically advantageous during this gas-crunching age and essential to protect the fragile wildness of the park itself, the shuttles are a great adventure for kids. Different shuttles go different places, though, and while navigating both the shuttle schedule and your kids can seem a little daunting, it doesn't have to be. Park service staff are great about answering questions, and both the *Alpenglow* and Denali National Park website are excellent resources for shuttle questions. Here are the basics:

Courtesy shuttle buses are free and provide transportation within the park's entrance area to make getting around a bit easier. Three shuttles, titled the Sled Dog Demonstration, Savage River, and Riley Loop, regularly swing into the bus stops scattered around these areas. Buses are wheelchair accessible and drivers will accommodate parents with stroller-bound kiddos.

Note: Do bring everything you need for adventures, since it could be some time until you get back to the car or hotel.

Shuttle buses also travel farther into the park along the 92-mile stretch of gravel road. The National Park Service sends at least 25 of these buses out each day during the peak of summer visitor season, and every time you

> ### PARENT PRO TIP
>
> We liked to take a shuttle bus to the Savage River Rest Area, then hike to Savage River from there. Our kids loved climbing the rocks and exploring trails near Savage Rocks and Healy Ridge behind it.
>
> —Steve, Anchorage father of two

turn around, there's a big, green converted school bus chugging along the Park Road. Shuttle buses are *not* tours but merely a mode of transportation farther into the park, providing get on–get off opportunities to hike, take photos, and explore the recently renovated Eielson Visitor Center at Mile 53. While a narrated tour is not provided, most drivers know this territory well and are happy to pull over for photos, talk up history, culture, and environment, and share what they know about the park. These shuttle buses require advance reservations and tickets, ranging anywhere from $13.50 for kids 15–17 to $46 for adults, depending upon the destination, which includes park admission. Kids 14 and younger are free. Call the park concessionaire (800-622-7275, 907-272-7275) for reservations and more information or visit the DNP website's Shuttle Bus page (www.nps.gov/dena/planyourvisit/shuttles).

Tour buses offer a bit more structure to the interior Denali National Park experience and are popular for those with limited time and accessibility issues, or those who truly want to immerse themselves in the park. Naturalists drive and narrate the entire tour, ranging in scope from natural history to an explanation of tundra and wildlife as part of an ever-evolving ecosystem. Tours cost approximately twice as much as a shuttle ticket and sell out fast, ranging from $33.25 for kids 14 and younger and $66.50 for 15 and older to take the Natural History Tour, for example. Tours can last anywhere from four hours to 12, so plan carefully when traveling with kids. The tour bus option can be great for older children and teens who have a keen interest in their surroundings, since naturalists are generally young adults who relate well to this age group. Make tour reservations via the park concessionaire in the Wilderness Access Center or by using the same number/website as for shuttles. Tour buses are all **TAN**.

MEET DENALI NATIONAL PARK

Denali National Park offers four in-park visitor information centers (the fifth is located in downtown Talkeetna) and all provide vital links to your wilderness adventure and how to recreate safely. Since the park is closed to most private vehicles, it is absolutely critical that visitors heed all signs, maps, and directions from park service staff.

Should We Hop on the Bus, Gus?
If So, What Should We Bring?

The eternal question among parents is whether or not a bus trip is worth the potential angst for both parents and kids. After all, small children will be forced to sit for hours on end watching grown-ups make fools of themselves in an attempt to capture photographs or videos of a far-off animal. I, too, lived in fear my son would pitch a holy hell-raising fit midtrip, my fellow passengers would cringe, and the bus driver would throw us to the wolves outside, left to our own devices for a return to the entrance area.

The short answer, grown-ups, is that you must know your children's personalities and capabilities when faced with (a) long car rides (b) tired, hungry, cranky antics due to the former and (c) how much said kids care about wildlife and beautiful scenery (at any age).

If you feel a shuttle ride longer than the 15 miles to Savage River could end badly, by all means, don't go any farther. Plenty of family fun can be had near the park entrance area and Savage River, and we'll talk about some options later on in this chapter. If, however, you do decide to take the shuttle, know the details. While shuttles do stop for rest breaks every 90 minutes or so, there are *no* services along the way. Bring enough food (and perhaps more) to feed your family for an entire day, including water

Denali Visitor Center is the largest of the five. Located at Mile 1.5 on the Park Road, this is the place to pay entrance fees, find a ranger-led program, have a meal, and explore the absolutely fantastic exhibits over two floors of space. All programs are free, including the usually interesting movies (for grown-ups, not so much for smaller kids). Children can grab a Discovery Pack at the entrance and independently explore the greater visitor center area with interactive, hands-on activities or participate in the always popular Junior Ranger program packet, available at the front desk. The park service also provides miles of level crushed-rock trails that bisect the entire

> **PARENT PRO TIP**
>
> Take several insulated bags with lunches, snacks, and beverages instead of an aisle-blocking cooler. With so many passengers scrambling to see wildlife, it saves barked shins and cranky looks while aboard the shuttle bus.
>
> —The author, mother of two hungry boys

and/or other beverages. Have an infant? Don't forget diapers, wipes, and bags for soiled items, and pack appropriate clothing for any sort of Alaska weather; it's been known to snow in June and be blistering hot in August. Kids should have their own little pack with books, crayons, and whatever else they need to last eight hours or longer.

If your children are of the age where car seats or boosters are a part of your luggage, do bring them with you, as all shuttle buses and/or tour buses require kids to be strapped in. However, a limited number of car seats and boosters are available with a prearrival registration. Inquire via the park website (www.nps.gov/dena).

Get on and off, if you wish, but be aware that buses operate on a space-available basis, so during peak times (i.e., the middle of the day) the bus you want may not be the bus you get after you flag it down and find it full of people. Be prepared to wait, sometimes as long as an hour, for another bus. I would strongly suggest this option only for older children who understand the concept of "maybe the next one."

All shuttle buses, whether courtesy or regular, are **GREEN**.

entrance area. Food can be purchased at the Morino Grill during the visitor center operating hours, and although it's a little pricey and always crowded, it is nice for a break. Sitting outside offers more room for families, we found. Open daily 8 a.m.–6 p.m. (mid-May through mid-September).

Murie Science and Learning Center (www.murieslc.org) is located across the parking lot from Denali Visitor Center, at Mile 1.4 on the Park Road (follow the pathway's painted dinosaur tracks to Murie from DVC). Named for brothers Olaus and Adolph Murie and their wives Mardy and Louise, Murie Science and Learning Center is dedicated to teaching visitors of all ages about the park's natural science. From hiking a wildflower-strewn trail to learning how Dall sheep survive and thrive in this subarctic environment, MSLC is a must-visit with children. Big kids will like the interactive computer programs and skulls and hides of Denali National Park's many critters. Smaller children (and parents) will appreciate the Children's Corner and a nice collection of books, coloring supplies, and pull-out drawers full of interesting discoveries. Operated through a partnership with Alaska Geographic and other agencies, the center also offers annual field seminars, including a number of seminars appropriate for families. Open daily 9:30 a.m.–5 p.m. (mid-May to mid-September).

> **KIDSPEAK**
>
> It was sort of quiet in the science center. I could work on the computer or read a book.
>
> —Owen, age seven

The Wilderness Access Center at Mile 1 on the Park Road is the place to go for bus reservations of any kind, campground reservations/check-in, to grab a quick snack, or fill up a water bottle. All shuttle and some tour buses originate at this facility, which is operated not by the National Park Service but rather Aramark/Doyon, the park's concessionaire. The ticket desk is open 7 a.m.–7 p.m.; the center itself is open 5 a.m.–7 p.m. for bus departures and coffee (you'll need it if you head out on that 5 a.m. bus).

Eielson Visitor Center at Mile 66 on the Denali Park Road is reached by taking either a park shuttle bus or the Kantishna Experience Tour bus. Opening later in the spring/summer seasons than the other centers purely out of weather-related practicality, Eielson offers families a host of daily ranger-led programs, a wonderful art gallery, hiking trails, and knock-out views of Mount McKinley and the Alaska Range. Many visitors simply utilize Eielson as a break spot as they travel to and from other activities, but it is worth spending a little extra time here. No food service is available, but you can fill up a water bottle and restrooms are left unlocked 24/7. Open 9 a.m.–7 p.m. (June through September, weather permitting).

There are approximately 1,760 caribou living within the Denali National Park boundaries, according to the National Park Service. During the 1920s and '30s, however, numbers were much greater, with about 20,000 caribou wandering the barren land of the park.

Alaska Fact

ACTIVITIES WITHIN THE PARK

Sled dog demonstrations showcase the only working canine team actively patrolling a United States national park. Integral to supporting efforts of researchers, rangers, and others who work within the two million acres of designated wilderness area, the teams are reminders of a rich history of dogsledding in Alaska. Sled dogs have been utilized in Denali National Park since it opened, and demonstrations are offered free of charge to park visitors thrice-daily at 10 a.m., 2 p.m., and 4 p.m., providing an up-close, paws-on chance to see these canine workers in action. Pick up a shuttle to the **Sled Dog Kennels** at the Denali Visitor Center 40 minutes prior to the demonstration and plan to spend at least an hour at the program, including dog cuddle time. This activity is suitable for the entire family. Demonstrations occur rain or shine, so bring a raincoat and hat. Before you visit, be sure and check out the "Puppy Paws" video series on YouTube (www.youtube.com/denalinps). It's full of pint-size sled dog antics and a great way to preview what you'll see in real life. Plus, those puppies are so danged cute.

Day hiking is outstanding within the park, thanks to incredible improvements made by trail crews over the last few years. Near the entrance area, all trails are wide, gravel pathways that work well for

A visit to the Denali sled dog kennels means time with these famous canines.

strollers or new walkers. At any of the park's visitor centers, you can pick up a map showing all trails, their mileage, surface, and any interpretive features.

I like the **Savage River Canyon** trails, located at the Savage River check station, 15 miles into the park, a two-mile hike along the river or a shorter, one-mile Nature Trail loop hike around the riverbed and surrounding tundra. The Canyon trail is narrow, rocky, and slippery in places, so strollers are out of the question, and toddlers should be in backpacks due to close proximity to the rushing Savage River. Look for a quaint footbridge at the river crossing and keep an eye out for Dall sheep on the rocky cliffs above.

For those wanting a short hike with plenty of wide-open beauty, try the **Mountain Vista** loop, adjacent to the Savage River Campground and Mountain Vista Day Use Area, around Mile 13. Picnic tables, restrooms, and a wide, level trail complete with interpretive signs allow everyone to explore at their own pace.

Near the park entrance, take hardier hikers on the two-mile-round-trip **Horseshoe Lake Trail**. Find the trailhead at Mile 1 of the Park Road, just as you cross the railroad tracks. Walk along the pathway adjacent to the tracks (watching for trains, of course), cross at the safety area, and head down to the lake. A few steep pitches exist on this trail, so parents of small children should hang on to their charges very carefully and consider carrying a walking stick or hiking pole. Horseshoe Lake is very buggy but busy with local beavers who are building enormous dams across the narrow lake sections and into the muddy shoreline. It is tons of fun to walk around the lake and see who's recently chewed on what tree. Benches for relaxing can be found on the north side.

Note: This trail crosses Alaska Railroad tracks, so stop, look, and listen!

Cycling is an increasingly popular mode for exploring the park. While it may be a bit difficult to navigate the entire 92 miles of dirt road into the park, families have a number of options available for some easy off-road

Winning the Lottery

Denali National Park offers its own special game of chance for those willing to visit later in the fall. Each September, after most of the tour companies have closed up shop for the season and autumn's breath begins to play upon the landscape, the park hosts a four-day bonanza of sightseeing known as Road Lottery. During this stretch of time (different dates every year, but generally in the middle of September), winners of the lottery are issued a single day-long permit to drive the entire Denali Park Road as far as weather will allow them to go. This is a highly coveted opportunity, and I know families who have applied each May for a chance to drive the road and witness the transition from fall to winter. Sadly, many of us have never received this opportunity and thus must either beg friends to take us along or suck it up until next year. It costs $10 to apply and the single permit, once awarded, is $25. Apply by phone at 877-444-6777 or via www.recreation.gov.

We head to the park early in May, before the crowds, and bike as far as we can go from Riley Creek check station. Biking in Denali is just so awesome, and the kids love it!

—Barb, mother of two

biking, beginning at Mile 1. The main entrance to Denali National Park offers parking spots for offloading bikes. With several gravel and paved trails at your disposal, some leading to the Glitter Gulch/Nenana Canyon area, families who bring bikes are guaranteed plenty of cruising time. Since trails are wide and generally flat, younger children on tagalongs and babies in trailers can have fun, too. The Denali Outdoor Center (www.denalioutdoorcenter.com, 888-303-1925) in Glitter Gulch rents bigger bikes at $7/hour with a two-hour minimum or six hours for $25. Kids' bikes and trailers can be rented in Anchorage via Downtown Bicycle Rental (www.alaska-bike-rentals.com, BicycleAlaska@aol.com, 907-279-5293) for a daily or weekly rate, if you have a way to get the equipment to the park.

If you do choose to venture beyond the Savage River check station (I wouldn't recommend riding up the hilly 15 miles out of the entrance area), be wary of kids and traffic. While the majority of motorized vehicles you'll see are likely to be shuttle or tour buses, a good many RVs and private cars are allowed to drive via permit to their campsites. Kids may become anxious at the sight of a two-ton bus barreling down the road, so parents should be extra cautious about bike safety. Helmets, gloves, and long pants/sleeves are a must. Don't forget bug spray, either; the tundra is a haven for mosquitoes.

Alaska Fact

Denali National Park has three dozen species of mammals, but no reptiles. So don't go looking for snakes, because you won't find any here, or in all of Alaska, for that matter.

Family Fun Outside Denali National Park

A host of activities awaits families with a little extra time to play beyond the interior area of the park. Catering to the adrenaline junkie in everyone (okay, almost everyone), the following businesses in the greater DNP area have cooked up a variety of fun adventures that hold the attention of children, especially those in the tween/teen category.

RIVER RAFTING

Nenana Raft Adventures
Mile 238 Parks Highway, AK 99743
(907) 683-7238

Nenana Raft Adventures offers a spectrum of 2.5-hour rafting adventures suitable for kids as young as five. Experienced guides will float your family down the scenic Nenana River, featuring rapids ranging from II to IV, depending upon your level of experience. Transportation, drysuits, life jackets, and river booties provided. **Note**: Inquire carefully about life preservers for younger children and be accurate about your child's weight/height. Trips start at $90/per person, adults, $80/per person for kids under 10.

Denali Outdoor Center
Mile 238.9 Parks Highway, AK 99743
(888) 303-1925, (907) 683-1925
www.denalioutdoorcenter.com, info@denalioutdoorcenter.com

Denali Outdoor Center is a longtime winner with locals who visit Denali. Their tours include a two-hour Canyon Run trip, suitable for hard-to-please older kids ages 14 and up. Let them paddle alongside the guide during this 11-mile float. For families with kids age five and up, the milder Scenic Wilderness float is two-hour trip that takes passengers through some lovely mountain landscape. All PFDs and drysuits are provided, but be sure to inquire about children's life vests.

FLIGHTSEEING

Era Helicopters

Mile 238 Parks Highway (just as you come over the Nenana River bridge), AK 99743
(800) 843-1947, (907) 683-2574
www.eraflightseeing.com

Era Helicopters is the premier vendor for flightseeing adventures over and through Denali National Park. Taking a helicopter up North America's highest peak then plopping down on a glacier for a little stroll is expensive, for sure, but if you haven't yet had the opportunity to view Alaska from above, this might be a good option. Flights range from two and a half hours to five hours, depending upon the tour, and kids who are old enough to sit still and appreciate the atmosphere are most welcome (four and up, in my opinion). A great time to consider a flightseeing trip is late summer, when leaves are beginning to turn yellow and wildlife are very active as they prepare for winter's arrival. Transportation provided from most hotels in the Denali National Park area. Excursions begin at $344/pp, based upon weight. Call for more information, including a fly/hike expedition and glacier landing tour.

DOG MUSHING

Husky Homestead

P.O. Box 48, Denali National Park and Preserve, AK 99743
(907) 683-2904
www.huskyhomestead.com, info@huskyhomestead.com

Husky Homestead, owned and operated by veteran musher and Iditarod champion Jeff King, remains one of the top attractions for visitors to Denali National Park. This three-hour tour is full of wiggling, barking, yowling energy (from the dogs, not Mr. King—at least, not usually). Transportation is provided to and from most lodging in the Glitter Gulch/greater DNP area and the tour includes puppy cuddling, a great history lesson, and a peek into the world of sled dog training (the journey of a thousand miles begins with a single paw print). Prices begin around

$60/adults, $40/kids 11 and under. **Note:** King does not recommend this tour for kids under three years of age.

ATV TOURS

Denali Tundra Tours

Mile 238.7 Parks Highway, Denali National Park, AK 99743
(907) 683-2746
www.denalitundratours.com, info@denalitundratours.com

Denali Tundra Tours, located in Healy (10 miles north of the park entrance), offers two separate opportunities for gearheads in the family to motor up these six-wheeled wonders and chug into the wild. Both provide lunch, drinks, equipment, and a guide as your kids witness the prime mode of transportation into Alaska's wilderness. The Stampede Wilderness Tour, at four and a half hours, is suitable for drivers 16 and older or passengers with a parent's permission. Great views and some fun terrain. The Tundra Picnic Tour is perfect for families or anyone who doesn't want to drive and includes a fireside picnic lunch in full view of the national park. Transportation to/from area hotels provided. Main office is located in Glitter Gulch. Tours begin around $125/person for the Stampede Wilderness trip and $75/person for the Tundra Picnic.

Black Diamond Resort

Mile 247 Parks Highway, Healy, AK 99743
(907) 683-4653
www.blackdiamondgolf.com, usbelli@mtaonline.net

Black Diamond Resort, also in Healy, has a variety of ATV tours to explore the back roads of this mountainous area. Some include breakfast, lunch, or dinner, some provide the opportunity to drive oneself, but all make sure the essence of Alaska's backcountry travel is clearly defined. Whether you choose an individual ATV to drive or select a group tour or the popular Geocaching Tour, your family will enjoy Black Diamond's hospitality. Tours start around $100. Transportation to and from hotels is provided.

OTHER ACTIVITIES

Black Diamond Resort

Mile 247 Parks Highway, Healy, AK 99743
(907) 683-4653
www.blackdiamondgolf.com, usbelli@mtaonline.net

Black Diamond Resort also offers golf, a Kids' Club, and the opportunity to take an authentic covered wagon ride through the Healy countryside. A truly "come and play all day" sort of place, Black Diamond caters to the family that may need to divide and conquer their outdoor adventures or to the individual who truly wants to do it all. The Kids' Club is available to children ages 4 to 14 and offers hikes, wagon rides, golf lessons, and nature crafts from 8 a.m. to 8 p.m. $25/three hours of care, per child. Transportation provided between area hotels and the resort. Packages for combo adventures are available.

ALASKA'S INTERIOR

> "The Yosemite Valley is beautiful, the Yellowstone Park is wonderful, the Canyon of the Colorado is colossal, and Alaska is all of these."
>
> —Burton Holmes (1917)

Alaskans commonly refer to the north-central section of Alaska as the Interior. Mostly vast wilderness, the Interior encompasses Denali National Park and the Richardson, Denali, and Parks Highways (see Chapter 12).

This is the Alaska people often view in magazines, with Mount McKinley looming large as a backdrop for birch forests and muskeg. Rural roads, when they exist, often consist of dirt or gravel, and travel is accomplished by four-wheeler in the summer and snowmachine in the winter. The Interior is home to the Athabascan people, proud shareholders of their land, stretching across much of the central areas of Alaska.

Fairbanks: "The Golden Heart City"

Fairbanks, a city of around 32,000 people, is usually as far north as most Alaska visitors dare to venture. Located roughly 360 miles from Anchorage, Fairbanks has a frontier-like atmosphere, partly from a rich gold-mining history but also due to the free-spirited attitude of residents and college students who live there. The community sits on both sides

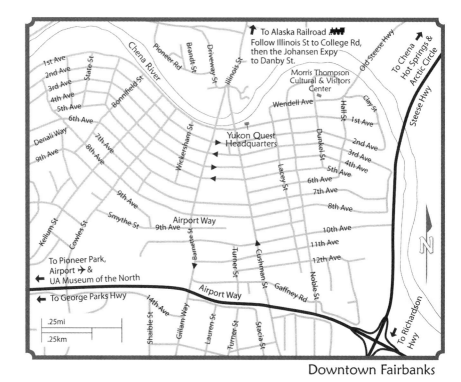

Downtown Fairbanks

Fairbanks

Population: 32,000 (2012 census)

Founded in: 1901 by Captain E. T. Barnette, who set up a trading post with the help of his friend, Judge James Wickersham. The city was named Fairbanks after then-Indiana Senator Charles Fairbanks, whom the good judge greatly admired. The city was formally incorporated in 1903.

Known for: Displays of the aurora borealis, or northern lights, especially during March and October.

Interesting fact: The Chena River usually freezes up in late October and stays that way until late April or early May.

Hot tip: If you're looking for an adventure, try visiting Fairbanks in late February or early March, when festivals celebrating ice, sled dog racing, or snowmachines provide lots of activity. Plus, the northern lights are amazing!

of the Chena River near its confluence with the Tanana River and holds an important place in Alaska's industrial progression. Gold mining, river commerce, and even farming in the Tanana Valley area were critical components to the evolution of Fairbanks. While the steamship era has sadly ended, mining, agriculture, and tourism keep Fairbanks alive and kicking with a vigorous energy.

Despite subarctic conditions (dry and cold in the winter and dry and hot in the summer), Fairbanks residents thrive in this outdoor paradise, managing freezing winters with layers of clothing and a sense of humor as gritty as the snow outside.

ARRIVING

By Air

Fairbanks International Airport (dot.alaska.gov/faiiap/index.shtml) is the hub for interior Alaska travel, though it's not a large airport. Taxi services are easily found just outside the main doors of the airport, and most hotels provide transportation. The cruise industry also provides transport for its passengers, picking up or dropping off with regularity. Fairbanks is also a hub for flights into bush Alaska, with smaller regional carriers serving these communities.

By Rail

The Alaska Railroad's passenger service (www.alaskarailroad.com, 800-544-0552) terminates in Fairbanks after a 12-hour trip from Anchorage, with stops in Talkeetna and Denali National Park. A beautiful, peaceful ride for most adults, the railroad journey from Anchorage to Fairbanks is often a stretch for most kids. Consider one of the Alaska Railroad's packages, whereby you can fly to Fairbanks and take the train south, or vice versa. It's a nice option for those who want the train experience without taking two full days up and back.

By Car/RV

Many people choose to drive to Fairbanks. Lots of interesting sights along the way mean plenty of wildlife, history, and activity, experienced at your own pace. Fairbanks can be approached one of two ways: by motor vehicle via the Parks Highway stretching from Wasilla to Fairbanks and going right through Denali National Park, or via the Richardson Highway, winding north past Glenallen and Tok and Delta Junction. Either way, allow at least a full day to arrive in the Golden Heart City, two days if you're not in a hurry (recommended). The landscape changes dramatically from Anchorage to Fairbanks, shifting from forested hills to tundra and back again, and the opportunity to mingle with Mother Nature among the birch and spruce trees is worth the extra time with kids.

GETTING AROUND

Fairbanks is not a large community by most Lower 48 standards, but the **Fairbanks Convention and Visitors Bureau,** located on Dunkel Street along the banks of the Chena River, provides an excellent map to make driving around pretty simple.

Local roadways establish a fairly consistent grid of main thoroughfares, with the Parks and Richardson Highways terminating near the fringes of town. North is the community of Fox and access to the Chena Hot Springs Road, the end of which is home to the famous Chena Hot Springs Resort. North of Fox are communities like Circle, where more and more tourists venture for a taste of the true Arctic. East of Fairbanks is the town of North Pole, where Santa Claus lives (we'll talk more about the big guy later in this chapter). West is the little town of Ester, where gardens grow and true frontier lifestyles exist. Fairbanks is situated in a borough, like most Alaska communities, but unlike others still has retained separation of borough and city government. Fairbanks is also home to the University of Alaska Fairbanks, perched on a hill overlooking the Tanana Valley.

Rental Cars

Fairbanks has a fair number of car and RV rental agencies for those who wish to explore on their own. Many are located at the Fairbanks International Airport, but a few are just a stone's throw from the runway and very convenient to reach. The advantage of independent exploring of the Fairbanks area with kids is the obvious flexibility a vehicle provides, given the nature of the area's widespread recreational opportunities.

Avis
Fairbanks International Airport, 6450 Airport Way, Ste. 5
(907) 474-0900
www.avisalaska.com

GoNorth Car Rental
3713 Lathrop St., Fairbanks, AK 99709
(907) 479-7272

Budget Rent A Car
Fairbanks International Airport, 6450 Airport Way, Ste. 15
(907) 474-0855

PUBLIC TRANSPORTATION

Bus service in Fairbanks is provided through MACS (Metro Area Commuter System) (www.co.fairbanks.ak.us/transportation). As the sole public transportation option, MACS takes riders throughout Fairbanks and out to the city of North Pole. Featuring eight different lines, MACS is a pretty reliable way to shuttle to and from many of Fairbanks's major attractions for a reasonable price. Fares begin at $1.50 per ride for adults, $.75 for students K–12, military, or disabled patrons. Kids five and under are free. A day pass costs $3 and can be an excellent value for families.

SHOPPING/GROCERIES

As a major hub for Interior and arctic Alaska travel and commerce, Fairbanks offers visitors many choices for shopping. All are within close proximity to the airport and surrounding hotels, in addition to being located on the bus lines.

Fred Meyer
3755 Airport Way, Fairbanks, AK 99701
(907) 474-1400
www.fredmeyer.com

Groceries, deli, pharmacy, banking, fuel station, souvenirs, and Starbucks coffee shop.

Safeway
3627 Airport Way, Fairbanks, AK 99701
(907) 374-4060

Groceries, deli, pharmacy, Starbucks coffee shop, fuel station, and some souvenirs.

MEDICAL CARE

Fairbanks Memorial Hospital
1650 Cowles St., Fairbanks, AK 99701
(907) 452-8181
www.bannerhealth.com/fairbanks

VISITOR INFORMATION

The **Fairbanks Convention and Visitors Bureau** (101 Dunkel St., Ste. 111, www.explorefairbanks.com, 907-456-5774) is housed inside the beautiful Morris Thompson Cultural and Visitor Center and shares space with the Alaska Public Lands Information Center, Tanana Valley Chiefs Conference, and Alaska Geographic, making this a perfect first stop for visitors. Plus, this facility also possesses some of the finest exhibits depicting life, culture, and history of the Interior and arctic communities of Alaska, including the various tribal groups. Interactive, fresh, and compelling, the building is a hub of activity any time of year. Plan to spend at least an hour wandering the exhibits or perusing the vast collection of maps and information available. Open daily 9 a.m.–9 p.m. during the summer months; hours vary during the winter.

Alaska Fact

A deposit of ice crystals on stationary objects exposed to free air is called "hoarfrost." This phenomenon is caused by direct condensation of water vapor to ice at temperatures below freezing, and occurs when air is brought to frost point by cooling.

LODGING

While a large number of Fairbanks visitors are part of an organized tour, and thus have little say in the matter of accommodations, independent travelers will find plenty of accommodations that welcome children.

Near Fairbanks International Airport

Alpine Lodge $$
4920 Dale Rd., Fairbanks, AK 99709
(800) 455-8851, (907) 328-6300
www.akalpinelodge.com

Alpine Lodge is a clean, affordable option for families looking for a quality stay without a lot of frills. Featuring 199 standard rooms, junior suites, and larger family suites, Alpine Lodge's rooms fit all budgets. Rooms come standard with full bath/shower, Wi-Fi, cable television, coffee maker, and refrigerator. A junior or family suite will include a kitchenette, small sink, and separate room for eating. The family suite also features a huge soaker tub in the main living/sleeping area, a bit odd but fun. Breakfast can be purchased for $3/person, with hot and cold cereals, toast and muffins, fruit, juice, and a hot entree. Coffee and tea are always available. An attached restaurant, The Finish Line, is a recent addition to the property, offering lunch and dinner during the summer months, with a well-balanced children's menu. A free shuttle service is provided to or from the airport or train station. Military upgrades are available.

Thumbs-up for: Low-key but attractive atmosphere, plenty of room for families, proximity to Fairbanks airport.

Pike's Lodge $$–$$$
1850 Hoselton Dr., Fairbanks, AK 99709
(877) 774-2400, (907) 456-4500
www.pikeslodge.com, info@pikeslodge.com

Pike's Lodge is a fun place for families. Set on the banks of the Chena River in a spot called Pike's Landing, the lodge and adjacent restaurant are known for true northern hospitality and Alaska decor. From the free ice cream offered nightly to all guests to the little putting green outside, Pike's provides great service in a resort-style atmosphere. The property features 180 rooms, including 25 sets of adjoining rooms, and accessible cabins with kitchenettes. A limited number of cribs are available for parents of small children. Continental breakfast is included. The lodge also shares property with Pike's Landing Restaurant and Lounge, whose enormous riverside deck is a great spot to have a cold beverage and a burger during the summer months. The restaurant provides high chairs. A complimentary shuttle is available to and from the train depot and/or airport.

Thumbs-up for: Alaska-themed atmosphere, proximity to outdoor activities, including a paved walking trail and miniature golf putting green. Free ice cream is a lovely touch.

North-Central Fairbanks

Hampton Inn $$-$$$
433 Harold Bentley Ave., Fairbanks, AK 99701
(907) 451-1502

One of the newer properties in Fairbanks, Hampton Inn (part of the Hilton chain) is fresh, clean, and decidedly businesslike. But don't let that throw you off—the hotel caters to kids in a big way, right down to the freshly baked cookies every day and the sparkling-clean swimming pool. All rooms feature fluffy bedding, huge televisions, a free hot breakfast, and lovely common area great for playing games or reading. Cribs and high chairs are readily available and transportation is available from the airport or train depot. Staff are gracious to families, and we return due to the warm welcome we always receive. Not set in the most picturesque of settings (across a busy parkway from a shopping center), the Hampton Inn nonetheless delivers in service and quality.

Thumbs-up for: Modern feel with kid-friendly appeal, excellent staff, swimming pool, snacks, and full breakfast.

Wedgewood Resort–Fountainhead Hotels $$-$$$
1501 Queens Way, Fairbanks, AK 99701
(800) 528-4916, (907) 456-3642
www.fountainheadhotels.com, hotels@fdifairbanks.com

Tucked between a wildlife sanctuary and College Road is Wedgewood Resort, a solid choice for families wanting more space for their traveling dollar. Part of the Fountainhead Hotels community, Wedgewood Resort is less fancy than other lodging options but provides more, more, more in the fun-and-games department. Located on 105 acres filled with trees, trails, and an antique automobile museum, Wedgewood has plenty to offer. Two options exist for family travelers: Bear Lodge, a 157-room hotel with large rooms, and the Wedgewood Suites, featuring apartment-style lodging in one- or two-room suites. A free trolley offers transportation around downtown Fairbanks (and to/from airport or train station, too), and everyone will enjoy the Fountainhead Antique Auto Museum and a hike around lovely Wander Lake. While not the most modern of properties, it does have very accommodating staff. Cribs and high chairs are limited in number, so do call ahead. A café in Bear Lodge is fair, food-wise, and rather expensive.

Thumbs-up for: Fabulous trails and activities on site, helpful staff, fun trolley ride. The property snugs up to Creamer's Field Migratory Bird Refuge and all trails from Wedgewood lead to the refuge, a wonderful spot for kids.

Alternative Accommodations

Fairbanks Association of Bed and Breakfasts
www.ptialaska.net/~fabb, fabb@ptialaska.net

The Fairbanks/Interior chapter of the Bed and Breakfast Association of Alaska offers a nice listing of B&Bs within the greater Fairbanks area. Ranging in style and price, these lodgings might be a great option for those who want an intimate, more personal Alaska experience.

CAMPING
Fairbanks is an awesome place to camp with the family, thanks to warm, sunny summer nights that (almost) never end, placid rivers and creeks, and shady birch forests. An advantage of Fairbanks's frontier appeal is that even in-town campgrounds feel like rural sites, a double win for convenience and amenities.

Note: Mosquitoes in Fairbanks are probably the ones you read about prior to heading north; they are relentless, ever-present, and a true nuisance to your family if you don't apply repellant.

Chena River Wayside State Recreation Park and Campground
221 University Ave., Fairbanks, AK 99701
(907) 452-PARK
www.fairbankscampground.com

Located on the banks of the placid Chena River, just off University Avenue and featuring five walk-in tent sites and 56 RV sites, most with water and power, this 26-acre park is a forested, relatively quiet option, save for the road right next door. The recently renovated park now features walkways, free Wi-Fi, and a swing set, volleyball, and horseshoe pitch for family fun. No reservations.

River's Edge RV Park and Campground
4140 Boat St., Fairbanks, AK 99709
(800) 770-3343, (907) 474-4286
www.riversedge.net

River's Edge offers a more modern "glamping" experience, with cable television, Wi-Fi, and tour arrangements on its 190-space property. Located on the Chena River, this is a popular place for RV travelers and fills up quickly. Kids will enjoy the walking trails.

Tanana Valley Campground and RV Park
1800 College Rd., Fairbanks, AK 99709
(907) 456-7956
www.fairbankscampgroundandrvpark.com

Tanana Valley Campground sits right next to the Tanana Valley Fairgrounds and is adjacent to Creamer's Field Migratory Bird Refuge. Set among tallish trees (for the Interior, anyway), the campground boasts a traditional campground feel. Featuring 50 sites, 30 of which accommodate RVs, the property is close to trails, a local farmer's market, and, of course, the annual Tanana Valley Fair, held each August. Find current rates or make reservations online.

Chena Lake Recreation Area
3780 Laurance Rd., North Pole, AK 99705
(907) 459-1070
co.fairbanks.ak.us/parksandrecreation/facilities/clra/clra.htm

Chena Lake Recreation Area is a short drive from downtown Fairbanks, near the community of North Pole. This 2,100-acre park shares space with the Chena River and Chena Lake, and miles and miles of outdoor biking, hiking, and camping can be found throughout the park. Popular camping areas include the Lake Park and River Park, each with 80 sites (some pull-throughs). A small island in the middle of the lake offers six boat-accessible tent sites, if you really feel adventurous. Chena Lake Recreation Area is a great value, too; tents are only $10 and campers/RVs a mere $12 per night. There are no reservations, so come early. Stays are limited to five days, or 10 days total within a consecutive 30-day period.

FEEDING THE FAMILY

Fairbanks is home to a variety of restaurants, coffee shops, and pubs that welcome children. One notable difference between dining in Interior Alaska and other areas of the state (that is, those with saltwater nearby) is a minimalist approach to seafood, which may or may not matter to your family. While many people can and do order the famous Alaska salmon, halibut, or crab dishes at Fairbanks restaurants, the resulting product will not be from a fish caught that very day, unless someone has a connection I don't know about. Interior Alaska is also catching on to the Alaska Grown movement, with local farms providing fresh produce, meat, and eggs to many restaurants, a lovely shift to homegrown products and sure to please the crowds of diners who arrive in Alaska each summer looking for unique experiences.

> **PARENT PRO TIP**
>
> If your family is up for a longer drive outside of Fairbanks, check out the resources at Chena River State Recreation Area (dnr.alaska.gov/parks/units/chena/index.htm). A variety of hiking trails, fishing, camping, cabins, and a picnic area. Do bring DEET, hoodies, and possibly head nets; it's a boggy area alive with mosquitoes.
>
> —James, Fairbanks father of one

Below are a few family favorites, based upon exhaustive (and digestive) research. All welcome children to their tables. All restaurants take credit cards unless otherwise noted.

Restaurants

FAIRBANKS CITY LIMITS

The Pump House $$$
796 Chena Pump Rd., Fairbanks, AK 99709
(907) 479-8452
www.pumphouse.com
Open daily 11:30 a.m.–1 a.m. (Memorial Day–Labor Day), Tuesday–Saturday, 4
p.m.–midnight, Sunday 10 a.m.–12 p.m. (winter hours starting Labor Day weekend)

Housed in an old pump house along the banks of the Chena River, the
Pump House restaurant has been serving up Alaska cuisine and rip-
roaring atmosphere since 1933 (most rip-roaring was done in the saloon,
I assure you). Reconstructed in 1978 to better accommodate diners who
actually wanted to sit down and eat, the Pump House is a popular establishment serving a healthy portion of everything, including steaks and a
variety of unique game dishes like musk ox and reindeer. This is the place
to go if you desire something different. Expensive, yes, but worth it for
the atmosphere and lovely riverside view, especially when kayakers and
boaters stop by and hang out on the deck.

Geraldo's Italian Restaurant $$$
701 College Rd., Fairbanks, AK 99701
(907) 452-2299
Open year-round for lunch and dinner. Call for current hours.

How about a nice Chianti and plate of ravioli after a busy day of exploring?
Family-owned Geraldo's is one of those restaurants that fits like a pair of
comfortable jeans—just right. It's not the place to go if you're in a hurry,
but we like the atmosphere here—walking in the door is a garlicky-sweet
trip, and we quickly forget about the longish wait for a table. Our son loves
the homemade ravioli, and my husband and I usually split an artichoke,
chicken, and garlic pizza. The food is typical Italian and not at all fancy,
but parents can let the kids scream for ice cream (gelato) afterwards.

The Cookie Jar $$
1006 Cadillac Ct., Fairbanks, AK 99701
(907) 479-8319
www.cookiejarfairbanks.com
Open Monday–Thursday 6:30 a.m.–8 p.m., Friday–Saturday 6:30 a.m.–9 p.m.,
Sunday 8:30 a.m.–4 p.m.

You can't go wrong steering kids into a restaurant named for dessert. We stumbled upon the Cookie Jar many years ago and find it to be a comforting, family-friendly place. Open early for breakfast and serving homemade scones, pancakes, and quiches, among other favorites, the Cookie Jar fills up fast, and by dinner, waitstaff are scrambling to fill orders for a variety of selections, including burgers, lasagna, salads, and wraps. It's a catchall menu, and kids love the variety, thankfully, with their own menu and coloring pages. Don't leave without buying a few (or a dozen) cookies.

Bulgogi Grill $$
400 College Rd., Fairbanks, AK, 99701
(907) 455-9116
www.ichibanalaska.com
Open daily until midnight during the summer months, variable during the winter. Call for specific hours/dates.

Our kid likes noodles. A lot. After driving past the little restaurant with its quaint deck and flower beds umpteen times and never stopping, we finally did one muggy, summer afternoon after a hiking trip. An hour later, we were fully immersed in pot stickers, chicken wings, and fresh, hot noodles. Service is delightful, portions are just right, and the tiny place has a truly family-friendly atmosphere. Non–noodle-eaters can find solace in some chicken strips and french fries. The only drawback might be the lack of beer or wine, but that is hardly a reason to avoid Bulgogi Grill.

Lemongrass $$
388 Old Chena Pump Plaza, Fairbanks, AK 99709
(907) 456-2200
www.lemongrassalaska.com
Open Monday–Saturday, serving lunch 11 a.m.–4 p.m. and dinner 5–10 p.m.

With a motto of "Making Alaska hotter since 1996," Lemongrass is a Thai restaurant located in a strip mall next to the Parks Highway. It's hot all right, and between hotness of spice and hotness of popularity, Lemongrass pleases a diverse crowd. A supporter of locally grown foods, the restaurant also prides itself on the freshest ingredients in its authentic Thai dishes. Look for satay, curries, and delicious soups. A vegetarian menu is also available. No specific children's menu, but staff are accommodating for orders of favorites like rice, chicken, and vegetables.

OUTSIDE FAIRBANKS

Silver Gulch Restaurant
2195 Old Steese Highway, Fox, AK, 99712
(907) 452-2739
www.silvergulch.com
Open Monday–Thursday 4–10 p.m., Friday 4–11 p.m., Saturday 11 a.m.–11 p.m.,
Sunday 11 a.m.–10 p.m.

A brewing-and-bottling company located in the small mining community of Fox, Silver Gulch's restaurant opened in 2007. Serving pub food with an Alaska twist, the restaurant is always busy, especially on the weekends. We love the gourmet burgers, pizzas, and bistro plates with things like zesty halibut tacos and beer-braised pork ribs. Partner any menu item with one of Silver Gulch's craft ales, and it's a celebration indeed. Kids have their own menu, too, with mini corn dogs, delicious fries, veggie platters, and lemonade on the list. Younger visitors are treated to coloring pages and crayons as well. Silver Gulch also serves brunch on the weekends.

FAMILY FUN IN FAIRBANKS

Fairbanks residents are a community of doers, whether the sun is blazing overhead or temperatures are plummeting far below zero. While Fairbanks has had its share of economic depression (and it shows in a somewhat drab downtown area), the city is nonetheless a vibrant example of just how determined Alaskans can be when it comes to making things happen. Miles of biking and walking trails, playgrounds, and a focus on Interior Alaska's history all play a role in the success of Fairbanks as a destination for visitors.

Museums and Cultural Experiences

University of Alaska Museum of the North
907 Yukon Dr., Fairbanks, AK 99775
(907) 474-7505
www.uaf.edu/museum, museum@uaf.edu
Open daily 9 a.m.–7 p.m. (May–September), Monday–Saturday 9 a.m.–5 p.m.
(late September–early May)
Admission: $12/general, $7/youth (1–14), $8/Alaska resident with ID (15+),
$5 Alaska resident youth (1–14).

The only museum in the state offering education, research, and cultural exploration of Alaska and the entire circumpolar North, the Museum of the North sits on a bluff at the University of Alaska Fairbanks campus. Known for its cultural history research, the museum's exhibits are quite detailed and intricate, so younger children may quickly become bored. Older kids, though, will have fun in the Gallery of Alaska, where an enormous bear greets visitors as they embark on an adventure through time. This is where I'd spend most of my time with kids; the art galleries, while incredibly beautiful, are simply not meant for younger visitors. Check out "The Place Where You Go to Listen" on the second floor, though. This small, blank space features sounds of earth's magnetic forces, both below and above. Always different, and quite intriguing, the room is a reminder that our environment is constantly changing. The museum offers regular family nights during the summer; check the website for dates and times. Also recently partnered up with the Fairbanks Children's Museum.

Fountainhead Antique Auto Museum
212 Wedgewood Dr., Fairbanks, AK 99701
(907) 450-2100
www.fountainheadmuseum.com, info@fountainheadmuseum.com
Open Sunday–Thursday 11 a.m.–10 p.m., Friday–Saturday, 11 a.m.–6 p.m. Winter hours vary, so contact museum for hours and dates.
Admission: $4/Fountainhead Hotels guest; otherwise $8/adult; $5/kids 3–12; free for kids under two.

Operating out of a large, spotlessly clean garage space at the far end of Wedgewood Resort, the Antique Auto Museum houses vehicles from early Victorian days through the Swing era. Kept in pristine condition, the automobiles, bikes, and snow cars all run (where applicable) and are regularly spun around the parking lot to keep their motors in tip-top shape. Sprinkled among the autos is a collection of vintage clothing, and many a photo op has been staged at the back of the facility,

> **PARENT PRO TIP**
>
> This is a great place to take teenagers, by the way. Young people will enjoy talking shop with manager Willy or swooning over the vintage clothing and shoes.
>
> —The author, mother of a sometimes-surly teen

where both grown-up- and kid-size dusters and hats are ready for dress up. Small kids have the chance to play cars with a floor mat and box of familiar toy cars, and if facility manager Willy is around, he might let them honk the big ka-hoo-ga horn. Suitable for the whole family, but tiny toddlers may have trouble keeping hands to themselves.

Pioneer Air Museum

2300 Airport Way, Fairbanks, AK 99701
(907) 451-0037
www.pioneerairmuseum.org, curator@pioneerairmuseum.org
Open daily noon–8 p.m.
Admission: $2/adults (12 and older), $5/family

Located in popular Pioneer Park, the Pioneer Air Museum is a quirky place to investigate the history of far northern air travel. Housed in a dome-shaped building, the museum's exhibits run the gamut of aviation parts, clothing, and log books, with a healthy number of full-size aircraft. Kids will enjoy the helicopter and vintage uniforms and a chance to chat with military veterans who often volunteer. Lots and lots to see inside the golden dome. Suitable for all ages, a playground is also adjacent to the museum for small children who become restless.

Tanana Valley Railroad Museum

2300 Airport Way, Fairbanks, AK 99701
(907) 459-1087
www.co.fairbanks.ak.us/pioneerpark
Open daily noon–8 p.m. (Memorial Day–Labor Day and also by appointment)
Admission: Free; train rides $1/person

Just across the playground from the Pioneer Air Museum is the quaint Tanana Valley Railroad Museum and Tanana Valley RR. Just the right size for kids, the museum houses a number of restoration projects, interesting gold rush artifacts, and for a mere dollar, families can ride on the steam-fueled train around the park's perimeter, complete with narration by a volunteer guide.

Fairbanks Children's Museum

www.fairbankschildrensmuseum.com
Various "Museum Without Walls" events at local businesses, held year-round.
Check website for complete schedule.

The newest kid on the block as far as museums go, the Fairbanks Children's Museum currently shares space with the Museum of the North on the UAF campus. With painting, music, nature exploration, and other activities specific to Alaska, this museum is destined to be a hot spot for visiting parents who are looking for a kids-only attraction.

Gold Dredge 8

1803 Old Steese Highway North, Fox, AK 99712
(907) 479-6673
www.golddredge8.com, reservations@golddredge8.com
Two-hour tours operate daily throughout the summer months, 10:30 a.m. and 1:45 p.m.

With so much history focusing on gold, the mining industry of Interior Alaska, and a few popular television reality shows in the hopper, Fairbanks has become a hot destination for those wanting to experience the local "color" (miner-speak for gold). Gold Dredge 8 is a recent addition to the popular Riverboat Discovery partnership, replacing the now-defunct El Dorado Gold Mine. Guests ride a replica of the Tanana Valley Railroad complete with singing conductor, learning all about mining along the way. At camp, visitors see how miners actually find and separate gold from the rest of the dirt, then get to try panning for themselves. It's fun, it's informative, and kids love it. Suitable for children preschool and up, but younger ones may simply take in all the commotion and machinery.

Note: The company did not offer shuttle transportation in 2012, providing instead a list of taxi services and rental car agencies.

Riverboat Discovery

1975 Discovery Dr., Fairbanks, AK 99709
(907) 479-6673
www.riverboatdiscovery.com, reservations@riverboatdiscovery.com
Open daily mid-May–late September
Rates: $54.95/adult; $37.95/kids 3–12; kids under 3 free
Daily tours at 9 a.m. and 2 p.m., reservations required.

The Chena was a crucial element to the evolution of Fairbanks, and nowhere else in Alaska will visitors witness the value of the wide, winding river to a growing community. The Binkley family welcomes passengers aboard the authentic riverboat—complete with paddle wheel—with free doughnuts and lemonade (they had me hooked with those) for a three-hour tour into the heart of Interior Alaska. Watch a float plane take off and land on the river's mirrored surface, stop by the kennel of Iditarod legend the late Susan Butcher, then take a break at an Athabascan fish camp and settlement. The narration on board is fabulous, the boat is authentic, and even though there is not a lot of wandering room for small children, there's enough eye candy to keep most kids settled down until they reach the settlement and can walk along the trails.

Creamer's Field Migratory Waterfowl Refuge

1300 College Rd., Fairbanks, AK 99701
(907) 459-7307
www.creamersfield.org
Open year-round for walking, skiing, and scheduled wildlife hikes. Farmhouse Visitor Center open daily in the summer, 9 a.m.–5 p.m.; open Saturdays during the winter, noon–4 p.m.
Admission: Free, but donations are always welcome.

Creamer's Field is a great place for children any time of year. With a 250-acre former dairy farm at their disposal, visitors can enjoy thousands of migrating waterfowl and a series of trails that wind in and out of a beautiful boreal forest. Named for the Creamer family, who purchased the farm in 1928 and eventually passed it on to the community of Fairbanks, the dairy fields now provide forage for various species of birds, like sand-hill cranes, geese, and ducks. Stop by the Farmhouse Visitor Center for a quick peek into the history of this lovely spot, then pick a grassy trail to wander, ending up at the short but informative Boreal Forest loop, with interpretive signs and tons of interesting woodland sights. Suitable for the whole family, and jogging strollers do just fine here. Toddlers will love to run across the fields in a very safe environment. Do bring bug repellent.

Sirius Sled Dogs

Murphy Dome, Fairbanks, AK
(907) 687-6656
siriussleddogs.net@gmail.com, www.siriussleddogs.net
Summer tours, $125/person, ages 10 and up, with a two-person minimum, 12-person maximum. Includes transportation from guests' place of lodging. Winter tours begin at $125/person for a one-hour tour. Email for current rates and dates.

This adventure should be called *Serious* Sled Dogs, because it doesn't get more authentic than this. Owners Nita and Josh have created the perfect storm of dog fur, licks, and tail-wagging mushing fun at their off-the-grid homestead 25 miles from Fairbanks. Summertime means a combination kennel tour/mushing school and a dog cart ride aboard the famous Beetlebombtrainer (a 1968 VW Beetle stripped down to bare metal). This is an excellent activity for older children; the combination of one-to-one partnership with a four-legged host and the opportunity to learn how much work is involved in raising 18 active canine athletes is a valuable life lesson. The cart ride is a wild trip around the meadow and guests can drive. Suitable for tweens and teens.

Outdoor Recreation

Fairbanks has the advantage of nearly 24 hours of daylight at summer solstice in mid-June, which translates into tons of opportunities for soaking up the famous midnight sun.

The city of Fairbanks has nearly 50 miles of paved bike trails and at least 50 community parks, making it easy to find a spot for a little unstructured running amok (www.co.fairbanks.ak.us/parksandrecreation). The best walking/biking trail, in my opinion, is along the Chena River, where kids can safely navigate the flat terrain within full distance of kayakers, ducks, river boats, and local parks.

Pioneer Park
2300 Airport Way, Fairbanks, AK 99701
(907) 459-1087
www.co.fairbanks.ak.us/ParksandRecreation/PioneerPark/about/
history_pioneer_park

A favorite among Fairbanks parents. Formerly known as Alaskaland, this 40-acre park was created in 1968 as a tourist attraction to show off Alaska's history. Renamed Pioneer Park in 2002 to remove the theme-park persona, the property still retains the charm of its early days, with a Gold Rush Village and related shops, several small museums (including the Pioneer Air Museum and Tanana Valley Railroad mentioned earlier), miniature golf, a carousel, and two playgrounds. Admission is free, and many a family has spent an entire day enjoying the music and interesting exhibits detailing the Far North's history and culture. Food vendors are available and picnic shelters are scattered throughout the park.

Biking

Fairbanks Paddle and Pedal

300 Front Street, Fairbanks, AK 99701
(907) 388-4480
www.fbxpp.com

Provides guided bike tours of Fairbanks or sends you off on your own for a day of exploring the city.

Alaska Outdoor Rentals and Guides

1101 Peger Rd., Fairbanks, AK 99709
(907) 457-2453
www.akbike.com

Offers bike rentals, maps of the area, and guided excursions.

EcoSegAlaska

(907) 328-3557
www.EcoSegAK.com

Now this is an interesting way to see Fairbanks with your teenagers. Guided tours aboard a Segway start at $50 for 90 minutes of riding and sightseeing and progress up to $75 for two hours. Self-riding opportunities are available for those who wish to explore on their own, at $45/hour. All participants, regardless of experience, are required to attend a 15-to-20-minute training session and must wear the provided helmets. Riders must be at least 14 years old (anyone under 18 must be accompanied by a parent or guardian) and weigh between 100 and 260 pounds. Tours take off rain or shine, so be

> **PARENT PRO TIP**
>
> We love exploring the Tanana Valley Farmer's Market in Fairbanks along College Road (www.tvfmarket.com). Besides the awesome and enormous vegetables, we also sample the baked goods, local honey, and kettle corn.
>
> —Lisa, former Fairbanks resident and mother of two

prepared for anything. The company is rather mobile, with usual meeting places behind the Morris Thompson Cultural and Visitor Center on Dunkel Street.

Canoeing and Kayaking

The Chena River winds through downtown Fairbanks and beyond and offers several hours of paddling bliss for canoe and kayak enthusiasts. **Alaska Outdoor Rentals and Guides** (www.2paddle1.com, 907-457-2453) will provide your family with everything required for a day on the water: lifejackets, canoe or kayak, paddles, and even an experienced guide if you wish. A popular excursion is the two-hour paddle from the rental office at Pioneer Park to the Pump House Restaurant, where you can enjoy a meal or snack on the deck while waiting for the shuttle to come pick you up. Nice. No reservations required for most trips.

> **PARENT PRO TIP**
>
> The Chena River is a great river for a leisurely family canoe or kayak ride. We actually like to head toward the Upper Chena just outside of town and float down, finding little gravel bars for a break. We spot many forms of wildlife, including moose, eagles, beavers, and lots and lots of birds.
>
> —Casey, father of three

Hiking

With gentle rolling hills that belie the craggy peaks of Denali National Park in the distance, the greater Fairbanks area is a wonderful place to hike with kids.

In town, try **Creamer's Field Migratory Waterfowl Refuge** (www.creamersfield.org) for a gentle, scenic hike appropriate for everyone (mentioned in the "Family Fun" section, above). All trails are under two miles and feature interpretive signs and/or feathered friends that capture the attention of pint-sized trekkers.

Linked to Creamer's Field is Wedgewood Resort (212 Wedgewood Drive, www.fountainheadhotels.com) and its revegetated **Wander Lake** trail, a former gravel pit brought back to life by a dedicated cadre of scouts,

The Trans-Alaska Pipeline stretches 800 miles from Prudhoe Bay to Valdez, and is visible near Fairbanks.

community members, and Wedgewood Resort staff. It's a delightful little lake with two viewing decks and level gravel tread suitable for strollers. Watch for a family of beavers that occasionally paddle past on their way to chewing through more willows along the shoreline. The trail system amounts to just about 1.5 miles. Jogging strollers are perfect for this terrain, and toddlers and preschoolers will do just fine around the gravel pathways.

Chena Lake Recreation Area (co.fairbanks.ak.us/parksandrecreation/ Forms/CLRA/CLRAMap.pdf) boasts a wide variety of trail systems available for family strolling or hiking, including the 2.5-mile self-guided nature trail along the Chena River at the River Park. Kids can follow the interpretive signs and spot different flora and fauna along the way, ending up near the campground at River Park.

Alaska Fact

Fairbanks has fewer clouds than anywhere else in the state, mostly due to moisture crossing the Alaska Range to the south instead of heading north to town. This funky weather means light rain and even lighter, fluffier snow.

Angel Rocks trail (dnr.alaska.gov/parks/units/chena/trails) is a popular hike with Fairbanks residents, who enjoy the option of a scenic 3.5-mile hike to a collection of interesting granite formations or continuing on another five or so miles along the Angel Rocks–Chena Hot Springs Traverse, winding along the upper reaches of the Chena Hot Springs road on its way to Chena Hot Springs at the end. Great views of the Alaska Range, Chena Dome, and Far Mountain can be seen from the ridgeline, and a small spring awaits about halfway through the traverse hike. Find the trailhead for both hikes at Milepost 48 of the Chena Hot Springs Road. This is not for jogging strollers; bring a backpack for small children and do watch older ones on the slippery surfaces.

Other Adventures

Running Reindeer Ranch
1470 Ivan's Alley, Fairbanks, AK 99709
(907) 455-4998
www.runningreindeer.com

A visit to the Far North wouldn't be complete without an up-close, nose-to-slobbery-nose visit with a real live reindeer; you know, the kind Santa Claus uses to fly all around the world. Ranch owner Jane will greet you and your family at her forested home and take you for a walk with her herd of very amicable reindeer. Yes, that's right: your kids will be able to take a hike with both adults and calves and Jane herself, who will give you a history of the species and a little background on how she came to be a reindeer wrangler, and offer plenty of photo-taking opportunities. Suitable for the whole family. Do bring insect repellent—it's pretty buggy out there—and a backpack or jogging stroller for tiny children.

Alyeska Pipeline Service Company
Milepost 8 Steese Highway, Fox, AK
(907) 450-5857
www.alyeska-pipe.com
Free roadside attraction, open 24/7

A sightseeing stop to view a pipe sticking out of the ground? Really? Yes, everyone, and for one simple reason: it's your oil flowing through that enormous insulated pipe some 10 feet off the ground. From Prudhoe Bay to Valdez, 800 miles total, bubbling crude glugs its way through one of the greatest engineering marvels of all time and everyone, kids included, should stop and take a look. Remember to follow directions for safety; no climbing around or under, but do take photos to show off at home.

It cost more than $8 billion to build the pipeline in 1974. Completed in 1977, the pipeline can hold 9.04 million barrels of oil when full, taking 4.5 days to travel the 800 miles from Prudhoe Bay to Valdez.

Alaska Fact

Calypso Farm and Ecology Center
Mile 5 Old Nenana Highway, Ester, AK 99725
(907) 451-0691
www.calypsofarm.org
Free to walk about the farm; produce available for purchase

Locally grown produce has been a priority for the founders of Calypso Farms since they opened up this wooded stand of birch trees in 2000. This hillside farm is home to a dynamic duo of sustainable agriculture, and taking time to walk among the lush green gardens is a treat, indeed. Complete with sheep, goats (ask if you can milk a nanny, very fun), cats, dogs, and chickens, Calypso Farms strives to educate Alaska on the value of knowing where, when, and how food arrives on our tables.

University of Alaska Large Animal Research Station (LARS)
2220 Yankovich Rd., Fairbanks, AK 99775
(907) 474-5724
www.uaf.edu/lars
Tours meet at the front entrance of the farm, Tuesdays–Saturdays, June 1–August 31, at 10 a.m., 12 p.m., and 2 p.m.
Admission: $10/adults, $9/seniors, $6/student, free for kids 5 and under

The Robert G. White Large Animal Research Station (or LARS) is located on a former homestead at the base of the UAF campus. A unique facility dedicated to research and education of high-latitude biology of large critters, LARS works hard to maintain colonies of musk ox, caribou, and reindeer and will give your family an up-close view of the amazing ability of these animals to survive and thrive in such harsh environments. Suitable for all families, but particularly those with school-aged children. Bring a backpack or jogging stroller for small kids.

Tours

A deep interest is developing among reality television show viewers to experience life in the far reaches of Alaska. Fairbanks is the closest major hub for travel to and from the Arctic Circle, and while many parents will find such travel prohibitively expensive, it is worth investigating if you have the time, funds, and transportation. Below are a few companies that offer guided tours of the arctic regions, for a day trip to cross the Arctic Circle or longer overnight excursions into such areas like Gates of the Arctic National Park.

Arctic Wild

P.O. Box 80562, Fairbanks, AK 99708
(888) 577-8203, (907) 479-8203
www.arcticwild.com, info@arcticwild.com
Rates begin around $3,000/person for a seven-day fly-in adventure. Costs cover all transportation to/from the site, meals, and guide services.

Sporting the tag line "adventures with latitude," Arctic Wild offers a number of family-friendly trips throughout the state, including base camp adventures that appeal to kids. Set up camp, then explore—that's how Arctic Wild rolls with families, and it's appreciated. From checking out Gates of the Arctic National Park and the Kobuk Valley to becoming acquainted with caribou, this is the way to introduce your children to one of the planet's most fascinating areas. Kids are welcome, but these trips are best suited for those age six and up. However, Arctic Wild staff are happy to discuss options for travel with smaller children of experienced hiking/camping parents; they can custom-build a trip just for you.

Northern Alaska Tour Company

P.O. Box 82991-W, Fairbanks, AK 99708
(800) 474-1986, (907) 474-8600
www.northernalaska.com, adventure@northernalaska.com
Fares: vary according to trip, but expect to spend close to $300/person for a seat.

Since 1986, Northern Alaska Tour Co. has schlepped tourists to the interior of Alaska aboard their touring vans for a detailed and very long day of exploring the tundra, Arctic Circle, and Native Alaska culture.

Note: These trips, while fantastic opportunities to expose kids to a truly wild Alaska, are very, very long, often departing Fairbanks at 5 a.m. and returning after midnight. We would recommend a tour of this nature for families with older children capable of managing their own bodies and minds for nearly 20 hours.

DAY TRIPS FROM FAIRBANKS

If you have access to transportation, exploring beyond the city limits of Fairbanks can be lots of fun. Below are a few great bets for road trips that aren't too far for youngsters.

Chena Hot Springs is a popular day or overnight trip from Fairbanks, offering activities meant to draw visitors from around the world. Located

60 miles northeast of downtown Fairbanks, Chena Hot Springs was founded more than 100 years ago as a small community, then transitioned into a full-service resort once word spread of the healing waters and wintertime aurora borealis displays. Today, the resort property features an 80-room lodge, campground, yurts, and activity center. The hot springs themselves consist of an adult outdoor pool (ages 18 and up) and indoor family pool. The resort is always busy, but day-trippers can easily snag some time in the pool, have lunch in the restaurant (featuring their own greenhouse produce), and perhaps hike a trail or two on the property. Do make sure you tour the Ice Museum, where temperatures are a chilly 20ºF and displays created completely out of ice will impress the kids.

> **PARENT PRO TIP**
>
> Really, our favorite time to visit Chena Hot Springs is during the winter months. When the weather is really cold, our kids like to sit in the outdoor pool and shape their hair into fantastic sculptures.
>
> —Lisa, former Fairbanksan and mother of two

While it's the sizzling water most people want to see, from a parent's perspective (mine) the pool layouts themselves are lacking in certain areas. The locker rooms are small, poorly laid out, and sometimes a bit unclean. If you can look past it, bring flip-flops and get in and out of there as fast as possible. That said, my son loves to play in both the pool and outdoor hot tub.

The resort is located at Mile 56.6 Chena Hot Springs Road (www .chenahotsprings.com, 907-451-8104). If you don't have your own wheels, the resort will gladly pick you up for $125/person with two or more people in the party. If you wish to stay at the resort in the lodge, rates begin at $189/night, with a special rate of $129/night for Alaskans. Family suites are also available for $289/night, with a maximum of six people ($229/ night for Alaskans). Camping is $20/night and yurts can be rented for $65/night.

Note: Do stop for breaks along Chena Hot Springs Road; many day-use areas exist for picnicking and photo taking.

North Pole (the community, not the actual pole) sits on the eastern fringe of Fairbanks, about 11 miles from downtown. Really more of a suburb of Fairbanks, North Pole incorporates the edge of Eielson Air Force Base and Fort Wainwright Army Base and both Tanana and Chena Rivers into its boundary and is a popular place to live. The real reason most tourists visit North Pole is, of course, to meet its most famous resident, Santa Claus, who keeps tabs on children all around the world, all the time.

Singing the motto "Where the spirit of Christmas lives all year round," North Pole's biggest attraction is Santa Claus House, a trading post–turned–St. Nick superpower and *the* place to visit with the big guy, live and in person, any time of year. Downtown streets are festooned with candy-cane light poles and decorated businesses and in front of Santa Claus House stands a 40-foot statue of you-know-who.

Santa Claus House (101 St. Nicholas Dr., www.santaclaushouse.com, info@santaclaushouse.com, 800-588-4078, 907-488-2200) is a gift shop and Christmas warehouse, but most kids who seize the opportunity to visit with Santa come away impressed. Santa is available for wish telling all year (wearing a Hawaiian shirt in the summertime) and makes every youngster feel important. If you believe, then you should go. Outside the store are some of Santa's reindeer, too, and it's fun to guess who's-who in the sleigh lineup.

> **KIDSPEAK**
>
> Santa sat in a big chair and wore a funny Hawaii shirt!
>
> —Owen, age seven

Alaska Fact

Every year, thousands of children from around the world send letters to Santa Claus in North Pole, Alaska. Since 1952, kids have sent heartfelt notes to 101 St. Nicholas Drive, North Pole, AK 99705—and they just might get a reply (*hint, hint*)!

14

SOUTHEAST ALASKA

"There ain't nothing like heading out on a gold rush to make folks feel their oats."

—Martha Ferguson McKeown,
The Trail Led North: Mont Hawthorne's Story (1948)

Southeast Alaska, with its drizzly weather and dense evergreen forests, is where many visitors capture a first glimpse of our state. Often confusing those who expected snow and ice, Southeast is hundreds of miles from the rest of the state; in fact, 557 air miles separate capital city Juneau from Anchorage.

While thousands of visitors arrive via cruise ship and stay for only a few hours, many fly in and out of Southeast's tiny airports or disembark the ferry to explore a history and culture very different from the rest of the state. Southeast Alaska is a diverse collection of communities scattered along the fringe of the state's panhandle. It is home to Native Alaskan groups like Tlingit, Haida, Tsimshian, and Eyak, all of whom rely upon a complex matriarchal clan system worth investigating. Southeast Alaska is also where you shall find the signature totem pole—a tool for storytelling and oral tradition unique to this region.

I've broken this section down by towns most visited by families, south to north, with activities and interesting points of significance to kids.

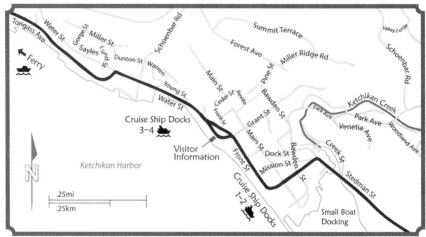

Downtown Ketchikan

Keep in mind that Southeast has no formal road system, other than the connection to mainland Alaska near Haines and Skagway, so any hopping between cities must be accomplished by boat or airplane.

Ketchikan: "Alaska's First City"

Salmon, rain, and cruise ships—that's what most people think about when discussing this island community. Located 700 miles from Seattle, on Revillagigedo Island, Ketchikan is the southernmost city in Alaska and

Ketchikan

Population: 13,938 (entire Ketchikan Gateway borough, 2012 census)

Founded in: 1900, as a salmon cannery and saltery.

Known for: Salmon fishing. In fact, Ketchikan is known as the salmon capital of the world.

Interesting fact: Ketchikan receives up to 200 inches of rain per year!

Hot tip: Explore the city on foot, away from the cruise ship docks. Hiking trails, small museums, and fascinating homes perched on steep hillsides are fun to see.

the first port cruise ships visit on their way up the Inside Passage, hence that "First City" moniker. Today, Ketchikan's seasonal tourism industry flourishes from May to September. Visitors flock to famous Creek Street, where both brothels and fish were plentiful in the early days of the city's history and where today kids can catch a salmon from a bridge linking one side of the street to the other (the brothels, thankfully, are gone, but an interesting tour still shows off the colorful history of Creek Street). Those desiring a true wilderness experience can hop aboard a float plane and visit Misty Fjords National Monument or kayak around the nooks and crannies of the Tongass National Forest, the largest in the country.

Revillagigedo Island is the 11th-largest island in the United States, but only some of it is available for housing and commerce; most belongs to the Tongass National Forest. At more than 730,000 acres, it's larger than the islands of Maui and Hawai'i. Too bad we don't have the temperatures to match.

Alaska Fact

ARRIVING

By Air

Getting to Ketchikan is interesting, since the airport (www.borough.ketchikan.ak.us/airport/airport.htm) is located half a mile away from the city on Gravina Island, accessible via tiny ferry. Alaska Airlines (www.alaskaair.com) is the only major air carrier serving Ketchikan, with daily flights to and from Seattle and Anchorage. If you choose to fly south from Anchorage, be forewarned that this is the aforementioned Milk Run we discussed in the beginning of this book. Bring snacks, amusements, and a positive attitude—you'll be on board for awhile. A few hotels offer shuttle service to and from the airport, and taxis are ready and waiting as

> **KIDSPEAK**
>
> Oh my gosh, that flight to Ketchikan took forever. Up, down, up and up, then down, down.
> —Owen, age seven

soon as you step out of the terminal. Don't worry, Ketchikan is dialed in to transportation, and most folks are well prepared for arriving visitors. The airport ferry departs on the hour and half-hour and fares are $5/adults, $6/vehicles one-way. Baggage carts are available if you're walking on a ferry directly from the airport.

By Boat

Refer back to Chapter 3 for cruise line options. Most cruise lines visit Ketchikan at some point, with smaller boat companies sometimes beginning or ending in this small city to maximize time spent in southeast Alaska. The Alaska Marine Highway System also visits Ketchikan on a regular basis, since many people rely on the ferries for transportation. Service is available year-round, but schedules do change, as do vessels. Visit the AMHS website or call the helpful reservation service for the most current information (www.ferryalaska.com, 800-642-0066). The ferry disembarks passengers near downtown and taxis are available, as is a free downtown shuttle.

GETTING AROUND

If you really want wheels, find Budget Rent-A-Car at 4950 N. Tongass Highway (907-225-8383) or Alaska Car Rental at the airport (800-662-0007).

Municipal bus service operates daily all around the Revilla Island area (how most people refer to Ketchikan's locale), with slightly reduced schedules on Sundays. Fares are $1/adults, $.50/kids and will get you to major attractions and sights supercheap. Find schedules and routes at www.kgbak.us/bus/info. A free downtown shuttle operates May through September on a 10-to-20-minute circuit from berth #4 (cruise ship central) around downtown attractions.

VISITOR INFORMATION

The **Ketchikan Visitors Bureau** (www.visit-ketchikan.com, 800-770-3300) has two locations in the greater downtown area: a satellite office at cruise ship berth #3 and a main office on Front Street. Both offer friendly service, a wealth of resources for activities, attractions, and directions, as well as providing public restrooms, an ATM, and Internet access.

SHOPPING/GROCERIES

Safeway
2417 Tongass Ave., Ketchikan, AK 99901
(907) 228-1900
Open daily 5 a.m.–midnight

Groceries, deli, pharmacy, bakery, fuel station.

MEDICAL CARE

PeaceHealth Ketchikan Medical Center
3100 Tongass Ave., Ketchikan, AK 99901
(907) 228-8300
www.peacehealth.org

LODGING

Although the majority of Ketchikan's visitors rest their heads upon cruise ship berths, a good many travelers require adequate space for an overnight visit. For such a small town, Ketchikan offers some pretty nice lodging, but make reservations early, since space is limited during the summer.

Cape Fox Lodge $$$
800 Venetia Way, Ketchikan, AK 99901
(866) 225-8001, (907) 225-8001
www.capefoxlodge.com

High above the city, Cape Fox Lodge is a tribally owned property featuring 72 guest rooms. Recent renovations replaced aging furniture with new comforters, white pine bedsteads, and in-room amenities like coffee makers and wireless Internet. A full-service restaurant and bar are located just off the spacious lobby, and a small coffee shop sells espresso and baked goods. The best part for kids, however, is the funicular, a chain-operated tram that carries guests to and from Creek St., free with a room key ($2/person otherwise). Shuttle to/from airport, ferry dock, and local events. Nonsmoking rooms available. Double-check when making reservations for cribs. Children under 12 stay free with a paying adult. Check website for current list of specials.

Thumbs-up for: Views, funicular transportation, Alaska Native heritage.

Best Western Plus Landing Hotel $$–$$$
3434 Tongass Ave., Ketchikan, AK 99901
(800) 428-8304, (907) 225-5166
www.landinghotel.com

Located across from the Alaska Marine Highway terminal and across the water from the Ketchikan airport, this hotel provides easy access. With 107 rooms, it's also one of the larger properties in town, offering standard rooms, suites, and common-area fireplaces to cozy up to after a rainy day exploring. The Landing restaurant is on-property. Complimentary shuttle service, free wireless Internet, cribs, fitness center, and accessible rooms available. Ask about special promotion rates. Children 12 and under stay free in the same room as a paying adult.

Thumbs-up for: Accessibility to ferry and airport, varying room size, and adjacent restaurant.

Super 8 $$
2151 Sea Level Dr., Ketchikan, AK 99901
(907) 225-9088
www.super8.com

One of the best deals in town, Super 8 has made a transformation over the last few years, renovating both interior and exterior. Super 8 also offers views of the waterfront area, and kids will enjoy watching the marine world go by from their window. Try one of the enormous family suites. Free breakfast, wireless Internet, cribs, shuttle transportation, early or late checkout, and access to local stores, restaurants, and the ferry dock/airport. Kids 17 and under stay free with a paying adult.

Thumbs-up for: Affordability, large family suites, free breakfast.

ALTERNATIVE ACCOMMODATIONS
Ketchikan Reservation Service (www.ketchikan-lodging.com, 800-987-5337, 907-247-5337) is a complete listing of alternative accommodations.

Downtown Ketchikan

From bed and breakfast to private vacation homes, this is a clearinghouse of everything that's available.

Camping

Seal the seams of your family tent and break out the hot chocolate, because while camping in Ketchikan is a little damp, it's still lots of fun. Try these spots for some outdoor overnights.

Last Chance Campground (877-844-6777) is located 10 miles out of town on Revilla Road in the Tongass National Forest. Pay just $10/night and enjoy one of 19 campsites close to hiking trails. Some sites are available for reservation. All unreserved sites are first-come, first-served.

Signal Creek Campground (877-844-6777) is in the Ward Lake Recreation Area of the Tongass National Forest, about seven miles from downtown Ketchikan and four miles from the ferry terminal. Great lake access, with fishing, hiking, and critter viewing. Camp for $10/night. Total of 24 campsites with some advance reservation possible.

Settlers Cove State Recreation Site

18 North Tongass Road, Ketchikan
http://dnr.alaska.gov/parks/aspunits/southeast/settlerscvsrs.htm

Offers 14 RV/tent sites near the water and is a popular spot with Ketchikan residents. Rates are $10/night, with nature trails, pit toilets, and access to fishing. No reservations, so get there early.

FEEDING THE FAMILY

Eating in Ketchikan is a seafood lover's delight. Everywhere signs proclaim the bounty of fresh, locally caught salmon, crab, or halibut and I, like most Alaskans, dance a little jig whenever I arrive in town. For such a little place, Ketchikan offers a surprisingly diverse lineup of eating establishments. Even with a picky eater in the family, we can usually find something to please everyone.

Restaurants

Alaska Fish House $$-$$$

3 Salmon Landing (right on the harbor, next to the Lumberjack Show),
Ketchikan, AK 99901
(907) 247-4055
www.alaskafishhouse.com
Open daily 6 a.m.–7 p.m. (April–October)

Steps away from the cruise ship dock and visitor center, the Fish House serves lots of seafood, including halibut, salmon, and spot prawns. My favorite menu item is the smoked salmon cornbread. Kids will enjoy fish and chips made with crunchy batter. They have great burgers, too. This restaurant can be crowded, so try early or late dining to maximize your seating options and thus the great view of the busy harbor.

O'Brien's Pub and Eatery $$

211 Steadman St., Ketchikan, AK 99901
(907) 247-2326
obrienspubandeatery@gmail.com
Open daily 11 a.m.–11 p.m.

I love the atmosphere of O'Brien's on a rainy afternoon. Lunch and dinner are served, along with great draft beer and excellent coffee. My son enjoys soup and a big pretzel, and my husband eats platter after platter of deep-fried salmon fritters the size of golf balls.

FAMILY FUN IN KETCHIKAN

Ketchikan is a city meant to be explored on foot as much as possible, so a pair of comfortable boots/shoes and excellent rain gear are a must. Don't let weather deter your family from enjoying this coastal Alaska town. Below are our best bets for kid-friendly attractions and activities.

Museums and Cultural Experiences

Tongass Historical Museum
629 Dock St., Ketchikan, AK 99901
(907) 225-5600
museum@city.ketchikan.ak.us
Open daily 8 a.m.–5 p.m. (May–September); varying hours other months.
Admission: $2/adults, free for kids 12 and under. Admission charged only during summer season.

This little museum is close to historic Creek Street, just a few blocks from the cruise ship dock and a cluster of downtown shops. Housing a collection of information and exhibits connected to the art, culture, and history of Ketchikan and southeast Alaska, the museum offers many public programs and events with family appeal. There is a great photography display archived in this museum, which might appeal to older kids fascinated with the way of life way back when. This museum is most appropriate for school-aged kids.

Southeast Alaska Discovery Center
50 Main St., Ketchikan, AK 99901
(907) 228-6220
www.alaskacenters.gov/ketchikan.cfm
Open Monday–Friday 8 a.m.–5 p.m., Saturday–Sunday 8 a.m.–4 p.m. (May–September); Thursday–Saturday 10 a.m.–4 p.m. (winter months)
Admission: $5/adults, free for kids 15 and under. $15/season pass.

Close to downtown, with plenty of hands-on exhibits and activities like a scavenger hunt for readers and nonreaders, this visitor center is great.

Swing in and check out the fabulous movie theater with full-size photos of southeast Alaska, see the difference between a rain forest and boreal forest, and let the kids catch an up-close view of the industries that made this region successful. This is a must-see facility. Suitable for the entire family.

Potlatch Totem Park
9809 Totem Bight Rd., Ketchikan, AK 99901
www.potlachpark.com, potlachpark@yahoo.com

Located 10 miles north of downtown Ketchikan and on the bus line, Potlatch Park is a great way to expand your exploration of southeast Alaska's Native culture. Featuring tribal houses, intricately carved totems, some very interesting dioramas of early Native Alaska villages, and a collection of antique cars and firearms, this park is fine for kids preschool and older.

Saxman Native Village
Tongass Highway, in Saxman village, 2.5 miles south of Ketchikan
Tours arranged by Cape Fox Tours
(907) 225-4846
www.capefoxtours.com
Guided tours $35/adults, $18/kids 12 and under. Unguided visits $3/person.

Similar to other native cultural parks in Ketchikan, Saxman offers a guided experience that may or may not appeal to your younger children. With a short video presentation preceding the tour, visitors can witness the history of the tribe and area before seeing a traditional dance demonstration and some totem carving. Catering mainly to the cruise ship crowd, this is an experience best for older kids, but if you don't have a chance to see other Native Alaska exhibits, it's worth a stop. Tours can be combined with the Lumberjack show and other various land/water excursions.

Great Alaskan Lumberjack Show
P.O. Box 23343, Ketchikan, AK 99901
Located near Pier One, downtown
(907) 225-9050
www.lumberjacksports.com
Open May–September, 3–5 shows daily
Admission: $34/adults, $17/kids.

Featuring a great cast of characters and a wonderful history of a dying industry in southeast Alaska, this one-hour show provides action for kids, including a ton of audience participation as real lumberjacks (who all seem to be 25 or younger) show off their skills in a quest to be Bull of the Woods. Our son has seen the show a number of

> ### KIDSPEAK
> The lumberjacks can *run* on the logs and I don't know how they don't fall off. They also carved me a stool to sit on with their chain saw, but I don't always use it because it gives me slivers.
> —Owen, age seven

times, and it's always a top request when we visit Ketchikan. Suitable for kids two and up. Try and sit near the front so your little lumberjack can yell a resounding "YoHo!" and possibly win a prize.

OUTDOOR RECREATION

Hiking

The best hiking trails in the Ketchikan area are located away from the downtown area, which means transportation can be an issue. If you have access to a car, here are a few favorites.

Settlers Cove State Recreation Area
Milepost 18 N. Tongass Highway, Ketchikan, AK 99901
dnr.alaska.gov/parks/aspunits/southeast/settlerscvsrs.htm

If you have time to drive the distance from town, hike around the Settlers Cove system of family-friendly trails. The Hollow Cedar Beach Trail is a fully accessible trail leading to a beach picnic shelter. For a longer, more challenging hike, take the Lunch Creek Falls Loop trail, connect with the Lunch Creek trail, and catch a view of the beautiful falls

> ### PARENT PRO TIP
> My boys love the Perseverance Trail. With only a slight elevation gain and the easy-to-navigate gravel or boardwalk paths, we can easily manage the five-mile round-trip hike with little protest.
> —Amy, Ketchikan mother of two

before heading back to the parking lot. Strollers will be no problem on the Hollow Cedar Beach hike, but you might want a backpack for the little ones on Lunch Creek.

Perseverance Trail—Tongass National Forest
www.fs.fed.us/r10/tongass/recreation/rec_facilities/ktnrec.html

Many local families enjoy the Perseverance Trail for its kid-friendliness. At a short 2.3 miles from trailhead to Lake Perseverance, this is a nice way to stretch legs and get to know Ketchikan's forests. Pick berries, go fishing, or just amble the gravel and boardwalk trail to its end.

Totem Bight State Historical Park
9883 N. Tongass Highway, Ketchikan, AK 99901
(907) 247-8574

The result of a 1983 mission to preserve and protect the many totem poles scattered around Ketchikan, Totem Bight State Park is a testament to the power of community. Visitors are treated to accessible trails, a clan house, and 14 totems that represent a variety of symbolic creatures of southeast Alaska. Restrooms and a gift shop are available. Suitable for the entire family, but smaller kids may not appreciate the clan house or totems. Thankfully, there is plenty of running-around room in the park. Public bus system stops right outside the park entrance.

> **PARENT PRO TIP**
>
> You gotta let kids explore things in their own way. Dropping a crab pot, pulling it up again, and then parking on a beach to cook the crabs teaches kids a whole lot more than going to a restaurant.
>
> —Captain Johnny, grandfather to a bunch

Experience One Charters
3857 Fairview, Ketchikan, AK 99901
(907) 225-2343
www.latitude56.com,
skipper@latitude56.com
Prices vary; call or email for rates.

Fishing, crabbing, and a grandpa's excellent personality—that's what families receive when they sail with Captain Johnny and Experience One Charters. Whether you want to fish, haul up a crab pot and have lunch in a secluded cove, or just cruise the Ketchikan harbor, Captain Johnny will make sure everyone is happy. He even provides snacks, drinks, and home-made cookies at no extra charge! Kids get to drive the boat, too. Suitable for preschoolers and older, since the boat is small and there's not a ton of extra room for babies and toddlers to cruise safely.

Alaska Rainforest Sanctuary
116 Wood Rd., Ketchikan, AK 99901
(877) 947-7557, (907) 225-5503
www.alaskarainforest.com, info@alaskarainforest.com
Open May–September
Begins around $85/person, depending on age and tour type

Traveling with a tween or teen? Zip with them on a three-hour tour of the forest, from the top down! Truly an awesome adventure, this company knows how to satisfy the adrenaline junkie, with crazy-cool zips, suspension bridges, and a 4X4 ascent up the mountain to get it all started. Kids must weigh a minimum of 90 pounds and be at least 10 years old to safely zip this trip. But a lovely forest walk and history tour is available at the same time, a great option for nonzippers and parents of young children.

Alaska Sea Cycle Tours
802 Monroe St., Ketchikan, AK 99901
(907) 821-2728
alaskaseacycletours@gmail.com
Tours start at $95 for a three-hour tour.

The sea cycle craze is just beginning to hit southeast Alaska after a strong showing in the Lower 48. Part bike, part paddleboat, a sea cycle is a great way to pedal around the calm waters of nearby Ward Cove, exploring the estuary, wildlife, and salmon cycle of the Ketchikan area. The three-hour tour spends time in Ward Cove and the four-hour tour combines pedaling with a tour of Totem Bight State Park. Both are great for kids of all ages, and guides promise they'll provide gear, snacks, and PFDs for varying size ranges and ages. Recommended for the whole family, but do be aware that infants and toddlers might not enjoy it as much due to the constraint of being in a tiny little boat, even if there are seats in back. Kids 12 and younger must be accompanied by an adult.

Ketchikan Kayaks

3 Salmon Landing, Ketchikan, AK 99901
(800) 287-1607, (907) 225-1258
www.kayakketchikan.com, paddle@kayakketchikan.com
Rates vary, but plan on spending around $60/day per boat.

Ketchikan Kayaks offers both rentals and guided tours. Take a serene paddle around a secluded cove for a few hours (usually four or so) or take a guided wilderness adventure for a few days. Kids must be six or older to participate, and parents should remember that they will provide much of the paddle-power for kids 10 and younger. Triple kayaks are available, in addition to doubles and singles. Ask about PFD sizing and be prepared to bring your own.

Ketchikan Walking Tour

Starts at Ketchikan Visitor Center, on cruise ship dock
www.visit-ketchikan.com

Some kids (like mine) enjoy being the guide whenever the family explores a new city, and fortunately, Ketchikan provides a great opportunity to tour the city. Grab a free walking tour map at the visitor center and hoof it around downtown, Creek St., and the outskirts of the city in a few hours. Marvel at the brightly colored houses on Creek St., see salmon swimming upstream near the hatchery, and climb tons of stairs on your way to a great view of the city and Gravina Island beyond.

Guided Tours

Bering Sea Crab Fishermen's Tour

P.O. Box 9619, Ketchikan, AK 99901
(888) 239-3816, (360) 642-4935
www.56degreesnorth.com, cfishadventures@56degreesnorth.com
Rates: For a 3.5-hour tour, about $160/adults, $100/kids 5–12, May–September

Ever since the debut of reality television show *Deadliest Catch*, visitors have clamored for a true-to-life experience aboard a crabbing vessel. The Bering Sea Crab tour offers a chance to spend a few hours getting to know this dangerous, chilly occupation. Stepping aboard the *Aleutian Ballad* (from season two of the show), guests will see how a crab pot is baited, flung over the side, then retrieved, hopefully filled with king or snow crab, and perhaps an octopus or two. Kids will get a chance to touch the tough crab shells, feel starfish, and truly experience life on the high seas. Suitable for kids in kindergarten and older. Plan for nasty weather.

Taquan Air Flightseeing/Venture Travel
4085 Tongass Ave., Ketchikan, AK 99901
(800) 770-8800, (907) 228-4616
www.taquanair.com, info@taquanair.com
Rates: Vary by length and destination, but begin around $250/person.

Offering flightseeing and adventure packages to areas like beautiful Misty Fjords National Monument or Anan Bear Preserve near Wrangell, Taquan Air has a long history of customer satisfaction and safety. While rainy weather may hamper some enjoyment of landlocked activities, a flightseeing trip can go on even if the clouds send rain. Look for mountain goats, moose, wolves, and the famous Alaska coastal brown bear as you soar above the trees. A variety of flightseeing trips are available—and remember, you're paying to experience untouched Alaska, so this is a definite memory maker for older kids. Suitable for children in kindergarten and older, in my opinion. Do poll the family to make sure a trip like this is on everyone's wish list.

Alaska Amphibious Tours/Ketchikan Duck Tour
5191 Borch Ave., Ketchikan, AK 99901
(866) 341-3825, (907) 225-9899
www.akduck.com

Pack your little quackers and climb aboard these amphibious vehicles for a 90-minute tour of Ketchikan, rain or shine. This fun tour is full of goofy humor and lots of interesting sights on land and in the Ketchikan harbor. If you're looking for a typical tourist attraction, and if you want a ride around town with a unique perspective, give it a whirl. Kids in particular will enjoy the amazing ability of these amphibious vehicles to suddenly take to water like a, well, duck.

Note: Consider carefully the purchase of those plastic duck lip whistles offered by guides, especially if you have more traveling to do. Trust me on this.

Wrangell: A Hidden Gem

Off the main track for many visitors, the community of Wrangell is 90 miles north of Ketchikan on picturesque and historic Wrangell Island. This southeast Alaska community relies upon fishing industries and tourism after an early 21st-century federal policy switch reduced the timber industry to sawdust. Wrangell is a great place to savor the essence of southeast Alaska.

ARRIVING

Like most southeast Alaska communities, Wrangell can be reached one of two ways: boat or airplane. Your mode of transportation will depend upon time, budget, and the type of activities you and your kids would like to experience.

By Air

Alaska Airlines (www.alaskaair.com) flies daily to Wrangell. Most Wrangell tour companies, hotels, etc. are well acquainted with the airline's schedule and will likely accommodate your needs for lodging and recreation. Pay attention to arrival/departure schedules if you wish to catch the ferry from Wrangell, as neither is likely to wait for a delayed flight/docking.

Wrangell

Population: 2,448 (2012 census)

Founded in: 1867 as a U.S. fort named Wrangel, after Alaska became a territory. However, the town originally began in 1834 as a Russian outpost, and was known before that as one of the most powerful Stikine Tlingit settlements.

Known for: An interesting governance, flying flags of the Tlingit Nation, Russia, Great Britain, and the United States.

Interesting fact: Wrangell is one of the oldest non-Native settlements in Alaska.

Hot tip: Make sure to take a charter tour of the Stikine River and surrounding areas. The geology, anthropology, and cultural history are fascinating.

By Boat

The **Alaska Marine Highway** (www.ferryalaska.com) sails to Wrangell a few times a week, and depending upon which boat arrives when, your family can opt to spend a few days in Wrangell before departing for other Inside Passage communities or stick around longer.

> **KIDSPEAK**
>
> The (Alaska ferries) are like a giant hotel that's on water and you can go outside and see all these animals you never see if you're on land.
>
> —Eryn, age seven

In 2013, **Rainforest Islands Ferry** (www.forestislandsferry.com, 907-329-2031) is due to begin service between Prince of Wales Island via Coffman Cove, Wrangell, Petersburg, and Ketchikan. This small company will accommodate both vehicles and foot passengers.

GETTING AROUND

Most of Wrangell can be explored via your own two feet or with the cooperation of lodging and tour operators. But if you feel the need for other transportation, Northern Lights Taxi service (907-874-4646) operates all day and most of the night, seven days a week. They accept credit cards or cash.

Stop in at the **Wrangell Convention and Visitor Bureau**, located near the waterfront in the James and Elsie Nolan Center (296 Campbell Dr., www.wrangellalaska.org, nolancenter@wrangellalaska.org, 907-874-3699). Find walking tour maps of the town, kid-friendly hikes, and a great museum with plenty of child-friendly exhibits and movies explaining the four-governments concept, a fascinating history lesson.

SHOPPING/GROCERIES

City Market Inc.
423 Front St., Wrangell, AK 99929
(907) 874-3333

Full grocery store, meat department, and some pretty good produce considering the length of time it had to travel. Fax/copy center and postal center. *Bonus:* The store makes free deliveries.

Bob's IGA
223 Brueger St., Wrangell, AK 99929
(907) 874-2341

Offers the basics, including produce, deli, and bakery. **Note**: Closed Sundays, so plan ahead.

MEDICAL CARE

Wrangell Medical Center
310 Bennett St., Wrangell, AK 99929
(907) 874-7000
www.wrangellmedicalcenter.com

Emergency room, lab, radiology services.

LODGING

Wrangell offers a few comfortable places to spend the night. Below are some options for families.

Hotels

Alaskan Sourdough Lodge $$
1104 Peninsula St., Wrangell, AK 99929
(800) 874-3613, (907) 874-3613
www.akgetaway.com

Owned by the sort-of-sour-but-harmless former mayor Bruce Harding, Sourdough Lodge offers comfortable lodging, access to meals (extra charge outside of the free continental breakfast), and plenty of space. The property has 16 rooms with wireless Internet, television, and a laundry area. Tours, fishing, and/or sightseeing trips can be arranged through Bruce's extensive connections and transportation to/from is provided with advance warning. Nonsmoking indoors. No cribs available.

Thumbs-up for: Lots of space, access to a laundry room, transportation to/from area activities. Also affordable is the Family Room, with four twins or one king and two twin beds.

Stikine Inn $$–$$$
P.O. Box 662, Wrangell, AK 99929
(888) 874-3388, (907) 874-3388
www.stikineinn.com

Located near the City Dock and bustling Front Street, within full view of Wrangell's waterways, the Stikine Inn offers great access to downtown and the area's outdoor recreation opportunities. Featuring singles, doubles, and suites, the hotel also has an in-house restaurant and coffee shop. A few cribs available with advance notice. Courtesy shuttle available.

Thumbs-up for: Access to activities, restaurants, shopping. Lovely views.

Bed and Breakfast

Fennimore's Bed and Breakfast $–$$
312 Stikine Ave., Wrangell, AK 99929
(907) 874-3012
www.fennimoresbbb.com, wrgbbb@gci.net

Owned by a retired teacher and her husband, Fennimore's offers clean, comfy lodging right across the street from the ferry terminal, making it extremely convenient for tired families who arrive late on the boat. Fennimore's provides a yummy breakfast, a trading post, bikes for borrowing, and great storytelling. Two types of rooms are available, kitchenette and standard.

Thumbs-up for: Awesome owners; clean, comfy, affordable rooms; and access to ferry.

Rooney's Roost B&B $$
206 McKinnon St., Wrangell, AK 99929
(907) 874-2026
www.rooneysroost.com

Located in downtown Wrangell, Rooney's offers guests a bit of history with their stay. A renovated 1900s-era home provides four rooms with private baths and televisions and a full, hot breakfast each morning. Find warm cookies every evening, too, making this a delightful stop for kids. Complimentary shuttle service and loaner bikes.

Thumbs-up for: Accessibility to town, friendly folks, and fresh cookies.

Wrangell residents read three times as many books as residents in other U.S. communities of similar size. Must be the weather.

Alaska Fact

CAMPING

City of Wrangell RV Park at Shoemaker Bay
Mile 5 Zimovia Highway (about five miles from center of town)
(907) 874-2444
parksrec@ak.net

This city-run campground offers 25 spaces for RVs; hook-ups $25/night and all others $15/night. There are six tent spaces for $15/night. Guests are able to use the nearby recreation center's swimming pool, showers, and weight room at no extra charge (except for a few weeks in August when routine maintenance is done). Stays at the RV park and/or campground are limited to 10 days.

Thumbs-up for: Free pool/shower usage.

The **Tongass National Forest** website (www.fs.fed.us/r10/tongass/districts/wrangell/index.shtml, 907-874-2323) offers a comprehensive listing of all Wrangell Island NF campgrounds. Some are very remote and with limited number of spaces, so plan ahead carefully.

FEEDING THE FAMILY
Eating in Wrangell is pretty simple. Kids will enjoy the lack of fuss with respect to food and grown-ups will appreciate a variety of options to fill up picky eaters. Below are a few options, besides the aforementioned Sourdough Lodge, which offers meals at the property.

Restaurants

Stikine Restaurant $$
Front St. and City Dock, downtown Wrangell (in the Stikine Inn building)
(888) 874-3388, (907) 874-3388

Fresh local favorites like clam chowder and fish and chips headline, but there's also a good number of steak entrees to keep carnivores happy. Great sandwiches, frybread pizzas (frybread is a Native staple), and an excellent selection of burgers. They also offer a great draft beer lineup, in case you need a happy hour. Try the berry lemonade; it's a fabulous treat the whole family can enjoy.

Diamond C Cafe $-$$
223 Front St., Wrangell, AK 99929
(907) 874-3322
dfarm@gci.net

Unpretentious but with a solid menu and local atmosphere, the Diamond C offers breakfast and lunch. We stopped in one rainy, cold afternoon and had an excellent bowl of soup and a great fish burger. A coffee shop next door serves espresso and blended drinks, in addition to gourmet coffee and tea.

FAMILY FUN IN WRANGELL

A wonderful way to explore Wrangell is through a **self-guided walking tour**, starting at the Nolan Center and Museum on Campbell Drive. Grab a Wrangell map and tour guide and let your feet do the storytelling as you wind through the industrial, historical, and cultural areas of this lovely town. Below are some interesting spots to stop along the way.

> The oldest known Tlingit carved house posts in existence, built in the 1700s, are on display at the Wrangell Museum (and are very cool).
>
> **Alaska Fact**

Museums and Cultural Experiences

Chief Shakes Tribal House (wcatribe@gmail.com, 907-874-4303), located on tiny Shakes Island in the middle of the Inner Harbor of town, is a replica of a 19th-century tribal house. Built in 1940, the house recently underwent extensive renovation, and visitors can feel the beat of the Native Alaska culture while attending daily performances. Pay careful attention to the totems standing outside and see if your kids can decipher the stories behind the characters. To reach the house on your own, take Front Street to Shakes Street, then turn left to Shakes Island. Call for performance times.

The grave of **Chief Shakes** himself sits at the top of a little hill just off Case Avenue. Look for the site's distinctive orca totems marking the area.

Totem Park is on Front Street, just past the City Market. Do stop by and view the Kahlteen totem at the front and wander the gravel pathways

Ancient petroglyphs dot the beach near Petroglyph Park in Wrangell.

around the back. You can feel the effort it took to create such wooden wonders and it's well worth the time to visit.

Farther out of town along Evergreen Avenue (a 20-minute walk along a local road) sits the famous **Petroglyph Beach**, a State Historic Site and a fascinating mystery of southeast Alaska. Read the interpretive signs at the accessible platform before hopping down onto the rocky beach and searching for the petroglyphs. Nobody really knows who carved these forms into the smooth, large rocks sitting shoreside, or why, and the closest guess of when places the carvings at 1,000 years old or more. A fun activity is to create rubbings of the mock petroglyphs at the platform and take some of the mystery home with you.

Note: Do not allow kids to climb on the actual petroglyph rocks—history needs care, you know. Also remember that all beach rocks are slippery with rain and an abundance of kelp.

Outdoor Recreation

It's an outdoor world in Wrangell. Everything centers around nature's bounty and that includes recreation. From kayaking to hiking to jet boat tours, the greater Wrangell area offers a wide variety of family fun.

HIKING

Search the Southeast Alaska Trail System's website (www.seatrails.org) for a complete listing of the area's hikes, broken down by day/overnight/accessible, etc.

Nemo Point Saltwater Trail is a scenic one-mile round-trip hike along a forested boardwalk. Children and adults will enjoy walking through the cedar, spruce, and hemlock forest to the beach at trail's end and the lovely views are a great bonus. Drive 13.4 miles from town to Nemo Loop Road (Forest Service Road 6267) and follow another 5.2 miles to the trailhead. Allow one to two hours, plus time at the beach. Bring rain gear and sturdy shoes/boots that accommodate slippery surfaces. Suitable for all ages and abilities. Strollers are appropriate.

Rainbow Falls Trail is located 4.5 miles from town along the Zimovia Highway. Many lodging establishments offer transportation to and from the trail, which offers great access to a waterfall along the way and occasional views of the Zimovia Strait. At a distance of 0.8 miles one-way, many families are deceived into thinking this is an easy-peasy hike for small kids, but some steep sections do make travel tough for toddlers and preschoolers, so do use caution. No jogging strollers here.

Mt. Dewey Trail is great for kids who want a chance to climb. This is a short trail (a quarter-mile one-way), but the views are super, and everyone, it seems, loves this spot. Head up Third Street from downtown, behind the high school, and follow the stairs leading up to Reid Street. Then bear left and follow the residential street to a dirt road and follow the sign. Take the camera for panoramic views of the city below. Suitable for kids who can ambulate themselves up the hill and back down again or take kids in a pack. **Note:** This is an awesome before-bed hike to run the wiggles out of kids, but watch for slippery steps on wet days.

KAYAKING

The calm waters of Zimovia Strait and surrounding coves make for wonderful kayaking and canoeing adventures. Heck, the downtown area alone is an interesting adventure in water exploration.

Breakaway Adventures
P.O. Box 2107, Wrangell, AK 99929
(888) 385-2488, (907) 874-2488
Kayak and canoe rentals starting at $60/day.

Alaska Vistas
P.O. Box 2245, Wrangell, AK 99929
(866) 874-3006, (907) 874-3006
www.alaskavistas.com

Guided kayak tours (some unguided opportunities available, but one must prove ability before setting out). Rates vary according to trip; call for current rates and offerings.

WILDLIFE

Anan Wildlife Observatory
Tongass National Forest
(907) 874-2323
www.fs.fed.us/r10/tongass/recreation/wildlife_viewing/ananobservatory

Located deep in the Tongass National Forest, accessible only by float plane or boat, the observatory can be experienced along the banks of Anan Creek, site of an ancient Tlingit fishing area. Boasting the largest pink salmon run in southeast Alaska, Anan attracts black and brown bears each summer, the only place you'll find both together. Managed by the Tongass National Forest, Anan Wildlife Observatory is tightly controlled by rangers May–September and access is limited to those with prearranged permits. A half-mile trail leads from the estuary near Anan Creek to the observation decks, and every step of the way visitors are able

> **KIDSPEAK**
>
> The bears were scary, but I got to see a mom bear catch fish and feed them to her really, really hungry cubs!
>
> —Owen, age seven

to witness the life and times of the area's bears, since they also use the trail for their own travels to and from fishing areas. Best suited for kids age seven and up, Anan is a close-up observation opportunity, but it does not come without some stressful moments, as bears cross in front of or behind hikers.

Wrangell's Children Shine in the Garnet Market

No lemonade stands here—Wrangell kids are too busy selling garnets. The beautiful burgundy-colored gems are sold all around town by local children in an impressive business venture that dates back to the late 1800s. The Wrangell garnet ledge was originally founded in 1881 by a group of men who soon discovered garnet mining was more difficult than the gold most prospectors sought, and ultimately the garnet ledge (located five miles north of Wrangell Island, on the mainland) was mined by a group of women from Minnesota. Tough, press-savvy, and pretty successful at their toils, the mining mamas, teachers, and businesswomen eventually drifted away, and individual garnet seekers began to step forward.

In 1962, Fred G. Hanford acquired the ledge with the intention of donating the entire site to the Boy Scouts of America, stipulating that "for only so long as the said grantee... shall use the land for Scouting purposes and shall permit the children of Wrangell to take garnets from there in reasonable quantities." Today, children of Wrangell make an annual pilgrimage to the garnet ledge, located at the mouth of the Stikine River, to try their hand at prying loose the rough, dirty-looking gemstones. No power tools are permitted, and only children under 18 and their parents can mine.

How much cash do these enterprising youngsters glean from their efforts? Some kids have paid for college educations. Children set up tables along the pier at City Dock and sell their shiny stones to passengers disembarking the Alaska ferry, sometimes making up to $2,000 every summer.

You can visit without a guide, but given the somewhat unpredictable nature of bears (and children), my recommendation is to travel to Anan under the supervision and helpful guidance of a charter outfit. Below are two excellent companies that have been guiding visitors to Anan for many years and also understand the needs of families. Trips last around five hours from start to finish and include lunch, guide services, and plenty of time for boating the beautiful waterways near Wrangell on the way to/from Anan. Plan on spending a few hundred dollars per person for a daylong excursion, but the cost is well worth the amazing experience.

Note: Anan Wildlife Observatory is 30 miles from Wrangell, so plan accordingly for weather, mealtimes, and bathroom protocol. Boats are noisy and small but fun to ride in, as our son discovered. Ask about PFDs for children.

Alaska Vistas
P.O. Box 2245, Wrangell, AK 99929 (City Dock)
(866) 874-3006, (907) 874-3006
www.alaskavistas.com, info@alaskavistas.com

Alaska Waters
P.O. Box 1978, Wrangell, AK 99929
(800) 347-4462, (907) 874-3138
www.alaskawaters.com, info@alaskawaters.com

Petersburg: "Alaska's Little Norway"

The blue ice of LeConte Glacier was more than just pretty to Norwegian Peter Buschmann. Ice was critical to the fish business, and Buschmann found the abundance of it to be a perfect reason to build a cannery, Icy Straits Packing Co., in the late 1800s. In 1910, the city of Petersburg was incorporated and began to thrive as its residents, many of them directly from Norway, enjoyed mountains, cold water, and deep fjords. Today, Petersburg is a delightful stop along the Alaska Marine Highway and smaller cruise itineraries, and its Norwegian heritage remains strong in both character and architecture.

For families, time spent in this community means low-key fun with fishing, kayaking, hiking, and cultural connections with local residents. Petersburg is located on Mitkof Island, a 23-mile-long stretch of muskeg bog and forested hillsides, where the Wrangell Narrows meets Frederick Sound.

ARRIVING

By Air

For such a small town, Petersburg is lucky to enjoy the services of Alaska Airlines (www.alaskaair.com), which provides twice-daily jet service from Seattle or Anchorage.

By Boat

The **Alaska Marine Highway** (www.ferryalaska.com, 800-642-0066) sails to and from Petersburg multiple times per week, taking passengers through the gorgeous Wrangell Narrows as it travels south. The **Rainforest Islands Ferry** (www.forestislandsferry.com, 907-329-2031) will commence sailing around smaller southeast Alaska communities by 2013.

Petersburg

Population: 3,937 (2012 census area)
Founded in: 1897 as a fish processing and packing site by young Peter Buschmann, a Norwegian.
Known for: Close ties to Norway and its culture.
Interesting fact: Much of downtown Petersburg has retained the charm of Norwegian culture. Homes and businesses are designed to model those of far-off Norway.
Hot tip: Arrive in Petersburg via the Alaska Marine Highway (ferry). The journey is as delightful as the destination!

GETTING AROUND

Walking or biking is the best way to see Petersburg. With a series of in-town trails and walking paths and with low traffic, Petersburg is perfect for strolling or pedaling with kids.

The Alaska ferry and small-ship cruise companies dock right downtown, leaving passengers with easy access to shops, restaurants, and trails. **Viking Cab** (907-518-9191) will transport you just about anywhere on the island, including to and from the Petersburg Airport.

Life Cyclery (907-650-7387) offers bicycle rentals, including trailers for kids and gear, at a cost of around $30/day and $10/day for each additional bike.

VISITOR INFORMATION

The **Petersburg Chamber of Commerce and Visitor Center** (www .petersburg.org, visitorinfo@alaska.com, 907-772-3646) is located on the corner of First and Fram Streets, an easy walk from the docks. Find information about all manner of lodging, food, and recreation here, as well as some free fun stuff for kids.

SHOPPING/GROCERIES

Hammer & Wikan Inc.
1300 Howkan, Petersburg, AK 99833
(907) 772-4246
www.hammerandwikan.com
Open Monday–Saturday 7 a.m.–8 p.m. Sunday 8 a.m.–7 p.m. (summer months)

Groceries, deli, produce, and some organic choices in one locally owned spot. Find a healthy dose of local goings-on, too. Also owners of a True Value convenience store on Main Street, where lattes and snacks can be purchased for last-minute needs. Free dockside delivery!

Petersburg Rexall Drug Inc.
215 North Nordic Dr., Petersburg, AK 99833
(907) 772-3265
www.petersburgrexall.com
Open daily, but hours vary. Call for seasonal hours.

Medical equipment, supplies, and prescriptions.

MEDICAL CARE

Petersburg Medical Center
103 Fram St., Petersburg, AK 99833
(907) 772-4291
www.pmc-health.com

A 13-bed hospital with emergency services.

LODGING
Petersburg welcomes children with open arms, especially those visiting for a short while. Local hospitality shines through with many options for lodging, even in this tiny community.

Hotels

Scandia House $$
110 Nordic Dr., Petersburg, AK 99833
(800) 722-5006, (907) 772-4281
www.scandiahousehotel.com, info@scandiahousehotel.com

Offering 33 rooms right in the heart of downtown, Scandia House is a short walk from the ferry dock. The hotel also has a private kitchen and offers a free continental breakfast. Families will enjoy rental skiffs available at a special rate, and parents will love that kids under 12 stay free. Smoking and nonsmoking rooms, so be specific when you make a reservation. A courtesy van is available, or rent a car and explore on your own.

Thumbs-up for: Great Norwegian atmosphere, excellent location, access to kitchen. Love the boats, too.

The Tides Inn $$
307 North First St., Petersburg, AK 99833
(800) 665-8433, (907) 772-4288
www.TidesInnAlaska.com, tidesinn@alaska.com

Also located downtown, the **Tides Inn** is affordable lodging, with 45 rooms, some with kitchenettes and a continental breakfast. Children 11 and under stay free. Access to Avis Car rental services is also an option. All rooms have wireless Internet. Walk to local restaurants, the museum, and ferry dock. This is a smoking and nonsmoking establishment.

Thumbs-up for: Affordability, access.

Bed and Breakfast/Vacation Rental

Alaska Sport Haven Lodge $$
301 South Nordic, Petersburg, AK 99833
(800) 772-4741
www.alaskasporthaven.com, alaskasporthaven@yahoo.com

Located just two blocks from the Petersburg harbor, the Sport Haven Lodge offers access to all sorts of family fun. Sleeping up to nine people, the lodge (a house, really) is perfect for multigenerational vacations, with a barbecue, coffee and tea bar, game room, and free bikes to pedal about town. Hosts can arrange tours and charters as well. A full breakfast is provided each morning. This is a smoking and nonsmoking property. You may need to bring your own portable crib.

Thumbs-up for: Access to town, free bikes, great breakfast.

Broom Hus Vacation Rental $$-$$$
411 South Nordic Dr., Petersburg, AK 99833
(907) 772-3459
www.broomhus.com, broomhus@aptalaska.net

Charming in every way, this home sleeps up to six people with private kitchens, baths, and a daily continental breakfast. Located approximately five minutes from the harbor and downtown area, the Broom Hus provides a nice retreat for busy travelers of any age. Transportation is available, too. Nonsmoking property.

Thumbs-up for: Old-town Petersburg charm, quiet location, full kitchen.

Camping

Ohmer Creek Campground
U.S. Forest Service
Mile 22 Mitkof Highway, Petersburg, AK 99833
(907) 772-3871
www.fs.fed.us/r10/tongass/recreation/rec_facilities/psgrec.htm
Fee structure changes per year, so see website for information/rates.

A 10-site RV/tent campground operated by the Tongass National Forest, this area offers no power or water for RVs. Pit toilets are available. Hike the short Ohmer Creek trail (.25 mile) through a temperate rain forest, a great way to show kids how large southeast Alaska's trees can grow.

Thumbs-up for: Nature trail; quiet, USFS-maintained sites.

FEEDING THE FAMILY

Petersburg has a nice lineup of kid-friendly eating establishments. From chowder to good old fish and chips, restaurants do a brisk business with both locals and visitors.

Restaurants

Coastal Cold Storage $–$$
306 N. Nordic Dr., Petersburg, AK 99833
(877) 257-4746, (907) 772-4177
Open Monday–Saturday 6 a.m.–7 p.m., Sunday 7 a.m.–2 p.m. (summer); Monday–Saturday 7 a.m.–2 p.m. (fall/winter)

"The *best* halibut and chips I've ever eaten." That's what people say about this local fish market and small restaurant. Featuring a grab-and-go sort of style, the menu at Coastal Cold Storage reads like a seafood lover's wish list: halibut, shrimp, clams, and sometimes oysters. Also a great location for free Internet. The seafood market can process and ship your fish, if you're a fortunate fisherperson.

Note: Not a lot of seating, so try relocating outdoors or heading to the docks to dine alfresco.

Inga's Galley $$
104 N. Nordic Dr., Petersburg, AK 99833
(907) 772-2090
www.ingasgalley@gmail.com
Open Monday–Friday 11 a.m.–8 p.m., Saturday 11 a.m.–7 p.m.

Hopefully you'll be in town for more than one meal, because just down the street from Coastal Cold Storage is another seafood gem worth a nosh. Inga's doesn't look like it would be a gourmet seafood establishment, housed in a tiny shack with outdoor seating, but it is. Rockfish and chips, excellent burgers, and smoked salmon chowder. Great fries, too. No children's menu, but our son did okay with the listed items. Mostly the fries.

Helse Restaurant $–$$
13 Sing Lee Alley, Petersburg, AK 99833
(907) 772-3444
Open Monday–Friday 8 a.m.–5 p.m., Saturday 10 a.m.–3 p.m.

The local hangout, Helse is open all year and features homemade bread, soups, sandwiches, and ice cream. Kids love the simple menu items and, of course, the ice cream. The establishment also has a nice espresso/coffee selection.

FAMILY FUN IN PETERSBURG

Whether you have a few hours or a few days, Petersburg has plenty of elbow room and fun places to explore.

Museums and Cultural Experiences

Clausen Memorial Museum

203 Fram St., Petersburg, AK 99833
(907) 772-3598
www.clausenmuseum.org, clausenmuseum@aptalaska.net
Open Monday–Saturday (May–September). Hours vary, so call ahead.

This museum offers a glimpse into the cultural history of fishing from the perspective of the ancient Native Alaskans and the enterprising white man. Not really designed for kids under the age of eight, it is still an interesting stop, and even little kids will enjoy the fountain out front. Watch an interesting video about Petersburg's rise to popularity within the fishing industry and see some of the tools needed to successfully catch salmon and halibut in the chilly waters of southeast Alaska. Suitable for school-agers, eight and up.

Sandy Beach Petroglyphs and Prehistoric Fish Traps

Located at Sandy Beach Park (Sandy Beach Road and Haugen Drive), these ancient symbols of life so long ago are important stops for families interested in Alaska's history. Managed by archeologists and anthropologists of the U.S. Forest Service, these artifacts are reminders that life in the Far North existed for many thousands of years before being "discovered" by the white man. Pick up a flyer about the fish traps and petroglyphs at the Petersburg Visitor Center and start exploring, and ask about guided tours of the area.

Note: The fish traps can be difficult to see without the flyer/map, but once you spot the layout, it's fascinating. Remind kids (and other grown-ups) to tread lightly; these are at least 2,000 years old! Contact the **Tongass National Forest Petersburg District** office (12 N. Nordic Dr., 907-772-3871) for summertime guided tour times.

Outdoor Recreation

WALKING AND HIKING

The town's careful planning for trails and pathways has created some nice venues for sightseeing that are mostly flat, with great views and interesting side trips. Try a short **walking tour** of town from the ferry terminal into the quaint downtown area. Visit the **Sons of Norway Hall** and its beautiful rosemaling designs (flowery decoration on the shutters), the cool Viking ship next door, and the interesting **Hammer Slough**, full of squawking seagulls and the occasional sea lion near the boat docks. Allow about an hour for kids to get their fill of the creatures, wooden roadways, and traditional architecture.

A longer walk takes visitors up Excel Street, past the old Lutheran Church, and up to the community ball fields and skate park. Here, two options are available: one takes a right onto a short **nature trail** and boardwalk that winds through a wetland for approximately 900 yards. Watch for Sitka black tail deer here. The other option is to head left at the ball fields and walk the **Hungry Point Trail**, through a muskeg meadow filled with skunk cabbage, wildflowers, and the occasional blueberry patch. Look for stunning views of the surrounding mountains as you amble the level gravel trail. Both are suitable for jogging strollers and early walkers. Hungry Point Trail takes about 40 minutes one way, so hikers can either make this an out-and-back or take a left upon arriving at Sandy Beach Road and return to town along the waterfront sidewalks.

If you have transportation, try the **Blind River Rapids boardwalk trail**, located at Mile 14 of the Mitkof Highway. Also a popular fishing spot, this boardwalk traverses a muskeg bog before reaching the rapids' fishing hole. Total length out and back is a mile or so, and the trailhead is

Fishermen's Memorial Park honors Petersburg's main industry.

meticulously maintained, with bathrooms, parking lot, and picnic shelter at the end of the trail.

Be sure to stop by **Outlook Park**, located along Sandy Beach Road, about halfway between Hungry Point and Sandy Beach Park. Take a picnic lunch to the timber-frame shelter built to model a Norwegian Stave church and peer through the telescopes for whales, icebergs, and busy sea lions. Also see if Devil's Thumb is sticking up from the Coast Mountain range, not always visible due to cloud cover.

KAYAKING

Tongass Kayak Adventures
P.O. Box 2169, Petersburg, AK 99833
(907) 772-4600
www.tongasskayak.com, info@tongasskayak.com

Trips range from four hours to four days, and include sightseeing paddles and whale watching. They'll also know the remote cabins to rent and drop you and your fam off and pick you up after a few days of paddling the calm coves in the Petersburg area. Day trips include PFDs, snacks, and guide services. Kids are welcome to hop in a double boat and paddle with Mom or Dad as they explore the harbor and Petersburg Creek area. Best for kids age six and up.

FISHING

The easiest way for kids to experience the thrill of hooking a fish is, honestly, to buy or bring gear and let them toss a line off the **harbor docks**. Besides being cheaper than a charter boat, fishing from the dock affords awesome creature viewing, as sea anemones, jellyfish, sea lions, and other marine life swims, floats, or flutters around. Pick up gear at any number of locations, including the Hammer & Wikan True Value store or the Trading Union, located on Nordic Drive. Kids under 14 don't need a license to fish in Alaska, so let 'em at it!

Note: South Harbor is a fun spot to fish; boats are lined up in a cornucopia of colors and styles and old-timers love to talk with young anglers.

FLIGHTSEEING

Temsco Helicopters
Petersburg James A. Johnson Airport
1504 Haugen Dr., Petersburg, AK 99833
(907) 772-4780
www.temscoair.com/petersburg

> ### PARENT PRO TIP
>
> Parents who will be kayaking in a double boat with kids should be aware that it is the grown-up who will be doing most of the work. Paddling is tough for little arms, even with child-sized paddles. Also ask ahead of time about PFDs and spray skirts, because not every outfit has them to fit smaller kids.
>
> —James, father of two

> ### KIDSPEAK
>
> The best part about fishing in Petersburg was the big sea lion that kept swimming around and barking at us. He had big teeth.
>
> —Owen, age seven

Try a flightseeing trip to Patterson Glacier or a combination of the glacier trip and Stikine Icefields. The Patterson Glacier trip is a one-hour experience that includes a glacier landing. Deep crevasses and ice spires become clear reminders of the fragile power of our earth, and stepping out for a photo op is a once-in-a-lifetime experience. The combo tour is about two hours from start to finish and includes a flyover of the southernmost active tidewater glacier in North America, LeConte. Best suited for kids of walking age and those who can sit still for the flight to the glacier(s).

Note: Be sure to wear weather-appropriate clothing—it's chilly on these rivers of ice!

TOURS

Viking Travel, located at 101 N. Nordic Drive (www.alaskaferry.com, 800-327-2571, 907-772-3818), provides the latest in local tour and travel and will be able to arrange last-minute charters, whale-watching trips, and many other activities. The one-stop shop for all things Petersburg, these friendly folks will also show off the **Petersburg Marine Mammal Center** exhibits (www.psgmmc.org), a collection of information and computer-based resources to learn more about the variety of mammals sharing the waterways.

Sitka: Blending of Cultures

Located on the western coast of Baranof Island, Sitka represents the best of a community full of opportunities for learning about a diverse and rich cultural history. The Tlingit people have thrived on Baranof Island for more than 10,000 years, finding the temperate rain forest ideal for living off the land and sea. When Vitus Bering arrived with his expedition team in 1741, he quickly saw the value of the sheltered bays and abundant game and planted the Russian flag. A fort quickly followed and so did the ire of the local Tlingits, who destroyed the New Archangel city in a bitter battle and led to a back-and-forth fight until 1808. Then Sitka was the capital of Russian America, a swath of land that extended from Fort Ross, California, all the way to the far northern reaches of Alaska.

Sitka is a wonderful destination for families. The combination of history, culture, and art means lots of accessible and interesting activities.

ARRIVING

Yep, you guessed it: Sitka is accessible only by boat or airplane. **Alaska Airlines** (www.alaskaair.com) has daily service from either Seattle or Anchorage, and the **Alaska Marine Highway** (www.ferryalaska.com, 800-642-0066) ferries stop by regularly.

GETTING AROUND

For a smallish town, Sitka has some great transportation options, mostly due to the arrival of a few large cruise ships each summer. Below are some ideas for navigating the island.

North Star Rent-A-Car
600 C. Airport Rd. (Sitka Airport), Sitka, AK 99835
(800) 722-6927, (907) 966-2552
www.northstarrentacar.com, nstar@alaska.net

Moore Taxi and Tours (907-738-3210, moorebusi@gci.net) operates from 4 a.m. to 11:30 p.m., providing taxi service to and from many Sitka destinations. They also provide a nice option for getting out of town and seeing sights without a formal tour company. Rates vary, so call ahead for pickup at the airport or ferry dock.

The **Visitor Transit Bus "UnTour"** (907-747-7290) operates only when the big cruise (i.e., those with 1,000 or more passengers) ships are in port. A free service to move people smoothly around town, this is a great way to see the city upon arrival and plan ahead for further adventures. Kids will enjoy stops at local attractions, too. The bus is available near the cruise ship tender docks (downtown waterfront, near the bridge) and operates until the final tenders arrive/depart each day. Call for the most current schedule, but buses generally rotate through the downtown area every 25 minutes or so. Look for the bright-yellow bus stop signs.

Sitka's public bus system, **Community Ride** (publictransit.sitkatribe.org, 907-747-7103), operates Monday–Friday, 6:30 a.m.–6:30 p.m. The hourly routes cover most of the commerce areas of town, including the ferry terminal. Visit the bus system's website for the latest schedule. All buses are accessible for wheelchairs/strollers.

VISITOR INFORMATION

Harrigan Centennial Hall (330 Harbor Dr., www.cityofsitka.com/government/departments/centennial, 907-747-3225) is the epicenter of Sitka visitor information. Located on the harbor, within full view of the beautiful scenery, this is where to find brochures, make tour arrangements, and pick up transportation for many land and sea tours. It's also close to the city's library, a great spot to relax and read for a bit with the kids for a little down time.

The **Sitka Convention and Visitors Bureau** maintains the information within Centennial Hall and on a fabulous website (www.sitka.org), which has information on everything from planning a trip to finding a restaurant, not to mention some awesome pictures of Sitka from its annual photography contest.

SHOPPING/GROCERIES

Market Center
210 Baranof St., Sitka, AK 99835
(907) 747-6686

Sitka

Population: 9,084 (2012 census)

Founded in: 1867 as capital of the new U.S. Territory of Alaska, but Russian traders jumped on land in 1741, and Tlingit Indians inhabited the prosperous land for thousands of years prior.

Known for: Incredibly rich Alaska Native cultural history, with 24 local attractions listed on the National Register of Historic Places.

Interesting fact: Sitka was known as the Paris of the Pacific during the 1800s, for its charming architecture and interesting allure of adventure for wealthy travelers.

Hot tip: Plan to spend at least three nights in Sitka, taking in some of that culture. Art, music, science, and Alaska Native traditions are worth the extra time.

A full-service grocery and convenience store, this is a good spot to stock up on kid-friendly snacks and drinks. They also have sandwiches, salads, and a coffee shop.

Harry Race Pharmacy
106 Lincoln St., Sitka, AK 99835
(907) 747-8006
www.whitesalaska.com, whites.inc@acsalaska.net

Medical supplies, medications, and personal items.

MEDICAL CARE

Sitka Community Hospital
209 Moller Ave., Sitka, AK 99835
(907) 747-3241
www.sitkahospital.org

Acute, outpatient, and emergency care.

LODGING
Plenty of downtown lodging options are available for visiting families. If you're using the Alaska Marine Highway ferry, do ask your hosts if they provide transportation to or from the ferry terminal, as arrival/departure times can be in the middle of the night, and it's best to know ahead of time for other arrangements if necessary.

Hotels

Sitka Hotel $$
118 Lincoln St., Sitka, AK 99835
(888) 757-3288
www.sitkahotel.net, stay@sitkahotel.net

With 50 rooms within walking distance to most of Sitka's attractions, the Sitka Hotel is clean and bright. Victoria's restaurant is also on-site, and kids under 12 stay free. Laundry, free wireless Internet, and 24-hour desk service. Front desk will assist with taxi/shuttle arrangements to airport or ferry.

Thumbs-up for: Location and affordability. Restaurant is a nice addition for families.

Shee Atika' Totem Square Inn $$–$$$
201 Katlian St., Sitka, AK 99835
(866) 300-1353, (907) 747-3693
www.sheeatika.com, totemsquare@sheeatika.com

This Native-owned hotel and conference center is large and usually busy, so make reservations well in advance. The 68-room property is located right on the waterfront, near a large patch of grassy parkland. Shee Atika' has 16 suites and provides wireless Internet, an on-site restaurant called the Dock Shack, a snack center, and shuttle service to many local attractions. This is a nonsmoking hotel. The hotel can arrange fishing charters and other tours.

Thumbs-up for: Proximity to Sitka attractions, full-service atmosphere, and transportation.

Super 8 Sitka $$
404 Sawmill Creek Rd., Sitka, AK 99835
(907) 747-8804
www.super8.com/hotels/alaska/sitka/super-8-sitka/hotel-overview

This 35-room hotel, located a short walk from downtown, offers clean rooms with typical budget hotel style. Kids 17 and under stay free. Free wireless Internet, laundry facilities, hot tub, and continental breakfast. Transportation must be arranged by you, however, so keep this in mind should you require a ride to or from attractions, ferry terminal or airport.

Thumbs-up for: Affordability, quiet location.

BED AND BREAKFASTS
The Sitka Bed and Breakfast Association offers a listing of B&Bs (www.accommodations-alaska.com), as does the Sitka Visitors Bureau.

Alaska Ocean View Bed and Breakfast Inn $$–$$$
1101 Edgecumbe Dr., Sitka, AK 99835
(888) 811-6870, (907) 747-8310
www.sitka-alaska-lodging.com, alaskaoceanview@gci.net

This one-suite property offers great views, a quiet atmosphere, and a non-smoking environment. It's a bit out of town, so you'll need transportation to get here. Full breakfast, dietary needs accommodated.

Vacation Rentals/Cottages

Fairweather Vacation Homes $$$
308 Monastery St., Sitka, AK 99835
(907) 747-8601
www.fairweatherdreams.com, fairweather308@gci.net

Actually two vacation rental properties near the downtown area, these are great options for families. Kitchens, living space, and easy access to all the fun stuff in Sitka make either the Fairweather or Dreaming Bear suites good choices. If you're catching a plane or ferry, you can store gear onsite.

Thumbs-up for: Location, ample space, kitchens, and deck at each property.

Home Away from Home Vacation Rentals $$–$$$
236 Lincoln St., Ste. 103, Sitka, AK 99835
(800) 478-8558, (907) 747-8558
www.vacationsitka.com, skipper@charteralaska.com

Choose from among five private, comfortable lodging options in the downtown area. Laundry facilities, full kitchen and related amenities, and access to sightseeing and fishing activities through their charter service. Rent by the day or by the week. Ask about nonsmoking options.

CAMPING

Sitka Sportsman's Association RV Park
5211 Halibut Point Rd., Sitka, AK 99835
(800) 750-4712
www.rvsitka.com

A nifty RV and tent park located next door to the Alaska Marine Highway ferry terminal, seven miles from town. Sixteen RV sites are available and a grassy area for tents, at a rate of $25/RV, $19/tents. Sewer hookups, bathrooms/showers, and wireless (most of the time). Families will enjoy access to a rocky beach and kayak put-in area.

Thumbs-up for: Great access to the ferry dock and waterfront, plus hot showers.

Starrigavan Campground
Tongass National Forest, Sitka Ranger District
(877) 444-6777
www.recreation.gov

Flush with opportunities to get completely away from town, Starrigavan features a loop of three camping areas. Of the three, only 18 offer space for RVs, so reserve early. Fees range from $12 to $16/night, with a 14-day limit. Lots of hiking nearby and a beautiful bird-viewing shelter. Also inquire about U.S. Forest Service cabins for rent. These bare-bones cabins are available for a nominal overnight fee to save sleeping in a fabric tent, if you so desire. They go fast, though. Do practice your bear-aware techniques and secure *all* trash and smelly items.

Thumbs-up for: Scenery, remote location, access to great hiking.

FEEDING THE FAMILY

We love eating in Sitka, that's all there is to it. Children are welcome in just about every establishment, but below are a few favorites among the home team.

Restaurants

The Bayview Restaurant and Pub $$–$$$
407 Lincoln St., Sitka, AK 99835
(907) 747-5300
www.sitkabayviewpub.com
Open Monday–Friday 11 a.m.–late, Saturday–Sunday 8 a.m.–late

Yes, it's a sports bar, but this is no ordinary pub-and-grub. Located near the harbor, with views, great food, and very kind staff, Bayview is a winning choice for lunch or dinner any day. Breakfast is added on the weekends, with waffles, egg dishes, and kid-pleasing French toast on the menu. Speaking of kids, they have their own lineup of dishes like mac 'n cheese, chicken tenders, and fish and chips. Bayview also has stacks and stacks of coloring books and piles of board games and puzzles to keep young people happily occupied.

Larkspur Cafe $-$$
2 Lincoln St., Ste. 1A, Sitka, AK 99835
(907) 966-2326
www.larkspurcafe.blogspot.com
Open Monday–Tuesday 11 a.m.–3 p.m., Wednesday–Sunday 11 a.m.–10 p.m.

Housed in a restored cable house, with creaky floors and a large back porch, the Larkspur offers fresh food with a view. In the same building as locally produced Raven Radio, the dining room often has small concerts in the funky space, so some kids might not like the loud atmosphere. But the music is fun, the food always excellent, and it's worth a visit. We love the halibut tacos (spicy and crunchy). Staff will adapt many items for kids, so don't be afraid to ask. My son loves to drink their fresh lemonade from a mason jar.

Pizza Express $-$$
1321 Sawmill Creek Rd., Sitka, AK 99835
(907) 966-2428
Open Monday–Saturday 11 a.m.–9 p.m., Sunday noon–9 p.m.

Heads up, the specialty here is Mexican food, but they do have pizza, too. Confused? We were, too, but ultimately found this restaurant to be perfect for our picky eater. Pizza Express is located in the Sawmill Creek Plaza, by the way, so look for a long strip mall. A bonus: they deliver Monday–Saturday until 10 p.m.

Need Coffee? Highliner Coffee Company Roasts Their Own Special Blend of Comfort
Yes, parents do need their coffee, and Highliner Coffee Company Café, located next to the Sitka Fire Hall (327 Seward St., www.highlinercoffee .com), is the perfect spot for a little pick-me-up or warmer, depending upon the weather and mood of your children. We love their bagels and muffins, too, in addition to some awesome gourmet espresso. Wireless Internet will allow you to keep in touch with social media world. A great place to take a break.

Dock Shack Café $$–$$$
201 Katlian St., Sitka, AK 99835
(907) 747-2755
www.dockshack.com
Open daily 6 a.m.–8 p.m.

Part of the Shee Atika' Totem Square Inn complex, the Dock Shack Café sells solid food for a family. Offering a Little Bear Bites menu for kids, both portions and prices are reasonable for breakfast, lunch, and dinner. The corn dog nuggets are always a hit, as is the Little Bear Breakfast of eggs, bacon, sausages, and hash browns. Parents will also like their menu, with calamari, halibut bites, and some excellent salads.

FAMILY FUN IN SITKA

The charm of Sitka is evident. From the distant mountains to up-close Russian influences, Sitka's natural and man-made sights are quite wonderful. Stroll the neighborhoods and paved pathways around town; it's here you'll discover the essence of kid-friendliness and hospitality. Take advantage of local playgrounds and fishing holes, too, and discover why so many families consider Sitka to be just about perfect.

Museums and Cultural Experiences

Sitka Historical Society and Museum
330 Harbor Dr.,Sitka, AK 99835
(907) 747-6455
www.sitkahistory.org
Open Monday–Friday 9 a.m.–5 p.m., Saturday 10 a.m.–4 p.m. (May–September)
Admission: $2

Located along the harbor front inside Centennial Hall (where you'll also find visitor information), the Sitka Historical Museum covers information and culture dating back to the community's Tlingit, Russian, and American past. A nice first stop, the museum doesn't have tons of exhibits that appeal to the under-10 crowd, but our son enjoyed the dioramas and U.S. Navy information regarding World War II, when a small air station was built on nearby Japonski Island as protection. Suitable for kids age eight and older.

Note: The nearby harbor, park, walking paths, and public library might be a good divide-and-conquer activity for little ones and a parent while olders get their museum fix.

Sitka National Historical Park and Sitka Cultural Center

National Park Service
103 Monastery St., Sitka, AK 99835
(907) 747-0110
www.nps.gov/sitk/
Admission: $4/person 16 and older; free October–April

The site of a bloody battle between invading Russian traders and the indigenous Tlingit Indians, the National Historical Park is a landmark place, and one appealing to a wide spectrum of visitors. Walk the 110-acre property, looking for towering totems that appear to be rising straight from the earth; explore the beach and imagine yourself immersed in a fight with strangers from so far way. Step inside the cultural center and get a Junior Ranger activity booklet that helps explain the reasons behind the battle and why this site is so sacred to Sitka. Local carvers and silversmiths are often on hand to share their skills with visitors.

Note: The trails on the property are fantastic for kids and parents; jogging strollers will be fine here. Do be bear-aware. Allow at least two hours for indoor and outdoor exploration, so pack snacks and drinks. The beach is awesome for looking under rocks.

Sheldon Jackson Museum

104 College Dr., Sitka, AK 99835
(907) 747-3004
www.museums.state.ak.us/sheldon_jackson
Open daily 9 a.m.–5 p.m. (mid-May–mid-September), Tuesday–Saturday 10 a.m.–4 p.m. (winter months)
Admission: $5/adults, $4/seniors 65+, free for kids 18 and under; $3/adults in winter

Part of the State of Alaska's museum system, Sheldon Jackson Museum presents a collection of items from the Reverend Jackson, a missionary who explored Alaska from the top down and eventually settled in Sitka to establish a now-closed college. The oldest museum in Alaska, the building alone is worth a visit; it's a round, rotunda sort of structure, and kids will enjoy peering up into its rooftop. Drawer after drawer of artifacts and

Castle Hill in downtown Sitka is the site where Alaska's transfer of ownership from Russia to the United States occurred in 1867.

specimens are available to gaze upon, and children can try their hand at mat weaving, writing, and wayfinding at various stations set up around the building. This museum is suitable for kids of school age, since many exhibits are fragile and/or involve reading. But it's like a big treasure box.

Castle Hill, located downtown at 100 Lincoln Street, is not a museum but rather the site of an early stronghold of the Tlingit tribe until it was taken over by the Russians and a series of structures were built upon the knob of a hill. The last, called Baranof's Castle, was the site of the transfer of Alaska to the United States in 1867, a date Sitka celebrates each year at Castle Hill. Climb the stairs or walk the graduated pathway, but however you get up there, do stop for the view and to see the old cannons. Suitable for all ages.

Outdoor Recreation

Like most southeast Alaska communities, Sitka receives a lot of rain, but many sunny days, too. If you're expecting to hoof it around town, consider footwear that will allow for a transition from rocky beach to pavement to wooded trail and back again, in any sort of weather.

We like to take a break at the **community park** along the waterfront, near the corner of Davis and Lincoln Streets. Across the street is the Sheldon Jackson campus and museum. Restrooms, playground equipment, and a long grassy area are at your disposal.

Whale Park is located six miles south of town, along Sawmill Creek Road. Built in 1995, the park provides an opportunity to spy humpback whales in the late fall and early spring as they migrate north or south. Featuring a boardwalk, small picnic shelter, and free viewing scopes. A nice bonus is the provided hydrophone to listen to whales "singing" with one another.

Kayaking is fabulous in Sitka. With tons of marine wildlife making their homes here, kayakers can explore a variety of sheltered areas with a guide or on their own (if experienced). Try **Sitka Sound Ocean Adventures** (www.kayaksitka.com) for a 2.5-hour paddle around the harbor and nearby islands with a guide. This trip is also affordable, at $69/adults, $49/kids 6–12, and it's tons of fun. The company has lots of other trips, too, so look for their signature blue bus just outside Crescent Harbor, on the dock.

Family-Friendly Hiking

Sitka is blessed with a wealth of trails for children, most of which are easily found within the city limits. Below are a few favorites.

Sitka National Historical Park (see also "Museums and Cultural Experiences") features a three-quarter-mile loop trail through a spruce and hemlock forest, showcasing the many totems brought here over the years. Begin at the National Park Service building and follow the Indian River, looping back to the parking lot. The area also extends across the Indian River and around to the other side, where a picnic shelter and more trails (totaling about 1.5 miles of walking) offer great views of spawning salmon toward July and August.

Sitka's Cross Trail can be accessed either at Keet Goosh Elementary School near Edgecumbe Street or Sitka High School, near Monastery Street. This refurbished trail is a wide, gravel trail that accommodates jogging strollers and new walkers nicely. It's also a great trail for mountain bikes. Spanning seven miles across the outskirts of town, this is a good choice for those who are seeking refuge from downtown and want to get in some serious miles. The trail ends at Indian River Road (another access point). Visit Sitka Trail Works (www.sitkatrailworks.org) for more information.

Note: Parents should remember their bear-aware techniques when hiking around Sitka.

Beaver Lake Trail is a wonderful first hilly hike for youngsters who have expressed interest in something other than walks along even terrain. Beaver Lake is located at the end of Sawmill Creek Road, where Blue Lake Road veers off to the left. Find this wonderfully maintained trail at the end, near Sawmill Creek itself. The first mile of this 2.9-mile hike (round-trip) is pretty easy but transitions into switchbacks, rocks to climb over and around, and some interesting formations created by volunteers from Sitka Trail Works. *Psst*—offer a treat to the one who spots the waterfall first. Suitable for kids age five and up. This is not a trail for wheels; infants/toddlers should be in packs.

Note: Watch smaller children as you near the lake—there is little shoreline to speak of and banks toward the water can be steep.

Alaska Fact

The Sitka black-tailed deer is one of the noisiest animals found in Alaska! These social animals sometimes sound like sheep, bleating and baaaahing their way through the dense coastal rain forests of southeast Alaska.

Guided Tours

While a family can easily explore Sitka on their own, if time is a factor or you'd like an interpretive approach to explore the community, we recommend **Sitka Tribal Tours** (www.sitkatours.com, 888-270-8687), who can arrange fast visits to such attractions as the Tlingit Clan House, the Alaska Raptor Center, Totem National Historical Park, and other stops of interest. Tours usually last three hours and come with narration by local Native residents.

Note: With its on-off fast pace, this tour is best for kids old enough to handle the crowded, busy atmosphere. Strollers are allowed, but front or backpacks would work best for infants.

Other Adventures

Sitka Sound Science Center
834 Lincoln St., Sitka, AK 99835
(907) 747-8878
www.sitkasoundsciencecenter.org
Open daily 9 a.m.–4 p.m. during the summer
Admission: By donation

The Sitka Sound Science Center is located in an aging concrete building along Lincoln Street, across from the Sheldon Jackson Museum, and is in the process of building itself into a top-notch facility for marine learning and research. The organization has outside tanks for young salmon and a few indoor touch tanks for closer exploration of the rich variety of marine creatures calling the Sitka Sound home. Young volunteers are on hand to help, making this a truly community-supported place. Great for all ages. Allow about an hour to touch and see all the fun stuff, indoors and out.

New Archangel Dancers
208 Smith St., Sitka, AK 99835
(907) 747-5516
www.newarchangeldancers.com
Admission: Ticket prices and show times vary; inquire via phone.

Promoting Sitka's strong Russian influence, the New Archangel Dancers are a fun, colorful, always-moving part of the community's history. This all-woman troupe is famous for their handmade costumes and difficult dance moves, and I was impressed by our son's interest. Perhaps it was the whirling spins or the "Heys!" that accompanied many of the leaps and jumps. Whatever the reason, this is one hour of compelling activity. Encourage kids to ask questions at the end of the show; many of these ladies are moms, too, and understand the need to inquire about why a girl is wearing boy clothes (the answer is fascinating, by the way).

Fortress of the Bear

4639 Sawmill Creek Rd., Sitka, AK 99835
(907) 747-3032
www.fortressofthebear.org
Open daily 9 a.m.–5 p.m. (April–September)
Admission: By donation.

Housing rescued brown bears that, as cubs, found themselves alone and too small to survive, the Fortress of the Bear facility is located outside of town. On a two-acre patch of land where bears frolic below and guests stand on a platform above, the facility is working to improve the area as the bears grow and require more space. If you're going to see bears at other southeast Alaska destinations or elsewhere in the state, I'd skip this, frankly. But if seeing brown bears up close is a must-do for your family, then stop. The bears are acclimated to their human family and can be quite funny when asking for a fish snack, much to the delight of youngsters in the crowd.

Alaska Raptor Center

1000 Raptor Way, Sitka, AK 99835
(800) 643-9425, (907) 747-8662
www.alaskaraptor.org
Open daily 8 a.m.–4 p.m. (May–September)
Admission: $12/adults, $6/kids 12 and under

Southeast Alaska's only rehabilitation center specifically for raptors, the Alaska Raptor Center houses eagles, hawks, owls, and other birds at its forested property outside of town. A popular stop on the cruise ship excursion route, the Raptor Center is best visited around the arrival of the motorcoach crowd (call ahead). A short introductory tour is required before you enter the rehabilitation area, where a large indoor flight center reintroduces injured birds to the concept of flying after illness or injury. If you join a formal tour group, staff will bring out a bird to view up close. Do walk around the outside area and wander a short trail to the creek; it's worth navigating and gets you away from the crowd.

Juneau: Our Most Remote Capital City

A visit to Juneau is a must for families touring Southeast, if for no other reason than to see the only capital in the United States inaccessible except by boat or plane. That's right, no roads lead to Juneau, which makes for interesting governing processes. Located on the shores of Gastineau Channel in the north-central area of the Alaska panhandle, Juneau is surrounded by high mountains, deep water, and a resourceful resident population who love their city and its quirky leadership of the rest of the state.

Juneau got an auspicious start as a gold mining camp. Two miners, Joe Juneau and Richard Harris, were sent by a Sitka mining mogul to explore the area and report back on the prospects, which were unusually good thanks to a local Tlingit chief by the name of Kowee. The Tlingit, Haida, and Tsimshian people had lived along the channel and surrounding forests for thousands of years, and were generally peaceful with the newcomers. Today, the Tlingit people are most numerous in the greater Juneau area. In 1880, the original town site was laid for a community by the name of Harrisburg, until Mr. Harris ticked off the local businessmen and Joe Juneau's name prevailed.

When Sitka lost clout in the early 1900s due to a decline in the fur and whaling industries, Juneau became the next in line as a territorial capital.

Juneau

Population: 32,832 (Juneau city and borough, 2012 census)

Founded in: 1880, originally as Harrisburg.

Known for: Alaska's capital city, accessible only by air or boat.

Interesting fact: The Juneau borough is larger than the state of Delaware.

Hot tip: Visit Mendenhall Glacier and the adjoining visitor center just before closing; bears are active and crowds are fewer. A rental car is a good idea.

A formal brick-and-mortar building was completed in 1929, and as Alaska grew, first as a territory then as a state, discussion began about the overall benefit of having a capital city so far from the major centers of Alaska commerce. With Anchorage as the state's largest city, many government officials split time between offices in both cities, and transportation costs soar ever higher each year. Yet Juneau remains Alaska's capital city, and families who live and work there are deeply involved in their community and its rich historical significance to Alaska as a whole.

ARRIVING

By Air

Alaska Airlines (www.alaskaair.com, 800-252-7522) offers daily jet service to and from Anchorage and Seattle. The gate area of Juneau International Airport (www.juneau.lib.ak.us/airport) provides a small play table and a few toys for smaller kids under five.

By Boat

The **Alaska Marine Highway System** (www.ferryalaska.com, 800-642-0066) regularly sails to and from Juneau. Sailing north from Bellingham, Washington, and Prince Rupert, British Columbia, the ferry is a great way to get to Juneau if you have the time. See Chapter 2, "How to Get Here," for more info about the ferry.

GETTING AROUND

Since Juneau has only 45 miles total of major roadway along the mountainous coastline, it's pretty easy to navigate the city and outlying areas. A great way to explore Juneau's outskirts is via rental car, offering both flexibility and opportunity to see the forests and beaches up close. Most of the rental agencies are located near the baggage claim of the Juneau airport, at 1873 Shell Simmons Drive.

Avis Car Rental (www.avis.com, 907-789-9450)
Budget (www.locations.budget.com/ak/juneau, 907-789-4111)
Hertz Rent A Car (www.hertz.com, 907-789-9494)

A **public bus system** is widely available throughout the borough of Juneau and into the bedroom community of Douglas, across the Gastineau Channel on Douglas Island. **Capital Transit** (www.juneau.org/capitaltransit, 907-789-6901) costs $2/adults, $1/kids 6–18, with transfers for free.

Note: Passengers must board with exact change, so carry some cash if you want to take the bus. Buses also are equipped with bike racks for those wanting to supplement their two-wheel tours with four on occasion.

Taxi service is available through a three-companies-in-one service. **EverGreen Taxi, Capital Cab**, and **Taku Taxi** offer one convenient number for three separate services (www.evergreentaxi.com, 907-586-2121 or 907-586-2772). Call 24 hours a day for a traditional sedan or vans to maximize passenger and gear transportation.

VISITOR INFORMATION

Juneau Convention and Visitors Bureau operates a welcome center along the cruise ship docks at 470 S. Franklin Street (www.traveljuneau.com). Hours of operation are 8 a.m.–5 p.m., May–September.

Information can also be found at the Juneau airport near the baggage claim area; the visitors bureau tries to keep a volunteer at the desk to answer any questions as passengers arrive in Juneau.

SHOPPING/GROCERIES

Foodland IGA (formerly Alaskan and Proud Grocery)
615 West Willoughby Ave., Juneau, AK 99801
(907) 586-3101

This new store offers an expanded produce, meat, and deli department to meet the needs of busy downtown shoppers. Within walking distance from most major hotels.

Safeway
3033 Vintage Blvd., Juneau, AK 99801
(907) 523-2000
local.safeway.com/ak/juneau-1820

Located along the Glacier Highway, near the Juneau airport. Offering full-service deli, coffee shop, bakery, and groceries. On the bus line as well.

MEDICAL CARE

Bartlett Regional Hospital
3260 Hospital Dr., Juneau, AK 99801
(907) 796-8900
www.bartletthospital.org

Emergency services, radiology, pharmacy, and medical supplies.

LODGING

Lodging in Juneau means either staying in the middle of downtown, convenient to many local attractions, or staying on the outskirts of town, where trails, scenic vistas, and access to air transportation is available. Both areas boast a fine assortment of options, and the decision rests largely upon your schedule of activities.

Downtown Juneau

Driftwood Lodge $-$$
435 Willoughby Ave., Juneau, AK 99801
(907) 586-2280
www.driftwoodalaska.com, driftwood@gci.net

The Driftwood is located next door to the Alaska State Museum, within walking distance of downtown attractions. Despite a dated appearance, the property's 63 units are a clean and affordable option for families who want some space. We usually stay in a kitchen suite, with dishes, sink and stove, and sitting room. The bedrooms are spacious and the bathrooms are clean. While nonsmoking rooms are available, there are indeed many smokers who frequent the Driftwood Lodge. Courtesy transportation to and from the airport or ferry and baggage storage available. Bike rentals for big kids and adults, no trailers at the time of this writing. In-room coffee, television, and wireless Internet (although Internet is slow, slow).

Thumbs-up for: Affordability and location. Open year-round.

Prospector Hotel $$
375 Whittier St., Juneau, AK 99801
(907) 586-3737
www.prospectorhotel.com

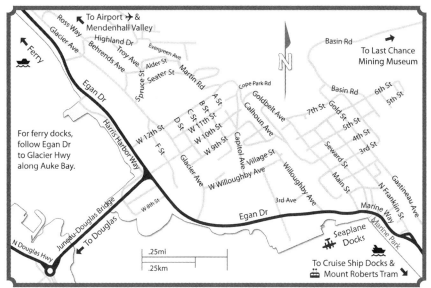

Downtown Juneau

Due to recent upgrades inside the Prospector bears mention. Located on a corner of land near Whittier Street, the Prospector offers affordable and spacious rooms with tons of convenience. A restaurant is on-site, rooms are huge, and staff is welcoming. The property is also next door to the Alaska State Museum, close to other downtown attractions. Refrigerators, microwaves, and wireless Internet available in all 62 rooms. Cribs upon request. No transportation, but it's on the local bus route, and taxi service is available.

Thumbs-up for: Attractive renovations, location, affordability, and space.

Goldbelt Hotel Juneau $$–$$$
51 Egan Dr., Juneau, AK 99801
(888) 478-6909, (907) 586-6909
www.goldbelthotel.com

With 106 rooms featuring standard and junior suites, Goldbelt Hotel is located near the waterfront, local transit station, small cruise ship dock, and attractions. An on-site restaurant, Zen, is a sort of Asian-fusion dining experience that my son loves. Complimentary transportation to and from the airport is available, as is in-room coffee, wireless, and, in the junior suites, a microwave and fridge. Cribs available upon request.

Thumbs-up for: Location, transportation, and a nice on-site dining option.

Mendenhall Valley Lodging

Best Western Country Lane Inn $$–$$$
9300 Glacier Highway, Juneau, AK 99801
(888) 781-5005, (907) 789-5005
www.countrylaneinn.com

Located eight miles from downtown Juneau and a short drive from the airport, the Country Lane Inn offers 65 nonsmoking rooms and suites to accommodate just about any family. The property is well decorated, with excellent service, a hot breakfast, and complimentary shuttle service to airport or ferry terminals and downtown. Cribs are available, as is a microwave, coffee maker, and high-speed Internet. We appreciated the kitchenette suites, where a simple meal could be made. A great choice for families with transportation or those who want to explore the valley area. Mileage plans available for frequent fliers.

Thumbs-up for: Great service, breakfast, and many amenities for guests.

Alternative Accommodations

A great listing of Juneau bed and breakfasts can be found at www .southeastalaskabnbs.com/juneau.html, but below is one of our favorites.

Silverbow Inn $$–$$$
120 Second St., Juneau, AK 99801
(800) 586-4146, (907) 586-4146
www.silverbowinn.com

In the heart of downtown Juneau, the Silverbow Inn has location and bagels on its side. Located in a prime spot for exploring the city, with museums, restaurants, and the waterfront close by, the Silverbow is also one of the best bagel shops this side of New York City. Guests in the 11 rooms receive a full breakfast, a bottomless cookie jar, and an evening wine and cheese social hour every day. Wireless Internet, a rooftop garden, and jacuzzi/sauna complete the package. No transportation provided, but the inn is on the bus line and taxis are very familiar with the location.

Note: Ask about parking options if you bring a rental car.

Thumbs-up for: Location, atmosphere, great food.

AK Cabin and Beach House $$$
3184 Indian Cove Dr., Juneau, AK 99801
(907) 523-1963
www.alaskabeachcabin.com, lodging@alaskabeachcabin.com

A more intimate option for families who want to be away from town, this cabin/beach house combination is located in Indian Cove, near the Alaska Marine Highway terminal. With an unobstructed view of a rocky beach and the water beyond, this is a peaceful location. Visit the local beach park or take the kids fishing. The house comes with a full kitchen, pots/pans, linens, private baths, and a host of other personal touches, which is why it's at the top end of our price range. However, for what you'll receive in hospitality, it's worth a second glance, especially if you'll be in Juneau more than just a few days. No transportation. Wireless Internet available. Crib upon request, well in advance.

Note: Parents of toddlers, the back yard area can be tricky with little ones, due to a lack of fencing and free-flowing tides coming in and going out.

Thumbs-up for: Remote, quiet location; outdoor recreation; full kitchen facilities.

CAMPING

Due to Juneau's small downtown area, campgrounds are generally located toward the Mendenhall Valley area, where the landscape is decidedly more spread out with lots more parks and trails.

Mendenhall Lake Campground
U.S. Forest Service, Tongass National Forest
(907) 586-5255
www.fs.fed.us/r10/tongass/recreation/rec_facilities/jnurec

Secluded and beautiful, this campground is located on Mendenhall Lake, a 13-mile drive from downtown Juneau. The 69-site property has a wide range of available areas, from walk-in tent sites to full-service RV slots. Each site has a fire grill, picnic table, dump site, and tent pad, with potable water and pit toilets nearby (no showers). Plan to purchase or bring your own firewood, since nothing can be removed from the forest. Open May–September. From $28/day for RVs to $10/day for basic tent sites.

Thumbs-up for: Lakeside location, variety of campsites. Lots to see nearby.

Spruce Meadow RV Park
10200 Mendenhall Loop Rd., Juneau, AK 99801
www.juneaurv.com

Spruce Meadow is near Mendenhall Glacier, just four miles away from the park. While it's outside the main downtown area, the city bus stops right outside the property and park hosts will assist you with schedules. The park has 47 sites in a forested location, and it's not uncommon to see local wildlife. Kids will enjoy the chance to play on the lawn and meet other young travelers, and grown-ups will like the Wi-Fi, laundry, and free showers. I personally love this place's connection with their community; guests who donate to a local charity receive $2 off their stay. Open all year. From $37/night for big rig spaces to $21/night for (limited) tent spaces.

Thumbs-up for: Clean facilities, excellent staff, access to downtown via the bus, and access to Mendenhall Glacier.

Alaska Fact
While only 32,000 people live in Juneau, southeast Alaska has 20,000 or more bald eagles! Our national bird is alive and well in Alaska.

FEEDING THE FAMILY
Since many visitors use Juneau as either a jumping-on or jumping-off point, showing up means a desire for fresh seafood. We understand. We also understand that many kids do not appreciate the finer points of dining on salmon or halibut (mine included), so we've offered up some variety in our Juneau restaurant section.

Restaurants

The Hangar $$-$$$

2 Marine Way, Ste. 106 (Merchants' Wharf Mall), Juneau, AK 99801
(907) 586-5018
www.hangaronthewharf.com, info@hangaronthewharf.com
Open Monday–Friday 11 a.m.–1 a.m., Saturday 11 a.m.–3 a.m., Sunday 11 a.m.–1 a.m.

The Hangar bar and grill is a popular hangout for hordes of visitors who, upon seeing the establishment's sign hanging waterside, run as fast as they can in the hopes of noshing on some fish and chips. They're right, for the seafood here is tasty, the atmosphere slightly nutty, and the variety just superb. Our son appreciates the simple handmade cheeseburgers, my husband likes the spicy halibut tacos, and I have a thing for the salmon burger.

Note: For the best seating (on the window side), call ahead to make reservations. This place gets crowded when ships are in port or when it's raining—pretty much all the time in the summer.

Silverbow Bakery $-$$

120 Second St., Juneau, AK 99801
(800) 586-4146, (907) 586-4146
www.silverbowinn.com, info@silverbowinn.com
Open daily

Fresh, fresh, and more fresh—that's the Silverbow. Trendy, hip, and totally the place to bring kids, the Silverbow offers homemade bagels, breads, waffles, soup/sandwiches, and yummy coffee. The lox and bagel combo is delish, grown-ups. Kids will love the PB&J bagel sandwich, too. Eat inside or go outdoors to the patio/deck area. This is also a great spot to access free Wi-Fi.

Sandpiper Cafe $$-$$$

429 Willoughby St., Juneau, AK 99801
(907) 586-3150
Hours vary, but generally from 6 a.m.–3 p.m., until 4 p.m. on Sundays

This restaurant, while operating under odd hours and occasional long waits, is still a favorite. Fresh ingredients and a creative menu mean a nice start to your day of sightseeing, so give it a chance. A nice menu for kids features items like French toast and pancakes. Be patient and try for a table during nonpeak hours. It's worth it.

Gold Creek Salmon Bake $$$
1061 Salmon Creek Lane, Juneau, AK 99801
(800) 791-2673, (907) 789-0052
www.bestofalaskatravel.com, info@bestofalaskatravel.com
Tickets for dinner and show $42/adult, $28/kids 12 and under.

Think Hawaiian luau, but in a Last Frontier setting and with musicians belting out songs about Alaska's history instead of the hula, and you've got the gist of the Salmon Bake. Geared to the cruise ship crowd but lots of fun for kids, the bake is full of silly antics, food, and lots of 49th-state kitsch. The meal features all-you-can-eat salmon, chicken, pasta, and sides plus entertainment. After dinner, wander to the campfire and roast marshmallows or try your hand at gold panning and give a pat on the head to the company's mascot, Mac, an enormous malamute who loves kids. Transportation provided from most downtown locations.

FAMILY FUN IN JUNEAU
As an Alaskan, I love Juneau because of its unique ability to serve as the seat of our state's government despite being located a good distance from the rest of the state. As a visitor, I love Juneau for its high-quality museums, walkability, and fascinating landscape. I even love the weather. Most cruise ships only spend a few hours or, at the most, a day in Alaska's capital city. Buck the trend if you can, stay for a few days, and get to know this community.

Museums and Cultural Experiences
History comes alive in Juneau, and hundreds of Alaska school kids make the pilgrimage here every year to see, in person, how their state was born through the efforts of a few dedicated individuals. I've listed the three best museums to visit with kids, offering a nice glimpse into the past lives of those who made the area home and those who came to find their fortune and glory.

Alaska State Museum
395 Whittier St., Juneau, AK 99801
(907) 465-2901
www.museums.state.ak.us/
Open daily 8:30 a.m.–5 p.m. (May–September)
Admission: $7/adults, $6/65 and older, free for kids 18 and under

Located a short walk from the cruise ship terminal/waterfront area of downtown, this state-run museum is crammed with interesting artifacts and exhibits about Alaska's diverse past. Climb the spiral staircase to explore the lives of Alaska's animals and birds in an enormous replica of an evergreen tree or hop aboard a merchant ship and sail the rough seas. Suitable for kids kindergarten and older. NOTE: At the time of this publication, the museum was undergoing a major renovation and is expected to be closed until early 2015.

Juneau-Douglas City Museum
114 West 4th St., Juneau, AK 99801
www.juneau.org/parkrec/museum
Open Monday–Friday 9 a.m.–6 p.m., Saturday 10 a.m.–5 p.m. (May through September)
Admission: $6/adults 13 and up, $5/65 and older, free for kids 12 and under

I like this museum. It's small, cozy, and easy to navigate with kids. We usually take about half an hour to explore the space, nice for younger children. For school-agers, ask for a copy of the activity page upon arrival; it's full of word searches, scrambles, and other fun stuff. While the old-time photos and information about the evolution of the city of Juneau and nearby Douglas is indeed interesting, it's the mining exhibit we like best. Hands-on, noisy, and completely kid-friendly—that's what draws us here. Great for kids preschool on up.

Last Chance Mining Museum
1001 Basin Rd., Juneau, AK 99801
(907) 586-5338
Open daily 9:30 a.m.–12:30 p.m. and 3:30–6:30 p.m.
Admission: $4/person

Visitors, check fancy-excursion expectations at the door. Last Chance is run by a former Juneau schoolteacher on a shoestring budget, because she believes everyone should know about mining in Alaska. The place is dusty and old but is the real deal as far as history is concerned. Let kids check out the old tools and machinery that once supported the efforts of the world's largest hard-rock gold mine. Pan for gold along the creek and take the short hike to the actual mine sites.

Note: The museum is reached via a 45-minute schlep from downtown via foot or by car, up Gold Street and through the mountain valley to Basin Road. Plan on a lot of walking, so bring the jogging stroller or pack for little ones. Watch youngsters on the trails and near the old mine buildings.

Walking and Hiking

Downtown Juneau is a fun place to explore. From steep streets crammed with vintage homes to the bustling cruise ship area, there's a lot to see on foot. Stop by the visitor kiosk at the cruise ship terminal and pick up a downtown Juneau map, which lists points of interest. Hot spots for kids include the Governor's House, Alaska State Capitol, and a number of bronze statues depicting the rich history of the city and state. Some areas are reached by steep stairways, but if you have little ones in a stroller, a nice access point to upper Juneau is near the bus depot at Main Street.

Mt. Roberts Tramway and trail system

409 South Franklin, Juneau, AK 99801
(888) 820-2628, (907) 463-3412
www.goldbelttours.com
Open Monday noon–9 p.m., Tuesday–Sunday 8 a.m.–9 p.m. (May–September)
Admission: $29/adult, $14.50/kids 6–12, free for kids five and under. Alaska
TourSaver coupon book 2-for-1 deals available (www.toursaver.com).

These bright-red, totem-marked trams whisk passengers to the top of beautiful Mount Roberts for a signature Alaska experience. Located along Franklin Street at the end of the cruise ship dock, the tram is always busy and especially so when ships are in port. Our advice? Head up later in the evening or first thing in the morning to escape the crowds, and pay heed to the number of ships tied up at the dock. Once up top, hike the beautiful trails, enjoying Alaska Native carvings, wildflowers, and an incredible view. The visitor center also offers films, a gift shop, and restaurant. Many trails are accessible, so do bring the jogging stroller for shorter hikes. But

Visitors aboard the Mount Roberts Tram enjoy bird's-eye views.

if you want to go up higher, plan on a pack for infants. Our son first hiked this trail at age five and did fine.

Mendenhall Glacier Visitor Center and Trails

Juneau Ranger District, 8510 Mendenhall Loop Rd., Juneau, AK 99801
(907) 789-0097
www.fs.fed.us/r10/tongass/districts/mendenhall
Open Tuesday–Sunday 8 a.m.–7:30 p.m., Monday 11:30 a.m.–7:30 p.m. (May–September); Thursday–Sunday 10 a.m.–4 p.m. (October–April)
Admission: $3/person (May–September) to enter the visitor center; all outside activities are free. Fall/winter season is free.

Mendenhall Glacier is often the first glacial view for Alaska visitors, and fortunately it's a great showoff. This towering wall of ice is fronted by a lake with bobbing blue icebergs and brave kayakers bundled against a chilly breeze. The U.S. Forest Service has done a super job of fixing up the trails around the property, most especially the Trail of Time, where a wide, completely accessible path is full of interpretive signs to show how the glacier has retreated over time. The visitor center staff can also provide a list of other, more challenging hikes in the area, worth it if you have the time. Do visit the creek, too, and watch for black bears fishing along the banks. Be bear-aware at all times! Everyone can enjoy this area.

Note: The Glacier Express shuttle runs from downtown Juneau; check at the visitor center kiosk for current running times and prices.

Outdoor Recreation

Juneau has a wonderful community playground on the outskirts of town along the **Twin Lakes** park area (www.juneau.org/parkrec), just off the Glacier Highway. Head toward the airport from downtown and the park will be on the right. A nice bike trail continues along the lakes and a local fishing hole is often popular with local kids.

ZIPLINING

Alaska Zipline Adventures
110 N. Franklin St., Juneau, AK 99801
(907) 321-0947
www.alaskazip.com
From $99/kids to $150/adults, more if jeep tour or glacier hikes are added.

Located across the Gastineau Channel from Juneau, near the community of Douglas, Alaska Zipline Adventures offers an exceptional canopy tour on the property of Eaglecrest Ski Area. Alaska Zipline is one of the few zipline companies allowing kids under 10 and/or 70 pounds to participate, and we love their accessibility and attention to families. Try the Original Zipline Tour, lasting four hours and sending guests through Alaska-themed platforms. Teens will love this experience, and parents can be secure in the knowledge base of staff, who strive to make every zip safe and enjoyable.

Alaska Fact
The greater Juneau area is only 45 miles end to end, but the borough boasts 130 miles of hiking trails!

KAYAKING

Alaska Boat and Kayak
P.O. Box 211202, Auke Bay, AK 99821
(907) 789-6886 (May–September only)
www.juneaukayak.com, info@juneaukayak.com

Offering kayaking adventures around the greater Juneau area, Alaska Boat and Kayak's most family-friendly adventure is its Mendenhall Lake paddle, a self-guided tour of the glacially fed lake. This four-hour trip includes transportation from downtown Juneau, all gear, a snack, and a map of the area. For a family who enjoys kayaking on their own, this is a great way to explore a glacier up close.

Note: Rates for this trip are around $110/person, with no child discounts, but if you love kayaking, this is a super trip. Children should be familiar with kayaks and proper safety techniques. The company also offers guided trips for those who'd like someone to lead the way. Check website for a list of current tours.

BIKE RENTALS

Cycle Alaska
1107 West 8th St., Juneau, AK 99801
(907) 780-2253
Open Sunday–Friday 10 a.m.–6 p.m., Saturday 9 a.m.–5 p.m.
Prices: Vary according to bike and duration of rental. Tours begin at $119/adults, $89/kids 10–12 for 4.5 hours of guided biking and sightseeing, plus helmets, gloves, rain gear, and water.

Juneau has a super bike trail system just waiting for your bigger kids to explore. Even though Cycle Alaska doesn't offer trailers or tagalongs (boo), kids from about 10 and up will enjoy a bike ride with Mom or Dad, either on a self-guided adventure or via one of their tours. If you're heading out on your own, ride along the waterfront of Franklin Street or head out the Glacier Highway on 12 miles of paved pathway. Whatever direction you choose, it's great.

GLACIER AND WILDLIFE CRUISES

ORCA Enterprises/Juneau Alaska Whale Watching
P.O. Box 35431, Juneau, AK 99803
(888) 733-7622, (907) 789-6801
www.alaskawhalewatching.com, orca@alaskawhalewatching.com
Tours generally run 3.5 hours, including transportation to/from. No bookings made via cruise ship tour desk.
From $62/children to $120/adults; call for most current price

No one could have a bad time aboard a boat named the *Awesome Orca*. Captain Larry Dupler, who has cruised the waterways of Juneau for more than 35 years, takes passengers on location in the Inside Passage to search for humpback whales, orca, and a variety of miscellaneous marine life. The *Awesome Orca* is a 42-foot jet boat suited for fast starts and a comfortable ride, with table seating, snacks, and an on-board naturalist. Its big-sister ship, the *Orca Odysea*, is even bigger, at 51 feet, and accommodates strollers and wheelchairs. Binoculars and indoor/outdoor viewing space provided. Recommended for kids four and up.

Dolphin Jet Boat Tours
9571 Meadow Lane, Juneau, AK 99801
(800) 719-3422, (907) 463-3422
www.dolphintours.com
Five tours per day
$110/adult, $85/child, free for kids two and under

At three hours, these tours are great for families with wiggly kids who may not be able to handle a full- or even half-day trip on the water. A great value as well, Dolphin tours will find the whales with their jet boats and hydrophones or you get some cash to pocket. An on-board naturalist will keep kids and adults engaged with stories and interesting whale facts. Restrooms, heated indoor space, and binoculars available. Recommended for kids four and up.

Allen Marine Tours
13391 Glacier Highway, Juneau, AK 99801
(888) 289-0081, (907) 789-0081
www.allenmarinetours.com, juneauinfo@allenmarine.com
Rates depend upon itinerary but average around $120/adults, slightly less for kiddos. Call for current price list.

Just in case you haven't seen enough of the glacial beauty that defines much of Alaska, Allen Marine will take you there. Their five-hour Tracy Arm Fjord and Glacier Explorer tour is just right for families with kids. On-board the company's high-speed, comfortable catamarans, everyone can relax inside if it's rainy or head up to the top decks to look at scenery unfolding off the bow. We love Allen Marine's attention to kids, with complimentary snacks and drinks, an on-board naturalist who knows how to engage youngsters, and lots of stops for photo ops. Watch for whales, seals, eagles, otters, and those beautiful blue icebergs. Suitable for all ages, but do watch nonwalkers/crawlers.

FLIGHTSEEING

Era Helicopters LLC
6910 N. Douglas Highway, Juneau, AK 99801
(800) 843-1947, (907) 586-2030
www.eraflightseeing.com
From $286/person to almost $500/person for dogsled tours. Call for current pricing.

Era Helicopters offers families many options for cozying up to a glacier, along with plenty of exciting activities. Choose from a glacier landing expedition or a dogsled tour and really give the kids something to talk about once they arrive back home. I'd recommend this tour for kids four and up, depending upon the child. Glacier Adventure tour is two hours; Dog Sled Tour approximately three hours and involves around 30 minutes of actual on-sled time with the dogs.

Temsco Helicopters Inc.
1650 Maplesden Way, Juneau, AK 99801
(877) 789-9501, (907) 789-9501
www.temscoair.com

In 1983, Temsco was the first helicopter tour company to figure out that folks might actually enjoy a trip to gaze at a huge hunk of ice. All grown up now, Temsco offers three tours out of Juneau, offering views of glaciers, the Inside Passage, and adventures with Alaska's beloved sled dogs. A great family tour is the fast but worthwhile Mendenhall Glacier Tour, at just under an hour. Guests will revel in the opportunity to actually stand atop the Juneau Ice Field at Mendenhall Glacier and see, feel, and hear the wondrous world of ice. Dog Sled Tours consist of the same fabulous flight plus a bit more time on Mendenhall Glacier for a pooch love-fest, a total of 1.5 hours. Glacier boots are provided. Kids over four will probably do well on either of these trips.

Alaska Fact The state sport is not hockey, as many people believe, but dog mushing.

BEAR VIEWING

Like Anan Wildlife Observatory in Wrangell, the Juneau area offers its own wild adventure. Pack Creek Brown Bear Sanctuary, located in the Tongass National Forest on Admiralty Island, is a permit-only site, meaning this area cannot be visited without the right papers. Like Anan, Pack Creek is full of busy, feeding, cub-raising bears, accessible by walking at least a mile and often two for clear observation of their activities. If you really want to see bears and won't be heading toward southcentral Alaska (see Chapter 10, "The Kenai Peninsula") or Wrangell/Anan, then do consider a bear viewing trip to Pack Creek.

Note: This is an expedition-type experience. Children should be at least 10, physically fit, able to follow directions to the letter, and confident about flying in small aircraft. Wear warm, weatherproof clothing and bring rubber boots or waders that fit your child.

Bear Creek Outfitters
2551 Vista Drive B301, Juneau, AK 99801
(907) 723-3914
www.juneauflyfishing.com, info@juneauflyfishing.com
Prices vary according to location and length of tour, so call for current year's rate.

Spend a half or full day with the guides of Bear Creek Outfitters, who will whisk you to the remote locales around Pack Creek, then hike with your party to view bears, eagles, deer, and, occasionally from the shoreline, whales. Tours include transportation, waders, or rain gear (but bring your own if you can), binoculars, a snack, and that awesome 40-minute flight, plus the company of a certified guide who knows his or her stuff. Have big kids? This is a truly awesome adventure and one they'll remember.

Note: Bear Creek Outfitters also offers fishing excursions, so if you've a hankering to catch a big one, they can help with that, too.

Gustavus and Glacier Bay

Just a hop by airplane across Icy Straight from Juneau (a mere 50 miles) sits the small community of Gustavus, doorway to Glacier Bay National Park. Built on the site of glacial outwash and a prime fishing and gathering ground for ancient Tlingit Indians, Gustavus offers visitors a chance to see remote Alaska, whether for a few days or just a few hours. While many cruise ship visitors and others do a quick in-and-out tour of the area, mostly to explore the national park, others wisely decide to spend a few nights. The scenic beauty and outdoor opportunities mean tons of quality outdoor time, especially for families who have been on the go and would like to establish a base camp for a little while. Since only about 400 year-round residents call Gustavus home, it's easy to capture a bit of Alaska's wonderful hospitality in this friendly community.

Getting to Gustavus and Glacier Bay National Park is pretty easy. **Alaska Airlines** (www.alaskaair.com, 800-252-7522) flies jet service from Juneau, a flight so short you'll barely have time to hand out snacks to the kids. **Air Excursions** (www.airexcursions.com, 800-354-2479, 907-789-5591), a small company with service to Juneau, Gustavus, Haines, and other southeast Alaska communities, will transport kit and kaboodle multiple times a day. They also offer flightseeing, by the way.

The **Alaska Marine Highway** ferry system (www.ferryalaska.com, 800-642-0066) also makes biweekly stops in Gustavus.

The **Gustavus Visitor Association** (www.gustavusak.com, 907-697-2454) can provide plenty of information about lodging, transportation, and nearby activities, both in town and around Glacier Bay National Park.

Gustavus has a number of suitable accommodations for families or groups. Try the **Gustavus Inn** (www.gustavusinn.com, 800-649-5220) for a truly Alaskan homestead experience. Inn hosts also own **Glacier Bay Tours and Charters** (same website) and can assist with arranging tours of the area, fishing trips, and kayak adventures. Borrow a bike and explore the countryside nearby or inspect the beautiful vegetable garden and flower beds. Transportation to/from airport and ferry dock are complimentary.

Blue Heron B&B (www.blueheronbnb.net, deb@blueheronbnb.net, 907-697-2337) has two cabins that lend themselves well to a family vacation. Both the Fireweed and Lupine cabins have kitchenettes, including microwaves, toaster ovens, and a fridge for easier overnights with kids. Guests also have the option of showing up for a full breakfast in the main house, featuring many Alaska favorites. Bikes are available to borrow. Transportation provided to and from the airport and ferry dock.

Another lodging option is the **Wild Alaska Inn** (www.glacierbay.biz, mail@glacier-bay.com, 800-225-0748, 907-697-2704), a 10-minute drive from the national park HQ. Inn owners will meet you at the ferry dock, spin you around the water for a whale-watching trip, and share their extensive knowledge of the area. Breakfast is included in the price, and dinner can be arranged in advance if you'd like to stay in for an evening. Take advantage of the bikes available for guests.

If you'd like to stay in the national park, one hotel is available. The **Glacier Bay Lodge** (www.visitglacierbay.com, 888-229-8687, 907-697-4000) is managed by Aramark, concessionaire of most Alaska national parks, and offers basic hotel rooms, a restaurant, gift shop, lovely lobby area with a rocky fireplace, and access to the park's activities. A park-operated day cruise also departs from this hotel, so a stay here can be worthwhile if exploring Glacier Bay National Park tops your list of must-dos.

Note: The national park is 10 miles from town, out the Park Road. Transportation can be arranged at the Gustavus Airport or by calling TLC Taxi (907-697-2239).

Gustavus delivers casual, family-friendly activities that can be as calm or wild as you desire. Kayaking is always popular here, so try **Glacier Bay Tours and Charters** (see above) or **Glacier Bay Sea Kayaks** (www.glacierbayseakayaks.com, info@glacierbayseakayaks.com, 907-697-2257). Plan on spending around $100/adults for a half day of guided paddling, about half that for kids. Bartlett Cove is a nice area for the less kayak-savvy; marine and land mammals frequent the area and water is usually pretty calm, especially in the late afternoon hours.

Beachcombing and tidepooling can be fabulous here, so dress the kids in their wet-weather gear (even if it's sunny) and have at it, remembering, of course, to handle living things with the utmost care. See any litter? Pick it up and pack it out, preserving the beach for future visitors. Start near the Gustavus Dock and wander from there.

Go hiking along the **Nagoonberry Loop Trail**, a 2.2-mile loop trail just off of Glen's Ditch Road, close to the airport. Scenic overlooks, a gravel tread, and the Gustavus Beach are wonderful motivators for kids of all ages. Do make some noise while hiking so bears and moose know you're coming.

Glacier Bay National Park (www.nps.gov/glba, 907-697-2230) is huge, bordering Canada on its northeastern side and boasting an impressive 3.3-million-acre landscape. Also one of the reasons people cruise to Alaska, Glacier Bay National Park is home to no fewer than 11 named glaciers, and thus the park brings thousands of visitors to its icy flanks each year. Don't forget to explore the park from the ground, beginning at the **Visitor Center**, located in the Glacier Bay Lodge. Here, kids can get their Junior Ranger activity book, take a guided nature walk, or investigate the interesting exhibits. Parents can receive assistance with planning their park adventure, find out about cruises, or relax in the restaurant. Local Alaska Native groups also perform on a regular basis; check at the front desk upon arrival.

A great walk or bike ride with kids is the (mostly) flat **Bartlett Lake Trail**, opened to bicycles in 2012. Follow all signage and stay on the old roadbed if you bike. If hiking, continue a loop to the Towers Trail and make a round-trip. Check at the Glacier Bay NP visitor center for a map. Be bear-aware.

Feed the kids sandwiches, fruit, chips, and a variety of other good stuff at the **Bear Track Mercantile and Deli** (907-697-2358), located on Dock Road downtown. The **Homeshore** café (907-697-2822), located at the Four Corners area of downtown, has awesome pizza to fill up even the heartiest eater. Or try the Glacier Bay Lodge restaurant, the national park's only concessionaire (800-451-5952).

Skagway: A Gold Rush, Reborn

The northernmost point of the Inside Passage takes visitors to the small town of Skagway. Living up to its Tlingit name meaning "windy place with white caps on the water," Skagway is on the itinerary for many cruise lines and road-trippers who venture south from Anchorage or north from Canada. In fact, Skagway is one of the only southeast Alaska cities to which one can drive (the other being nearby Haines), making the community accessible from all angles.

It's a frontier town redux, with false-front buildings, a narrow-gauge railroad, and lots of wild behavior. The famous Wyatt Earp showed up to be sheriff for a time, only to say a fast "no way" to the lawlessness of would-be gold seekers and merchants who were out to make a fast buck. Skagway swelled to almost 10,000 people in 1898, and I often wonder what the local Tlingit people thought of all this craziness, they who had lived in this windy corner of the world for thousands of years.

Skagway is full of stories and interesting historical attractions that capture the active imagination of children, with enough adventure to keep them busy dawn to dark.

Alaska Fact — Skagway is the setting for author Jack London's famous *Call of the Wild*, which most of us had to read in school. Remember?

ARRIVING

If you're already aboard a cruise ship with Skagway on the itinerary, you're in luck. Occasionally, cruise ships will swap ports of call with Haines, a community located about 30 minutes south of Skagway. If so, take the fast ferry (located at the cruise ship dock) and spend the day in Skagway, returning the same way (www.hainesskagwayfastferry.com, 888-766-2103, 907-766-2100). The ferry ride is about 45 lovely minutes.

The **Alaska Marine Highway** (www.ferryalaska.com, 800-642-0066) offers regular service from Juneau to Skagway, with a stop in Haines. At nearly five hours, the trip is beautiful and offers plenty of opportunities for whale watching and relaxing.

Driving to Skagway involves a pretty extensive itinerary (see Chapter 15, "Road Tripping with the Fam"), but the basic directions involve taking the **Alaska Highway** (Hwy. 1) north or south, then picking up the **Klondike Highway** in Whitehorse for 112 miles to town. Be aware that you'll be crossing the Canada–United States border, so make sure you heed all regulations and suggestions as mentioned in Chapter 2, "How to Get Here." Watch for wildlife, tour buses, bikes, and roadwork.

GETTING AROUND

Skagway can easily be visited without a car. It's a small community, and so many tour operators provide transportation that a vehicle is not necessary. Rent bikes from **Sockeye Cycle Company** (www.cyclealaska.com, 907-983-2851) on Fifth Street. Our family was pleased to find bikes for bigger kids, tagalongs for little ones, and helmets, gloves, and water bottles for extended rides. Biking is a great way to see the community, and Sockeye Cycle will also take guests on a guided tour as part of their package trips.

SHOPPING/GROCERIES

Fairway Market IGA
Fourth and State St., Skagway, AK 99840
(907) 983-2220
www.fairwaymarket.iga.com

The usual grocery items, produce, baby products, and a bakery/deli.

Skagway

Population: 961 (full-time residents, from 2012 census)
Founded in: 1897, when a steamship arrived from Seattle full of gold seekers ready to find their fortunes in the mountains.
Known for: Unscrupulous activities by Randolph "Soapy" Smith, who tried to outwit local business owners and swindle them out of hard-earned money through gambling schemes, prostitution rings, and other debauchery.
Interesting fact: Skagway has one K-12 school with about 125 students.
Hot tip: Make time to travel to the former settlement of Dyea, approximately nine miles from town, for hiking, mountain biking, and a history lesson.

MEDICAL

Rasmuson Community Health Center
350 14th Ave., Skagway, AK 9840
(907) 983-2255
Open 8 a.m.–5 p.m. for basic health care needs.

VISITOR INFORMATION

Skagway Convention and Visitors Bureau
P.O. Box 1029 (Second and Broadway), Skagway, AK 99840
(907) 983-2854
www.skagway.com, skagwayinfo@gmail.com
Open daily 8 a.m.–5 p.m. during the summer months

Visit with local volunteers and pick up information and walking tour maps. The visitor's bureau is located right downtown, in an interesting building covered with varnished tree branches, a conversation piece for sure. Ask to meet Buckwheat, the director and a local actor, writer, and voice of many Jack London recorded books.

LODGING

Just about every overnight establishment features some of the historical aspects of Skagway's charm, but some are more appropriate for kids than others. Below are a few options, both in the downtown district and on the fringe of activities, shops, and restaurants.

Historic Skagway Inn $$–$$$
P.O. Box 500 (Seventh and Broadway), Skagway, AK 99840
(888) 752-4929, (907) 983-2289
www.skagwayinn.com, stay@skagwayinn.com

Great downtown location, old-world charm, and a family-run establishment. Guests can choose a room with a private bath (most expensive) or shared bath. Beautiful gardens outside, steps away from shops and activities. Complimentary transportation. Kids 12 and under are free. Portable crib and/or rollaway available, small DVD player for children to borrow. Near the local park, too. Full hot breakfast included and Olivia's Restaurant is on-site.

Thumbs-up for: Location, historic furnishings, attention to kids.

Chilkoot Trail Outpost $$$
P.O. Box 286 (Mile 7 Dyea Rd. along the Chilkoot Trail), Skagway, AK 99840
(907) 983-3799
www.chilkoottrailoutpost.com, info@chilkoottrailoutpost.com

Stay in cabins or suites nestled within forested land near the Chilkoot Trail, the place that started the famous gold rush, with views of Long Bay and beautiful Lyn Canal. Located seven miles from downtown Skagway, but bikes are made available and hitching a ride into town is easy. Check out the campfire pit with s'mores makings every night, or take a hike on the Chilkoot. A great option for those looking for seclusion and outdoor recreation and worth every penny. Breakfast included.

Thumbs-up for: Fabulous wooded location, access to outdoor recreation, plenty of space indoors and out.

Sgt. Preston's Lodge $$–$$$
P.O. Box 538 (Sixth and State St.), Skagway, AK 99840
(866) 983-2521, (907) 983-2521
www.stprestons.eskagway.com

Sgt. Preston's is an affordable downtown lodging option. Just a block off the main downtown area, the property offers 40 rooms, some larger than others but all featuring private baths. Complimentary transportation to the ferry is available and kids 12 and under stay free.

Note: This is a popular place for travelers with pets, so if your kids have animal allergies, ask about cleaning procedures.

Thumbs-up for: Location, shuttle to ferry dock, kids stay free.

CAMPING
The **Dyea Campground** (pronounced "Die-ee") is a National Park Service site and is open all year. Fees are charged Memorial Day to Labor Day. With 22 sites of lovely sand/gravel/small-treed sites, this is a fun campground with lots of free roaming areas for kids. $10/night May–September and don't forget the bug spray (www.nps.gov/klgo/planyourvisit/campgrounds, 907-983-9200). No hookups, but pit toilets, picnic tables, and fire rings are provided. The campground is located nine miles from downtown Skagway.

FEEDING THE FAMILY

Most visitors are part of an organized tour from cruise ships, but if you'd like to dine on your own, Skagway delivers some delightful restaurants.

Restaurants

Sweet Tooth Café $$
315 Broadway, Skagway, AK 99840
(907) 983-2405
Open daily from 6 a.m. for breakfast and lunch

Any restaurant with a name like Sweet Tooth must be good, right? And the Sweet Tooth Café has wonderful sweet treats like donuts, pancakes, and sausage muffins for breakfast. Lunch features great burgers and soup, too, and excellent milkshakes. We also had fun listening to local old-timers complain about stuff.

Starfire $$
Fourth Ave., between Broadway and Spring Sts., Skagway, AK 99840
(907) 983-3663
Open Monday–Friday 11 a.m.–10 p.m., Saturday–Sunday 4–10 p.m.
(summer months)

After a busy day of biking, hiking, and sightseeing, our family fell into chairs at Starfire, hoping for something offering a little pep. This small restaurant may not look like much, but the perfectly seasoned Thai food turned us into believers. Patio seating in nice weather. Great service and portions are nicely presented for kids.

The Stowaway Cafe $$–$$$
205 Congress Way, Skagway, AK 99840
www.stowawaycafe.com
Open daily 10 a.m.–9 p.m.

Set in a little green house on the waterfront, the Stowaway serves diners fresh food, professional service, and hip ambiance. Our son loved the busy but happy atmosphere and I loved the halibut-bacon wrap.

FAMILY FUN IN SKAGWAY

There's a lot of action in Skagway, most of it naturally centered around the gold rush. As a major cruise ship port, activities are definitely geared toward the city's younger visitors.

Museums and Cultural Experiences

Klondike Gold Rush National Historical Park
P.O. Box 517 (inside the White Pass Yukon Route depot), Skagway, AK 99840
(907) 983-2921
www.nps.gov/klgo
Open daily (May–September)

The National Park Service has its brand upon many a historic building in Skagway and Dyea and with positive (I think) results for families. Four buildings—the **White Pass Yukon Railroad Depot, Mascot Saloon Exhibit, Moore House,** and **Chilkoot Trail Center**—are all open to the public and showcase life back in the crazy 1890s, when gold was all anybody thought about. Check out an adventure backpack filled with interesting activities that take your family all around the community on a walking tour/scavenger hunt. Kids will love the **Junior Ranger Activity Center** on Fourth and Broadway (open Monday–Friday 10 a.m.–12 p.m. and 1–3 p.m.). An interpretive ranger staffs the center and kids can play games from the late 1800s, try on clothes, feel a real fur pelt, and work on that cool Junior Ranger badge.

Between 1897 and 1898, the Royal Northwest Mounted Police referred to Skagway as "little better than hell on earth." It's gotten way better than that since then.

Alaska Fact

White Pass Yukon Route
231 Second Ave., Skagway, AK 99840
(907) 983-2734
www.wpyr.com, info@wpyr.com
Open May–September
Tickets from $113/adult to $56.50/kids for three-hour round-trip to White Pass

One of the marvels of modern engineering, the White Pass Yukon Route is an authentic narrow-gauge railroad that climbs 3,000 feet in a mere 20 miles. Steaming through canyons, over bridges, and through tunnels to the summit of White Pass on the Canada–U.S. border, where some excursions turn around and others continue on to Carcross, British Columbia, and the Yukon community of Whitehorse. Most families choose the

Waiting for the White Pass Yukon Railroad to board passengers in Skagway.

three-hour tour to the summit and back, since there's plenty to experience. Are your kids train-crazy? They'll love the chance to sit on authentic train benches or stand on the outdoor platform, smelling the coal-fired steam engine and feeling the rock and roll of the cars.

Note: This could be a tough trip for kids under three, due to the lack of services and the sway-ing, noisy cars. Ask when cruise ships come in and choose a trip at a quiet time. Two trips per day; 8:15 a.m. and 12:45 p.m. for the three-hour White Pass trip.

> **PARENT PRO TIP**
>
> If you take the White Pass Yukon Railroad, take advantage of the opportunity to stand outside on the car's platform. The combination of chugging and puffing noise from the engine and the creaking of the car takes you back in history.
>
> —James, father of two

OUTDOOR RECREATION

Chilkoot Horseback Adventure
P.O. Box 440, Skagway, AK 99840
(906) 983-4444
www.alaskaexcursions.com
Around $160/person for horseback tour and transportation

Saddle up, tween and teen buckaroos, for a 3.5-hour adventure along the historic trails of yesteryear. Operated by tour company Alaska Excursions at a little ranch in the townsite of Dyea, riders are transported from down-town Skagway to the corrals and spend almost two hours riding their own horses through Klondike National Historic Park. Your own horse? Yep. (I can almost hear the screaming of cowgirls everywhere.) Guides know the area, their horses, and how best to accompany experienced and inexperienced riders. End the tour with a sit by the fireside and some refreshments. Suitable for kids at least 4'10" (58 inches). Riders must weigh less than 250 pounds. Wear long pants and long sleeves (trust me, I'm a cowgirl from way back).

Skagway Float Tours

P.O. Box 1321, Skagway, AK 99840
(907) 983-3688
www.skagwayfloat.com, info@skagwayfloat.com
Rafting and raft/hike, raft/railroad combo tours start at $75/adults, $55/kids 12
and under. Check website for frequent Internet specials.

A unique way to see the power of mother nature with respect to the gold rush days, Skagway Float Tours offers a pretty nice view from their stable rafts. A great trip with kids is the approximately two-hour Scenic River Float, a trip that takes passengers down the Tayia River, ending with a snack at journey's end. Look for wildlife. Two departures per day, 9 a.m. and 1:30 p.m. Suitable for all ages and stages. Do prepare younger kids for at least 20 minutes of drive time to the put in, and 45 minutes of on-water time.

WALKS AND HIKES

The Skagway Convention and Visitors Bureau has three maps to show visitors the way: a Broadway Street map with fun facts and interesting buildings, a Trail map showcasing the accessible trails from town and farther out, and a true Walking Tour map for those who want to know more about the city's hot spots.

Our family enjoyed walking beyond the old rail yard to the **Gold Rush Cemetery**, where Soapy Smith and other notable (and not-so-notable) people are buried. It was a nice stroll and an interesting look at the community's history. Find it near Lower Reid Falls on any Skagway map.

Another nice walk takes visitors along Terminal Way (waterfront) to the Taiya Inlet bridge, adjacent to the little Skagway airport. Walk the bridge, then take a left onto the **Yakutania Point Trail**, hugging the coastline for almost seven miles, eventually ending up near Dyea.

> **KIDSPEAK**
>
> My favorite thing about Skagway was watching the tide come in to the flats near Dyea. Buckwheat (of the Skagway Visitors Bureau) helped us build a dam.
>
> —Owen, age seven

Kids might like to use up a little energy at the playground on the **Skagway School** property, on the corner of 15th and Main. It's a bit of a walk from downtown but easy on bikes, and our son loved playing on the standard school play equipment.

The **Chilkoot Trail** begins along the road to Dyea, along the Taiya River. If you wish to day hike, take plenty of water, snacks, extra clothing, and bug spray and remember bear-aware tactics. Hike this historic trail along the river, noting the difficult tread and talking about how tough it must have been for gold seekers to do this with a year's worth of "outfit" (food and supplies required by the Canadian government), horses, and terrible weather. Find more information and permits for camping at the National Park Service Trail Center on First and Broadway (www.nps .gov/klgo).

Skagway was one of only a few Alaska towns (including Seward and Petersburg) to endorse a 1939 report on territory development through immigration, especially that of Jews from Germany and Austria.

Alaska Fact

Haines: Family Adventure Away from the Crowds

Haines is one of those Alaska destinations that immediately captures the soul, even if you're staying only a few hours. Culturally significant to the history of southeast Alaska from both a Native and non-Native perspective and full of outdoor recreation, Haines is a very grounded community. But the charm of this town is its people, who know each other in a neighborly way many of us have forgotten. I highly encourage at least a few hours' time in Haines, if only to walk the streets and get to know its timeless character.

I mentioned earlier that Haines is one of the few southeast Alaska cities accessible by car, either from the Skagway side (see "Getting Here" in the Skagway section) or via the Haines Highway from the Yukon town of Whitehorse. *The Milepost* (www.milepost.com) is an excellent tool for driving to and from Haines, providing up-to-date information about road conditions and border crossings (there will be two).

If your cruise ship stops in Skagway, do consider hopping the fast ferry to Haines. It's short (only 45 minutes) and full of jaw-dropping scenery and, occasionally, whales.

Once you arrive in town, stop by the **Haines Convention and Visitors Bureau** (www.haines.ak.us, hcvb@haines.ak.us), a little building at 122 Second Avenue (conveniently located near a coffee stand). Here, local volunteers and staff will point you and your kids to all sorts of low-key family fun.

A great way to become acquainted with Haines is to explore on your own, either by foot or bicycle. Visitor center staff will provide a great map of interesting sights. Rent bikes from **Sockeye Cycles** (www.cyclealaska .com, sockeye@cyclealaska.com, 877-292-4154, 907-766-2869) and pedal around Portage Cove, along Front Street, stopping at the fantastic **Tlingit Park** and the community playground, an awesome place to picnic. Walk along Front Street to Mud Bay Road and explore the historic **Fort Seward** grounds, where the U.S. government established a military presence in 1902 to counteract ongoing border disputes between Canada and the United States. Decommissioned in the mid-1940s, the fort buildings are now private homes, an inn, restaurant, and a few shops and art galleries. Super views can be had from the upper grounds, making the uphill ride worth it.

KIDSPEAK

A museum with only hammers was kind of weird, but I liked it anyway.

—Owen, age seven

If it's museums you seek, try the **Hammer Museum**, housed in a little white house in the downtown district. Hammers big, small, old and modern are everywhere in this place and it's pretty interesting to ponder the importance of the hammer over the past thousand years or so. The Hammer Museum (www.hammermuseum.org, 907-766-2374) is located at 108 Main Street and is open May–September, Monday–Friday 10 a.m.–5 p.m. Admission is $3/adults, free for kids 12 and under.

The **American Bald Eagle Foundation** center (www.baldeagles .org, info@baldeagles.org, 907-766-3094) is a look into the life and habits of these majestic raptors and a few of their smaller friends as well as the natural history of southeast Alaska. This is a must-do for kids, if only to meet founder Dave Olerud, a passionate voice for the facility's museum and cultural center. Located within walking distance of downtown at 113 Haines Highway, the property is open daily during the summer months from 9 a.m. to 5 p.m. Admission is $10/adults, $5/seniors and kids ages eight through 17. Free to children age seven and under.

The largest concentration of bald eagles is found near Haines, usually in the late fall months as they gather to feast on dead salmon along the riverbeds near town. People come from all over the world to see our national bird in its natural habitat.

Alaska Fact

A great place to capture an overall view of the Chilkat Valley's history and culture is the **Sheldon Museum and Cultural Center** (www.sheldonmuseum.org, director@sheldonmuseum.net, 907-766-2366), at the corner of Main and First, just up from the small boat harbor. Full of Native art, fascinating photographs from Haines's early days, and lots of local information about the geography of Haines, the Chilkat Valley, and Lyn Canal. Open Monday–Friday 10 a.m.–5 p.m., Saturday–Sunday 1–4 p.m. Admission is $5/adults, free for children 12 and under. I like this museum for kids age eight and up; some of the exhibits are not as interesting for little ones. Allow about an hour.

GUIDED TOURS

If you have only a short time to spend in Haines and want to see as much of rugged Southeast as you can, it might be prudent to take a guided tour. **Rainbow Glacier Adventures** (www.tourhaines.com, joe@tourhaines.com, 877-766-3516, 907-766-3576) has a variety of tour packages, from kayaking to hiking to exploring the gold-mining community of Porcupine, home to the Discovery Channel's *Alaska Gold Rush*.

OUTDOOR RECREATION

Hiking is fantastic in Haines. The combination of water and enormous evergreen trees means lots of great views and some pretty fantastic terrain upon which to ply your boots. Most trailheads require transportation, but if you stop in at the visitor center for a map and a "Haines Is for Hikes" pamphlet, staff can direct you toward appropriate means.

Battery Point Trail is just right for kids. At 1.2 miles each way, this trail wanders the shoreline to a lovely beach that also provides access to the more challenging Mount Riley summit. Follow Beach Road south around Portage Cove, to the end of the road. Park at the Mount Riley Trailhead junction to Kelgaya Point picnic area. Watch for humpback whales feeding near the shoreline.

Note: The trail, while mostly level, is uneven and may be tough for little legs, although our son did this hike when he was three and loved it. Bring back or front packs for little ones.

Mt. Riley is longer and offers some fabulous views if the weather cooperates. For those who love to hike, this is a great option from the same trailhead as Battery Point. Kids should be decked out in hiking boots, and have extra water, clothing, and food. Allow several hours to hike the entire seven miles round-trip. Be bear-aware.

Alaska Fact	The movie *White Fang,* starring Ethan Hawke, was filmed in and around Haines in the 1990s, using both natural settings and a set that serves as a tourist attraction today, near the southeast Alaska fairgrounds.

Chilkoot State Recreation Site is located 10 miles northeast of Haines and five miles past the Alaska ferry terminal. Situated at the south end of Chilkoot Lake at the mouth of the Chilkoot River, this is a peaceful location to kayak, canoe, fish, and watch bears enjoy the bounty of salmon spawning in the river.

Note: During the summer months, be very aware of bears, especially along the riverbed, in dense brush, and near the mouth of the river.

CONTINUE THE FUN

"When you come to a fork
in the road, take it."

—Yogi Berra

Road-tripping is an extremely popular way to see Alaska—so popular, in fact, that we Alaskans often wonder if anyone *but* tourists are on our roadways May through September.

This section outlines a few crucial guidelines for driving around the state. We'll also discuss some valuable tips we've discovered after traveling hour after hour in a vehicle with our children (and other people's children, too) with nothing but passing scenery and the occasional wild critter to divert their attention. Finally, we'll offer up our favorite Alaska road trips, places we love for their beauty or kid appeal or just good food (hey, sometimes you gotta count your blessings in rural Alaska).

ROAD-TRIPPING WITH THE FAM

Here's the thing about driving around or across Alaska: it's unlike any traditional car-camping, interstate-following sort of family trip. While Alaska has a lot of real estate, it does not have an equally vast road system—just enough major highways to be interesting and a bunch of little byways with exciting twists and turns. Road-tripping Alaska is not difficult from a navigation standpoint; all you need is a map and a keen sense of discipline when faced with the unfamiliar, but Alaska does have a few unique attributes.

Alaskans joke about the state's two seasons—winter and construction—both presenting challenges for automobile travelers. Winter means slow travel due to icy roads, heavy snowfall, snow-removal equipment, and frequent moose encounters. As soon as all this snow melts and the ground thaws, work crews are dispatched to tackle issues left behind, and thus begins construction season. Delays are inevitable, roadways sometimes consist of nothing more than dirt (or mud), and there are few options for detours. Some roadside stops can last two hours while crews scramble to resurface a road, replace a culvert dislodged by freezing and expanding surfaces (known as frost heaves), or eat lunch. Travelers are often stuck without benefit of any services for the duration, so the key is preparation, whether driving for two hours or two weeks.

Know Before You Go

We covered the basics of automobile travel in Chapter 2, "How to Get Here." Alaska's roads are often two-lane affairs with a fair amount of distance between services (gas, food, lodging). As mentioned previously, *The Milepost* (www.milepost.com) is the most important tool you will possess in your vehicle, even more crucial than *Dora the Explorer* books. Buy one if you are contemplating a drive longer than 100 miles in Alaska. Heck, buy one even if you're not; the information alone is worth reading, especially while waiting at one of those aforementioned roadblocks. *The Milepost* is available at all Alaska Costco stores (www.costco.com) (one in Juneau, two in Anchorage), so purchase when you arrive, if desired. Get a good map of Alaska's roadways, either from your local AAA travel office or bookstore.

It is also prudent to check the Alaska Department of Transportation's frequently updated website, called 511 (www.511.alaska.gov). Here, you'll see where delays and other issues may impede your progress and have a better understanding of road conditions in real time.

Safety is an important factor of any road trip, but especially so in Alaska, where aid is often far away if something goes amiss. We Alaskans like to be prepared for anything, and it serves us well. Most drivers, from the minivan mom to the dad in a big truck, have an emergency kit stashed

"Hey There, Which Way to Highway 1?"

Alaska actually has 12 official highways, each featuring both a number and a name, which can cause unnecessary angst among visitors. Alaskans rarely, if ever, refer to their roadways by anything other than their name. Ask any resident how to get to Highway 8 and you might be met by a blank stare and a scratching of the head. Compounding matters is the merging of one roadway into the next, maddening for travelers who blink and miss the transition. To alleviate such confusion, purchase a detailed map of Alaska or utilize *The Milepost* for the dual-moniker format of our state roads.

away in the car and you should, too, *even if* you flew to Alaska from another state and don't have a ton of room for extra stuff. *Hear me now*—a driving tour means you must be responsible for your own family's welfare.

The Mechanics of Driving Around Alaska

Unless you've driven to Alaska in your own vehicle, which we talk about in Chapter 2, "How to Get Here," you'll have to find reliable transportation upon arrival. There are many, many options, most of which do fall under the definition of "reliable," but it pays to ask a few questions of any rental agency before you sign on the dotted line or even leave home.

- What repairs/mechanical breakdowns are covered under my rental agreement if we get stranded?
- Do you offer unlimited mileage or a pay-by-mile system?
- Am I allowed to take this car/RV off the standard paved roadways?
- What equipment/supplies are included in our rental? (for RV rentals)
- Are towing charges included in the rental price? If so, from what distance?
- Do you have car seats available? If so, what is their make/model/age?
- What is the average year of your vehicles? What inspections do you perform before we drive away?
- Will you pick us up at the airport, train station, or hotel?

Driving Alaska means your family has two options: renting a standard vehicle similar to that which you regularly use at home or renting an RV as a lodging/transportation combo. I listed some options for auto rentals in the Anchorage and Fairbanks sections, since most families begin or end their road-travel vacations in one of the two cities. The remainder of this section is dedicated to explaining RV rental options and a few recommendations for smoother RV travel with children.

Recreational Vehicles and Children

Recreational vehicle manufacturers enjoy touting the value of RVing as an unforgettable opportunity for family bonding, and they're generally correct. It's camping with benefits, and many parents agree: no leaky tents, a working kitchen to create culinary masterpieces, and the cool experience of seeing Alaska whiz by at 45 miles per hour from the comfort of a dinette seat.

Size matters. As a general rule, rental RVs come in lengths of 22 feet to 32 feet (novice drivers don't want to go much bigger than that), with a few sizes in between. A good rental agency will provide a blueprint of the vehicle's layout, including recommendations for sleeping arrangements, and offer either an online video or in-person short course on driving an RV upon pickup. Take a spin around the neighborhood before venturing out on the highway—our family can attest to the fact that everything

Road-Trip Supplies

Most car rental agencies will include a kit of some kind in their vehicles, consisting of basic breakdown (vehicle, not parental) aids: flares, reflectors, manual, etc. Consider adding the following:

Sleeping bags. We bring an older model that zips completely flat; in an emergency it will cover all of us and is also quite handy as a picnic spread during rest stops.

Extra nonperishable, high-energy food items. Granola bars, dried fruit, nuts, and shelf-stable milk all work well.

Water. Bring empty water bottles and fill up at your hotel or purchase a jug of water and stash in the car. Either way, keep about a quart of water for each person available at all times.

Cash. It may be hard to believe, but some Alaska businesses do not accept credit cards. Carry at least $100 in cash (small bills, please, some businesses may not be able to change that C-note) in a zip-type bag, tucked away inside the emergency kit.

Plastic garbage bags. Since you are traveling with kids, you'll need them anyway. Large bags are useful as shelters, rain gear, storage for wet clothing, and for their intended use.

Duct tape. The Alaskan solution to every problem, duct tape is useful for patching shoes, preventing blisters, and sticking the portable DVD seems different when viewed from the looming dashboard of an RV (sorry, local store, about that retaining wall; I assure you I told my husband *not* to turn there).

Safety first. Although recreational vehicles come with compulsory seat belts in specific areas of the coach, imagine our surprise when my husband attempted to install a car seat for our then-toddler. Duh-oh! Today's car seats are big, bulky, and do not usually fit where you want or, at least, not where you think they should. That dinette where older kids will thrive on card games, snacks, and movies is not the place for your infant or toddler, thanks to a very narrow space between seat and table. We had similar problems with our next option, a long, narrow bench seat complete with

player back together. It's waterproof, barfproof, and even has reflective qualities. Buy some—I promise you'll bow down and thank me at the end of your trip.

Chemical hand warmers. It is highly unlikely you will need to build a fire while stranded alongside an Alaska roadway, but you could get a little chilly while waiting for help to arrive. Thus, the nifty Little Hotties (or similar brand) hand/foot warmers are helpful additions to the emergency stash. Keep in a zipper bag to ensure they don't get wet.

Cellphone car charger. When you do have cell service in Alaska (we talked earlier about the lack of towers in some areas), I guarantee there will be a higher-than-normal rate of texting, uploading, Tweeting, Pinning, and/or Facebooking updates and photos, thereby sucking battery life out of a smartphone in record time. Wouldn't it be a bummer to have a dead cellphone while stranded? Buy a car charger if you don't already have one.

All of these items should be kept in a waterproof container or bag. We've been known to swing by a thrift store and purchase a plastic snap-top container or cheap cooler that doubles as a souvenir holder for the return trip, but a bag you bring from home works equally well and saves space.

a four-inch-thick foam cushion. Comfy? Sure, but try securing a car seat to *that*. After a puzzling half-hour of schematics involving the rental company staff and our own ingenuity, we ended up taking off the pad and fastened said car seat to the plywood bench underneath. Lesson: Don't leave the parking lot until you're satisfied with safety.

Location, location. Given the amount of traffic in the popular Alaska communities during the summer months, roadways, parking lots, and downtown areas can be full of people just like you searching for a place to park that motorized behemoth. While I do encourage staying in RV parks and campgrounds away from the hustle and bustle of daily (or nightly) life, it is also important to consider the drawbacks for transportation upon arrival at your destination. One way to mitigate the issue is to take advantage of shuttle services, water taxis, or your own two feet. Ask around at local visitor service offices or at your RV park. Many of the larger facilities are keenly aware of this problem and provide their guests with access to town.

Sleeping in. Just like tent camping, RVing exacerbates the internal clock shift of children so they are wide, wide awake when the sun comes up. Stick to your usual family routine as much as possible and wind the kids down before putting them to bed in your moving home away from home. Even though many RVs are equipped with blackout shades, they never seem to be adequate, so we bring a few extra blankets (ask the RV agency for more) and drape them over the windows of the vehicle with clothespins.

Recreational Vehicle Companies

ANCHORAGE

ABC Motorhomes
3875 Old International Airport Rd., Anchorage, AK 99502
(800) 421-7456, (907) 279-2000
www.abcmotorhome.com

The only agency located within a stone's throw of the Anchorage International Airport runways, ABC offers a wide variety of options for RV travelers, including cars, vans, truck campers, and motorhomes. They also offer a multitude of specials, including the one-way fall special to deliver RVs to the Lower 48. Free shuttle service to/from hotel or airport.

Great Alaskan Holidays
9800 Old Seward Highway, Anchorage, AK 99515
(888) 2-Alaska, (907) 248-7777
www.greatalaskanholidays.com

A vast selection of RV choices await you at Great Alaskan Holidays, so be clear about your family's needs. It is likely this company has something for you. One-way specials available, plus deals for prepaid mileage. Free shuttle service from just about anyplace in Anchorage.

Clippership RV
5401 Old Seward Highway, Anchorage, AK 99518
(800) 421-3456
www.clippershiprv.com

Four categories of RVs to rent, ranging from Platinum, with 2013 model units with all sorts of upgrades, to Copper, with 2004–05 model units with standard features. While not as flashy as the two aforementioned companies, Clippership is nonetheless a solid agency that operates year-round. Vehicles are clean and in good condition, and a family needs only to choose the level that suits their needs. Generator thrown in for free, by the way.

Choosing an Itinerary

Resist the temptation to develop itinerary envy among other RV aficionados you'll meet along the way. If you have but one week in Alaska, determine what fits your family's lifestyle, age range, and road-trip tolerance. Refer back to Part 1, "Planning Your Alaska Adventure," for a layout of the state's unique areas and go from there. Remember that driving Alaska's roadways will be slower than driving back home due to conditions, road width, and traffic volume; don't fall into the trap of mistaking miles on a map for ease of travel. You'll be sadly disappointed, not to mention exhausted.

GO NORTH, SOUTH, EAST, AND SOMETIMES WEST: GETTING STARTED

Despite Alaska's enormous size, road-trips are fairly simple affairs from a practical standpoint of determining a beginning and end point for your travels. Below are a few great options with family-friendly appeal. Some trips we've already outlined in greater detail; these are identified with a handy chapter reference. Some families, of course, will want to expand their explorations, but for most, the following options provide plenty of scenery, wildlife, and drive time.

One-Way Fly/Drive

Flying, then driving, is an excellent way to see Alaska from the top down or bottom up, especially when time is precious. Jet into either Anchorage or Fairbanks on Alaska Airlines (www.alaskaair.com) or through one of the smaller commuter airlines like Era Alaska (www.flyera.com) and rent a vehicle.

From Fairbanks, travel south on the Parks Highway (Route 3) and witness the splendor of interior Alaska, with Mount McKinley as your reference point. Be sure to read our chapter on Denali National Park (Chapter 12) for a guide to family-friendly activities, lodging, and travel within the park.

Some road-trip warriors prefer the **Richardson Highway** south, swinging through Delta Junction on the way to Glenallen, then moving west on the Glenn Highway to Anchorage. Beautiful in its own right but without the splendor of a 23,320-foot mountain in the mirror, the Richardson Highway is full of other vehicles that have arrived via the Alaska-Canada Highway (or Alcan), commercial trucks, and a fair number of Alaskans who are on their way to Valdez. The Alaska Range provides a breathtaking view of snowy peaks and raw, wild wilderness; opportunities for camping, hiking, and boating are plentiful. Visit the Delta Junction Chamber and Visitor Center (www.deltachamber.org/visitorcenter) for a complete listing of camping/recreation options.

> **PARENT PRO TIP**
>
> When we road-trip with our kids, I do a ton of research before we leave home about our overnight destination. I look for everything from lakes that lend themselves to rock throwing to nearby playgrounds and restaurants. We also look for destinations that have easy access for walking around and use a collapsible wagon to transport our small children—much less bulky than a double stroller!
>
> —Ashley, Anchorage mother of two

Delta Junction, around 100 miles from Fairbanks, sits at the confluence of the Tanana and Big Delta Rivers and is also the intersection of the Richardson Highway (Route 2 from Fairbanks to Delta Junction) and Alcan Highway (Route 2 and the end of the Alcan). Home to fewer than 1,000 residents, Delta Junction nonetheless thrives as a home base for nearby Fort Greely, a missile installation, and in the business of farming, where crops like barley, potatoes, carrots, and other hardy veggies survive in the chilly soil. The Alaska Pipeline emerges from the ground a few miles from town and parallels the Richardson Highway on its way to Valdez. The 800-mile-long pipeline crosses the Tanana River via a suspension bridge at Big Delta, a worthwhile sight to stop and see, especially with kids, who thrill at the sight of an enormous pipe carrying oil way, way over their heads. Stop in at the Delta Junction Information Center, located at the junction of Richardson and Alaska Highways, and gather some info about this curious section of Alaska. Don't forget to take a photo at the monument marking the end of the Alaska Highway.

One of the few worthy spots to eat in Delta Junction is **Pizza Bella** (907-895-4841), located across from the visitor center on the highway. Open daily 4 p.m–midnight. The **Buffalo Center Drive-In** (Milepost 266.5, 907-895-4055) is open seasonally, May–September, and offers great buffalo burgers, fries, and other kid-pleasers.

If you need to overnight in Delta Junction, rest assured your family will be offered clean, comfortable lodging. The **Alaska 7 Motel** (www .alaska7motel.com, 907-895-4848) has nonsmoking rooms, wireless Internet, and double beds. Rates start at $99/night and kids 10 and under stay free in their parents' room. Located at Mile 270.3 of the Richardson Highway, about four miles from downtown Delta Junction.

Another option is **Kelly's Alaska Country Inn**, a charming, three-generations-owned motel that has operated since the 1960s and recently underwent a renovation toward a more modern facility (http://www .kellysalaskacountryinn.com/, (moteloffice@kellysalaskacountryinn.com,) 907-895-4667). Now completely nonsmoking, the inn is located at 1616 Richardson Highway, a short walk from the true end of the Alaska Highway and within striking distance of shops and restaurants. Rooms are single or double, most with queen beds, and feature a television, refrigerator, and coffee maker. Rates begin at $99/night. Children under 12 stay for free in their parents' room.

Sail/Drive with the Alaska Marine Highway

This is my favorite way to travel between southeast Alaska and the Lower 48, or to get within reach of southcentral Alaska destinations with a car. The Alaska Marine Highway is the only designated Scenic Byway that doesn't feature blacktop or gravel and is an extremely popular and sometimes essential method of road-tripping the 49th state (see Chapter 2 for more info about the ferries).

The Alaska Marine Highway System (www.ferryalaska.com) also offers a popular discount program called Driver Goes Free, through which the driver of your family will travel for free on a round-trip sailing. Children under six are always free aboard AMHS, and kids 6–11 receive half off the adult fare. There are discounts available for seniors, too. Below are a few of our family's favorite jaunts on the ferry, using Anchorage as a "home base."

ANCHORAGE TO VALDEZ

Drive south along the Seward Highway to Whittier (described in Chapter 8) and catch either the fast ferry, MV *Chenega*, which will get you to Valdez in a speedy three hours, or the MV *Aurora*, which takes almost seven. Both ferries pass through gorgeous Prince William Sound on the way to Port Valdez, a deep fjord with steep mountains that begin right at the waterline. We'll talk more about the little town of Valdez below (www.valdezalaska.org), but rest assured your family will find plenty of fun before you head back to Anchorage via the Richardson Highway

Valdez, Prince William Sound Playground

Our family loves Valdez, both for the friends we've made over the years and for the amazing variety of activities we enjoy. Located in a natural fjord 11 miles from the vast waters of Prince William Sound, Valdez was originally home to the Chugach Eskimo people, who found the area's abundant wildlife and food sources to be perfect for their maritime and hunting lifestyle.

With the rush of gold seekers in 1898 pushing travelers from Port Valdez over the Chugach mountains via Valdez glacier, the city flourished, gradually increasing in size and importance as a fishing and trade route to Interior Alaska. When black gold was discovered in the North Slope area of Prudhoe Bay in the late 1960s, Valdez was recognized as an ice-free deepwater port to support a pipeline terminus. In the late 1970s, it became the end point for that 800-mile-long Trans-Alaska Pipeline.

Valdez has not escaped tragedy, however. A devastating tsunami hit Valdez after the great earthquake of 1964, a 9.1 temblor that shook almost the entire state and caused what is now Old Town Valdez to be wiped from its foundation. Then, in 1989, the famous *Exxon Valdez* oil spill caused millions of dollars in damage, and took the lives of as many fish and marine mammals. The city regrouped after each of these events, and is a testament to both the human spirit and hard work.

(Route 4 from Valdez to Delta Junction) and Glenn Highway, a gorgeous, mountain-and-waterfall trek that takes you through some pretty spectacular and spectacularly remote Alaska wilderness.

The **Valdez Convention and Visitor Center** (www.valdezalaska.org) is a good first stop to pick up literature. It's located on the corner of Fairbanks Drive and Chenega Avenue.

Stop in at the **Remembering Old Valdez Exhibit** at 436 Hazelet Street (www.valdezmuseum.org, 907-835-2764) and see the scale model of the city, pre-earthquake, and an interesting video about the earthquake itself. The **Valdez Museum** at 217 Egan Drive (www.valdezmuseum.org, 907-835-2764) offers some insight into the oil spill but is better suited for older children.

The **Maxine and Jesse Whitney Museum** (www.mjwhitneymuseum .org, 800-478-8800), located on the Prince William Sound College

Can We Really Camp Anywhere We Want?

One of the most exciting things about exploring Alaska by vehicle is the variety of options available for overnight stops. Alaskans have an independent streak a million miles long and it shows in an imaginary *Road Trip Rule Book*. For the most part, pullouts and slightly off-the-road areas are up for grabs by weary motorists and/or campers. It is not at all unusual to view a mishmash of expensive RVs and less-expensive trailers at remote roadside destinations. Formal campgrounds can be full or nonexistent, depending where you are, so the open road is considered open, as long as you leave the area cleaner than when you arrived.

Note: Some pullouts and rest areas prohibit stays longer than five to eight hours, so respect the sign and move along. Watch kids along busy roadways—drivers are not always looking out for pedestrians or campers—and be prepared for no services of any kind; you *are* in the wilderness. Treat your roadside campsite like any other. Put away all food and personal items to deter bears, refrain from starting a campfire, and be respectful of others who also want to view that beautiful glacier or scenic vista.

campus, showcases the collections of this intrepid couple, including some amazing mounted animals, beadwork, and Native art. Free admission.

If you have time, drive out to the **Old Town Valdez** site and walk the gravel grid of streets at the head of Port Valdez. A few interpretive signs posted at the entrance to the site provide photo documentation of the town pre-earthquake, and it's quite sobering to stand on the foundations of homes and businesses that were wiped away. Follow the Richardson Highway six miles out of town, and turn right just past the flashing yellow light. Follow the gravel road to the first set of interpretive signs to roadside parking.

For a glimpse into the rich marine life near Valdez, try a day on the water with **Stan Stephens Glacier and Wildlife Tours** (www.stanstephenscruises .com, 866-867-1297), one of the oldest day cruise companies in Alaska and an excellent choice for families. Choose from a 6.5- or 9.5-hour cruise (lunch is included), and see wildlife, glaciers, and the stunning scenery of Prince William Sound. Our son enjoyed the shorter cruise as a preschooler, and did fine a year later on the long cruise. Bring plenty to amuse kids, though, since wildlife is not a given.

Kayaking is excellent in and around Valdez. **Pangea Adventures** (www .alaskasummer.com, 800-660-9637) offers day and overnight kayak trips for all ability levels, and welcomes kids six and up. Our favorite is the Duck Flats paddle, an easy three-hour trip that cruises around the harbor area near town.

Anadyr Adventures (www.anadyradventures.com, 800-TO-KAYAK) also offers day and overnight kayak trips, with the addition of multiday "mothership" tours that provide yacht accommodations and daytime paddling. Kids age six and up are welcome on these adventures, and no experience is necessary.

Valdez has some excellent family-friendly **walking/biking/hiking trails**, including the 12-mile paved trail from city center out the Richardson Highway. We walk to the Forest Service Visitor Center just outside of town to see salmon spawning and hear the busy creek next door. Pick up a trail map here, or grab one at the visitor center. Stroller-friendly trail, but do watch for the occasional black bear feeding near Duck Flats.

Fishing is big in Valdez, either from the banks or aboard a boat. A great place to toss a line is near the **Solomon Gulch Fish Hatchery**, where people and bears share a common goal—fish. Pay attention to the rules and fish only where allowed, and watch for those bears! Find the hatchery at 1815 Loop Road, near the Alaska Pipeline Terminus, about 10 total miles from downtown Valdez, across the harbor. Even if you don't fish, it's fun to watch thousands of pink or coho salmon jostle their way upstream to spawn.

We like to stay at the **Eagle's Rest RV Park and Cabins** (www .eaglesrestrv.com, 800-553-7275). The cabins are tiny little things but are clean, cozy, and affordable. The **Best Western Valdez Harbor Inn** (www .valdezharborinn.com, 888-222-3440) is located right on the waterfront, and offers on-site dining and access to all the downtown fun.

Our favorite place to eat is **The Harbor Cafe** (907-835-4776), a trendy spot located at 255 N. Harbor Drive downtown. The food is fresh, the scene hip, and when the sun is shining, boy, is the ambiance fantastic. I am a rockfish taco fan, my husband loves the burgers, and our kiddo, the chicken strips. The ginger lemonade is a dream, too.

ANCHORAGE TO SOUTHEAST ALASKA (OR VICE VERSA)

Several options exist for those wanting a driving-ferry adventure through the rugged wilderness of Alaska. Best attempted as a one-way journey, unless you have tons of time and a rather large budget.

Driving from Anchorage, travel north on the **Glenn Highway** (Route 1 from Anchorage to Tok), a National Scenic Byway (www.glennhighway .org), to its terminus in Glenallen. Then swing northeast to Tok, connect with the Alaska Highway (Route 2 from Delta Junction to the U.S.-Canada border) and, eventually, the Haines Highway to Haines or the Klondike Highway to the historic town of Skagway (see Chapter 14, "Southeast Alaska"). The total distance measures in the neighborhood of 800 miles and means two hard days at the wheel, passing through Canada's Yukon Territory after a border crossing in Beaver. The Glenn Highway is a gorgeous, picture-perfect example of what many people envision when they think about Alaska, so plan for stops along the way. Gather more information about your trip at the Mat-Su Valley Visitor Center, located at the junction of Glenn and Parks Highways (www.alaskavisit.com).

The **Matanuska Glacier** (dnr.alaska.gov/parks/aspunits/matsu/matsuglsrs) at Milepost 101 is the largest glacier in the United States accessible by car. It's visible from the road but less so than in previous years due to receding ice. The state recreation area around the glacier offers hiking, picnicking, and camping options. Take the camera along the Edge Nature Trail, where overlooks provide stunning backdrops for family photos.

Just up the road from the Matanuska Glacier, at Milepost 113, sits the historic **Sheep Mountain Lodge** (www.sheepmountain.com, info@sheepmountain.com, 877-645-5121). Home to Iditarod mushers Zack and Anjanette Steer, the lodge is a perfect place to savor the Alaskan hospitality for which this family is known. Open year-round for lodging and boasting a fabulous restaurant during the summer months (mid-May to mid-September), Sheep Mountain is a favorite destination. Log cabins, a trail system, incredible views, and the food—it's all here and with the added bonus of a wide, grassy lawn upon which to play. Want to spend the night? Better make reservations early; the 11 cabins go quickly during the summer and on holiday weekends during the off-season. We like the Classic Cabins with their full kitchen and lovely front porches, but all are clean, cozy, and perfectly Alaskan. No reservations required for the excellent restaurant.

We usually stop in the community of Tok, staying overnight at **Young's Motel** (www.youngsmotel.com) and eating at the adjoining **Fast Eddy's Restaurant** (www.fasteddysrestaurant.com), both owned by very accommodating people who truly understand kids. Stop in at the Tok School and play on the playground, letting your kids mingle with local youngsters. Visit the Tok office of the Alaska Information Center (www.alaskacenters.gov/tok, 907-883-5667, 888-256-6784), where all things related to history, wildlife, and outdoor recreation options around Tok can be discovered. Find the center at Milepost 1314 of the Alaska Highway.

Once in Haines (www.haines.ak.us) or Skagway (www.skagway.com), hop aboard an Alaska Marine Highway System ferry and float your way to any number of delightful southeast Alaska destinations, including a return aboard the MV *Columbia* to Whittier, if you like.

ANCHORAGE TO THE KENAI PENINSULA

We covered this drive in Chapter 8. Of all road trips taken by visitors, this is one of the most popular, featuring all of the required components (moose, bears, accessibility, fish, and recreation). It involves a drive south along the Seward Highway (Route 1 to Tern Lake, then Route 9 to Seward) and/or a turn at Tern Lake to the Sterling Highway (Route 1) toward Homer.

ANCHORAGE TO TALKEETNA

An easy 120 miles north of Anchorage lies the village of Talkeetna, mentioned in Chapter 12, "Denali National Park." Travel north on the Glenn Highway to Wasilla, then continue through Wasilla to the George Parks Highway (Route 3) and Milepost 98.7. Here, turn right onto the Talkeetna Spur Road 14 miles to the town. On a good day, a drive to Talkeetna takes around two hours, making it a great destination for families. The Talkeetna Chamber (www.talkeetnachamber.org) offers a great lineup of family-friendly events and itineraries, plus lodging ideas if you want to spend the night.

WHY YOU SHOULD (OR SHOULDN'T) TAKE THE KIDS

While it's relatively easy to escape into backcountry during a typical Alaska vacation, it's quite another thing entirely to expose children to a truly remote wilderness existence for several days. However, with the advent of better equipment, increased access, and independent parents who want to show their kids the world, Alaska is ranking ever higher on family bucket lists.

Parents, however, do have a number of considerations to ponder before signing on the dotted line of Alaska adventure.

Cost

As you've undoubtedly noticed, Alaska is an expensive place to visit. Between paying nearly $4 a gallon for gas and $5 for a gallon of milk, many touring families struggle with finding affordable activities near the more populated areas, never mind hopping a floatplane to watch bears fishing for a few hours. That said, many people, including me, operate under a belief that Alaska is full of valuable moments of indescribable joy. Alaska *is* priceless, and if you have always wanted to experience a particular activity of interest, this might be a good time. But, as you'll see later on in this chapter, cost is not the only obstacle. Pencil out a budget, and read on.

Services

Depending upon your style of adventure travel, access to services may or may not be a glaring issue, but knowing what will or won't be available should be an important topic of discussion. For example, many companies offering overnight excursions in Alaska's backcountry provide comfortable yet rugged accommodations consisting of a sleeping bag, cot, and simple, family-style meals with no chicken nuggets or chocolate milk. Lattes are decidedly absent from the picture as well, as is the presence of an electrical outlet, meaning that the DS or iPad will eventually lose its charge (you can clap your hands with glee or wring them with angst now, parents).

Lodging in rural Alaska runs the gamut. High costs for materials and labor dictate how fancy a hotel, bed and breakfast, or cabin shall look and function definitely rules. Availability is also a factor to consider; with few spaces open at peak times of the year, visitors who show up expecting to find a room will be disappointed.

Activities

For the independent traveling family who requires little supervision and guidance, far-flung Alaska presents a world of interesting, educational, and exciting activities. From fly-in fishing to backpacking a historic trail,

Questions?

Ask yourself (and any company you do business with) the following questions before making arrangements for any over-the-top Alaska adventure:

- Is it safe for all ages? (Environment and/or landscape)
- Will each of my children enjoy this experience? (Fun is, after all, the hallmark of a great family vacation.)
- Will my partner and I enjoy ourselves? (If you're constantly worrying, rescuing, or placating kids, how can the two of you have fun?)
- What would we like our children to glean from this particular activity? (A sense of how other people live, work, or play? A time-out from busy lives back home? Merit badges?)

wild Alaska is truly at your disposal. Do be cognizant of smaller children's abilities, however, and make decisions based upon overall enjoyment of everyone.

Far-Flung Family Fun

Not sure how to begin the search for wild Alaska nirvana? Here are some options, broken down by geographical area. I've also included local visitor centers, outfitters/tour companies, and other helpful resources to assist parents with practicalities.

ADVENTURE TOUR COMPANIES

Alaska Alpine Adventures (www.alaskaalpineadventures.com, 877-525-2577) offers multiday guided trips arranged from their Anchorage office. Traveling families can explore via kayak, floatplane, backpack, and base camp. Trips include Denali National Park, Lake Clark National Park, Kenai Fjords National Park, Wrangell, Prince William Sound, and more. All trip prices include lodging, food, transportation, and some equipment.

Alaska Wildland Adventures (www.alaskawildland.com, 800-334-8730, 907-783-2928) is based in the small town of Girdwood and sells upscale adventures that include rafting, hiking, fishing, and bear viewing, either based from one of four Kenai Peninsula lodges or via bus or van transport. While Alaska Wildland does not offer family trips per se, they do accommodate kids and will adapt itineraries for group travel. Day trips are also available.

Specializing in small tours with tons of opportunities for kids and parents to explore Alaska, **Planet Earth Adventures** (www.discoverak .com, info@discoverak.com, 907-717-9666) is a very popular choice with adventure-minded families. Owner Albert Marquez operates under the belief that to truly understand Alaska, one must become immersed in its ever-changing landscape and culture—and this filters down to guests. Planet Earth Adventures offers a wide variety of tours, ranging from simple to more elaborate, and Albert and crew specialize in wintertime trips to view the northern lights and see the famous Iditarod Sled Dog Race.

Flying the Alaska Bush

Perhaps no other mode of transportation is as exciting as the Alaska bush plane. Rugged, versatile, and a vital link for residents of rural areas, these small aircraft deliver mail, carry groceries, and transport all manner of cargo hither and yon throughout the Bush. Ever since it was made available to Alaskans, the airplane has offered a connection to larger centers of commerce, with more than 10,500 registered pilots at last count.

Visitors to Alaska will utilize the services of an authentic bush pilot whenever travel requires remote access. Flightseeing, fly-in fishing, and/or bear viewing are just a few of the opportunities through which vacationers will be able to experience the thrill of flying.

A number of regional air carriers exist to connect the dots between Alaska's small communities. Depending upon the company and destination, aircraft vary between 20-seat twin-engine planes and single-engine jobs that carry five or fewer souls and a bit of cargo. Anchorage's Ted Stevens International Airport is home to three regional airlines: **Era Alaska** (www.flyera.com), serving the southcentral, far north, and southwest areas of the state; **PenAir** (www.penair.com), with service to southwest, far north, and the community of Kenai; or **Grant Aviation** (www.flygrant.com), serving the southcentral region. Well versed in rural Alaska travel, all three companies can assist travelers with itineraries and schedules that jive with larger carriers.

Small Alaska airports can also be a bit of a surprise to out-of-town guests. Designed strictly as indoor waiting areas for passengers, airports in rural areas will have no latte stands or restaurants. Bring everything you might need for comfort, including the DVD player/iPhone/iPad (in case your flight is delayed, a common occurrence), food, beverages, and warm clothing, even in the summer.

What can you expect once on board? A lack of space, for one, and no team of flight attendants, either. Small planes are, for lack of a better explanation, flying buses, with little attention paid to special touches, only safety. In fact, some of these planes are so small your kids are likely to sit ahead of or behind you unless they meet the lap child (under 2) rule. Weight plays a crucial role in small airplane travel, so don't be surprised if your current poundage is questioned prior to climbing through the door. Small planes are noisy, too, so prepare your kids ahead of time

Small planes are utilized for glacier and wildlife flightseeing experiences.

and accept the offered earplugs. If your child won't stick the small, squishy plugs into his or her ears, bring over-the-ear headphones.

Safety Rules in the Air!

As mentioned above, safety of both aircraft and passengers is on everyone's mind, especially the Federal Aviation Administration (FAA), the regulatory agency in charge of all aircraft soaring around Alaska and the rest of the United States. Alaska officials have worked hard to establish ground rules of flying in or piloting small airplanes, and this well-known "Circle of Safety" is posted everywhere in rural Alaska. In essence, it outlines the rights and responsibilities of passengers and pilots, including:

- **Don't distract a pilot during takeoff or landing.** Instruct children to stay seated and relatively quiet, especially during these times.
- **Pay attention during the safety briefing.** In a small plane, it could be you who responds first during an emergency.
- **Know the location of safety equipment.** Take a minute to find the survival kit, life jackets, signal beacons, etc. Ask your kids to do the same.

There's no reason to be particularly concerned about the safety or integrity of small aircraft in Alaska; it does, however, behoove the savvy traveler to be self-responsible.

SOUTHCENTRAL ALASKA

Kennecott Mines National Historic Landmark and McCarthy
Mile 106.8 Richardson Highway, Copper Center, AK 99573
(907) 822-5234
www.nps.gov/wrst/historyculture/kennecott

One of our favorite, and definitely most interesting, road trips is the long drive from Anchorage to Kennecott Mines National Historic Landmark, deep in the heart of Wrangell–St. Elias National Park. A long day's journey even by Alaska standards, driving to Kennecott and the small town of McCarthy is nonetheless worth every bone-jarring, single-lane minute.

Located 200-plus miles from Anchorage, the McCarthy-Kennecott duo can be reached via ferry ride from Whittier to Valdez, then up the Richardson Highway to Chitina and the Edgerton Highway; or, as we do, via the Glenn Highway to Glennallen and then Richardson Highway to Chitina. From Chitina, the road melds into a single, bumpy gravel lane for 61 miles until its terminus at a footbridge along the banks of the Kennicott River (the mine is Kennecott and the river is Kennicott).

Note: Most car rental agencies will not allow their vehicles to be driven on this road—it's an old railroad bed left over from the Kennecott Mine Company days of the 1920s and '30s, and spikes, ties, and other junk can still poke up and threaten tires. In addition, it's a jumpy, bumpy ride, even with recent improvements, so check before you plunge on ahead in someone else's vehicle. (See our RV rental information in Chapter 2, "How to Get Here," for options.)

Bring your trusty *Milepost* for up-to-date information about the road, current construction, and potential trouble spots.

We like to stay at the wonderfully restored **Kennicott Glacier Lodge** (www.kennicottlodge.com) right in the heart of the Kennecott Mines

Kennecott Mines National Historic Landmark near McCarthy is a step back in time.

townsite. With rustic charm partnered with wonderful service, this is a delightful place to use as a base camp for hiking, mountain biking, and exploring the Kennecott/McCarthy area. Our son, at seven years of age, found it to be the most exciting place he'd ever been, with mine tours, bears, skinny trails, and awesome glacial views. Plan to stay at least three nights in the Kennecott/McCarthy area; after an all-day drive, you'll need some down time.

Appropriate for: All family members, but do recognize the long and bumpy drive might be tough on infants or toddlers.

Cost: Fuel is expensive and difficult to find between Glennallen and Chitina, so plan ahead and bring plenty of cash (lots of places don't take credit cards). Lodging at Kennicott Glacier Lodge ranges from $99 to $150/night, not including meals. Four days of meals for three of us cost $400, so consider bringing snacks and the trusty jar of peanut butter to maximize your value.

Special considerations: There are **no services** along the 61-mile road between Chitina and McCarthy. Plan for every possible scenario, from flat tires to carsickness. Bring food for the trip, water for everyone, and go slow. Allow eight hours from Anchorage. Cell service is spotty at best, so assume all self-responsibility. That said, this is a fabulous trip.

Alaska Fact

In 1998, the National Park Service acquired many of the historical buildings and land around the historic mining town of Kennecott. Considered to be the best remaining example of early 20th-century copper mining, its buildings are now being restored for future generations of visitors. And yes, there are two different spellings for the lodge and mine community.

Hallo Bay Bear Camp
P.O. Box 2904, Homer, AK 99603
(888) 535-2237, (907) 235-9461
www.hallobay.com, bears@hallobay.com

Located 120 air miles southwest of Homer, on the fringe of Katmai National Park, Hallo Bay Bear Camp is more than a typical bear-viewing experience. Offering both day and overnight trips, Hallo Bay feels like an interactive safari rather than an observatory. Eco-sensitive, totally self-sufficient, and staffed with experienced guides, Hallo Bay combines wildlife with humans in a most thoughtful manner. It was the location for the 2014 Disney nature film *Bears*. For maximum benefit, stay at least two nights and truly capture the essence of nature's delicate balance.

Note: Hallo Bay Bear Camp now offers a five-hour day trip for families with kids eight and up. With more flexibility for beachcombing, shorter hiking distances, and snacks, the tour is available for an affordable $250/person, including a scenic flight to and from the site.

Appropriate for: Kids age 12 and up (eight and up for family day adventure).

Cost: Overnight tours begin at $900/person for one night; includes airfare to/from camp, food, bedding, and guide services.

Special considerations: Children must be able to walk up to five miles per day, follow explicit directions, and sit quietly for long periods of time (more than one hour). Multiday trips involve rustic accommodations with no frills. Guests must make their own arrangements to/from the small community of Homer (www.homeralaska.org).

SOUTHEAST ALASKA

Chilkoot Trail, Klondike National Historical Park
(Skagway, Alaska, to Lake Bennett area, Canada)
P.O. Box 517, Skagway, AK 99840
(907) 983-2921
www.nps.gov/klgo

One of two main routes to the Klondike during the gold rush of the late 1800s, the Chilkoot Trail was a major thoroughfare for Tlingit Indians long before the nuttiness of gold fever struck thousands. This 33-mile trail, traversable only on foot, is rugged and tough, but still worth the effort for families of tweens or teens who want to become part of living history. Allow three to five days for the whole thing (take your time, you're on a historic route, remember!), beginning near the Dyea townsite just outside Skagway and ending at Lake Bennett in Canada (www.pc.gc.ca/eng/lhn-nhs/yt/chilkoot/index).

Have younger kids? Take a few days to explore and camp along the way, turning around midtrail and heading back to the fun town of Skagway.

Appropriate for: Kids 12 and up (entire trail); kids eight and up (partial trail); or any age if you are prepared to carry them and/or their gear.

Cost: Transportation to/from Skagway and Lake Bennett, Canada (ferry, bus, air; varies in cost; the NPS can help you figure out the best route). Backcountry permits are required for each member of a party, starting at $25/ages 5–16 and $50/adult for the entire trail. Permits are also available for U.S.-only and Canada-only travel and vary per year. An additional reservation fee of $12 per hiker is required.

Special considerations: Reserve early—this is a popular trail. Call (800) 661-0486. Families attempting the Chilkoot should be aware of ever-changing weather and trail conditions and should check with the NPS before and upon arrival in Skagway. Bring bug repellent, bear spray, rain gear, and warm, noncotton clothing. Sturdy hiking boots with lug soles are a must.

INTERIOR ALASKA

Dalton Highway: The Ultimate Road Trip

Bureau of Land Management, Central Yukon Field Office
1150 University Ave., Fairbanks, AK 99709
(800) 437-7021, (907) 474-2200
www.blm.gov/ak/st/en/prog/recreation/dalton_hwy/central_yukon_field,
CentralYukon@blm.gov

The Dalton Highway is 414 miles of the roughest, toughest dirt and gravel you'll ever meet. It's also one of the most unique places to experience with children, with abundant wildlife, spectacular scenery, and millions of years of archaeological history. The highway actually begins in Livengood (84 miles north of Fairbanks) and extends to Deadhorse, eight miles from the end of earth and the Prudhoe Bay oil fields. Part of the 1970s Alaska pipeline boom, the Dalton is known as a haul road for truckers who must get goods to the North Slope on time and in good condition. It's also become quite popular due to the overwhelming viewership of the Discovery Channel's *Ice Road Truckers*. Drivers who attempt the highway must be aware of tricky conditions, fast trucks, and vicious mosquitoes. That said, the corridor of land managed by BLM provides mountains, tundra, and mile after mile of forestland. Camping is available at BLM's Marion Creek campground, just north of Coldfoot (six or more hours from Fairbanks), with a small fee charged to maintain this excellent location, complete with volunteer hosts. Otherwise, campers can free-for-all along the roadway, but be sure to pull off a good distance to avoid large rocks from passing trucks.

> **PARENT PRO TIP**
>
> If you're going to drive all the way up toward the Arctic Circle, keep in mind it's a long, long way. Take your time, enjoy the scenery, and make sure you hop out of the car once in a while. The Alyeska Pipeline has access points all along the road, and Finger Rock is a great place to allow kids to climb and play for a bit of a break.
>
> —Casey, Fairbanks father of three

Hike in the nearby Brooks Range (maps available via BLM) and the Arctic National Wildlife Refuge (commonly referred to as "An-wahr," the phonetic pronunciation of its acronym ANWR), made famous for its oil-rich dirt thousands of feet below the surface (a GPS is quite handy here). Hit up the visitor center in Coldfoot for information and some awesome interpretive exhibits (907-678-5209 or 907-678-2014). They're open 10 a.m.–10 p.m.

Appropriate for: All ages, with proper preparation.

Cost: Campground fee (around $20/night), fuel (prices vary), food/ beverages.

Special considerations: Visit the BLM's website for a complete list of cautionary supplies and important information concerning a drive along the Dalton Highway (www.blm.gov/ak/st/en/prog/recreation/dalton_ hwy/dalton_know). There are no grocery stores, gas stations/towing facilities, banks, or medical facilities. Cell service ends about 35 miles north of Fairbanks, with spotty service in Deadhorse. Be prepared in every way for every possible situation, and plan ahead far, far in advance. The Fairbanks Convention and Visitors Bureau can assist travelers with needed preparations (www.explorefairbanks.com).

ARCTIC/ FAR NORTH

Nome

Nome Discovery Tours
(907) 304-1453, (907) 443-2814

There's no place like Nome, especially when seen through the eyes of Richard Benneville, former Broadway actor and a shining star of Nome's tourism industry. Richard and his trusty (albeit rusty) van will meet you at the Nome airport, shuttle your family around the area, and regale your kids with endless tales of history and culture of this far northern community made famous by a diphtheria outbreak and subsequent epic dogsled journey in 1925. Walk a windy beach, go find some musk ox, or bask in the famous midnight sun while being entertained by Richard at the famous

Swanberg Gold Dredge. The Nome Convention and Visitors Bureau can offer some insight into the few lodging opportunities available, but we like the **Aurora Inn and Suites** (www.aurorainnnome.com, aurorainn@gci .net, 800-354-4606, 907-443-3838) on Front Street. Clean, comfy, and accessible to the beach. The **Nugget Inn** (877-443-2323, 907-443-4189), also on Front Street, is acceptable, with a decided historical decor. This is where a lot of visitors choose to stay, since the property is located at the edge of lapping waves in Norton Sound, but it is dated, albeit clean. Day trips from Anchorage or Fairbanks can also be arranged, saving you the high cost of overnight lodging. Our favorite place to eat is **Airport Pizza** (www.airportpizza.com, 907-443-7992), where Tex-Mex, Italian, and bush Alaska–delivered pizza take center stage, as well as a pretty good breakfast. Microbrews, wine, and fancy espresso can also be purchased, and kids will like the friendly, noisy crowd. They also have free Wi-Fi.

| Alaska Fact | Wyatt Earp, famous sheriff of the American Wild West, lived in Nome for a short time, in a cabin outside of town. |

Appropriate for: All ages.

Cost: Airfare to/from Nome ranges from $600/person round-trip. Richard Benneville's tours start at $100/person, but he'll sometimes arrange a tour around financial boundaries, if he has time. Lunch and other meals/snacks are on you, however.

Special considerations: Nome is remote, expensive, and not at all urban. Be prepared for changing weather, dusty, dirty streets, and interesting people. Kids and adults can learn a heck of a lot in one day, so open your minds and listen to Richard. Bring your own car seat for kids, if needed, plus extra warm clothing, boots, and snacks and ask to stop by the store for supplies.

PARTY ON—SPECIAL EVENTS WITH KID APPEAL

Alaskans love to have fun and it shows in the wide variety of fairs, festivals, and special events that capture an infectious spirit. No matter the season, visitors to Alaska can usually find some sort of community event celebrating everything from berries to gold panning. The best part about Alaska festivals is complete immersion into the local flavor, with music, food, and activities geared toward the whole family. Below are festivals with kid appeal organized by geographic area. This is by no means a complete calendar of events, merely a guideline by which your family can make a stop or two.

Southeast Alaska

KETCHIKAN

Blueberry Arts Festival, first week of August. Blueberry-themed activities, parade, activities, and tons of musical acts. (ketchikanarts.org/events-programs/blueberry-arts-festival/blueberry-arts-festival)

SITKA

Alaska Day Festival, mid-October. Celebrating the transfer of Alaska from Russia to the United States, this is a festival rooted in history. Lots of activities, including a parade, kayak and running races, music, and cultural arts reflecting the diversity of the state. (www.alaskadayfestival.org)

Sitka Fine Arts Camp, multiple weeks June–July. A wonderful opportunity for kids elementary through high school who love music, drama, or visual arts. Family camp available and new family housing for out-of-town participants. (www.fineartscamp.org)

JUNEAU

Alaska Folk Festival, mid-April. Seven days of folk music, dances, and workshops. (www.akfolkfest.org)

Juneau Maritime Festival, mid-May. Free day of events centered around boats, maritime history, and industry. Lots of boats and ships to tour, fun food to eat, and music to hear. (www.juneaumaritimefestival.org)

Juneau Gold Rush Days, end of June. Several days of celebrations for Juneau's industrial history, including mining, logging, and fishing. (www.traveljuneau.com/events)

Juneau 4th of July Parade, July 4. Join Alaska's capital city for a down-home parade and community celebration. Fireworks, too, from the nearby community of Douglas! (www.juneau4thofjuly.net)

SKAGWAY

Independence Day, July 4. A tradition in Skagway since Soapy Smith led the way in 1898. Don't miss the pie-eating contest and slow bike race—both are a hoot. (www.skagwaychamber.org/events.html)

Buckwheat Ski Classic, end of March. Fast becoming an international event, this race features a course through the White Mountains, along the gold-seekers' route.

Special race for kids and kids-at-heart. (www.skagwaychamber.org/events)

HAINES

Southeast Alaska State Fair, end of July. Four days of traditional fair fun, including animals, rides, crafts, and lots of Alaska-themed products, produce, and 4-H projects. (www.seakfair.org)

Prince William Sound

VALDEZ

May Day Fly-In and Air Show, mid-May. Full of color and skyward activity, the air show and fly-in represents the best of Alaska bush pilots and planes. Hundreds of small planes and a few big ones head to the Valdez airport for a weekend of flying and flight-related activities. You can even take a helicopter ride. (www.valdezalaska.org/events/valdez-fly-in-and-air-show)

Note: Weather is still chilly, so bundle up. Make reservations for lodging early, too.

Valdez July 4th Pink Salmon Festival, July 4 and a few days on either side. With thousands of pink salmon arriving to spawn, Valdez celebrates in tandem with Independence Day, featuring a parade, pink salmon cook-off, fireworks, and lots of great food. (www.ci.valdez.ak.us)

Southcentral Alaska

WHITTIER

Whittier July 4th Celebration, July 3–4. Lots of free family activities all day, including an all-hands parade and kids' games. (www .whittieralaskachcamber.org)

KODIAK

Kodiak Crab Festival, end of May, usually around Memorial Day weekend. Celebrating all things crustacean, with a Grand Parade (Shrimp Parade for kids), games, music, lots of U.S. Coast Guard demonstrations, and tons of crab-themed activities for all ages. (www.kodiak.org)

Kenai Peninsula

NINILCHIK

Kenai Peninsula Fair, mid-August. Another opportunity to see small-town Alaska with a rodeo, cotton candy, rides, and kid-friendly activities all in the little fishing village of Ninilchik, between Homer and Soldotna. (www.kenaipeninsulafair.com)

HOMER

Kachemak Bay Shorebird Festival, mid-May. A week of shorebird-related activities, lectures, hikes, and kids' activities. The whole family will enjoy the guided hikes and community atmosphere of Homer. (www .homeralaska.org)

SOLDOTNA/KENAI

Kenai River Festival, mid-June. A weekend event centered around the Kenai River and all her bounty, the festival is great fun for all ages, with a kids' zone, concert series, arts and crafts, and tons of festival food with a decided salmon theme. (www.kenaiwatershed.org/kenairiverfestival.html)

SEWARD

Polar Bear Jump, mid-January. A crazy weekend of icy water, the Polar Bear Jump is an institution for southcentral Alaska residents to raise money in support of children with cancer. Join the fun by donating then watching costumed folks leap into frigid Resurrection Bay, then participate in many other events. (www.sewardchamber.org)

Seward 4th of July, July 4. Yes, the fireworks, parade, and food are terrific. The activities for kids are fun, but it's really the Mount Marathon Race people come to see—a grueling climb up, then down the rocky, steep, and potentially dangerous mountain standing guard over Seward. This event causes Seward's population to triple, so make reservations far in advance if you'd like to go. (www.sewardchamber.org)

GIRDWOOD

Girdwood Forest Fair, early July. Get your tie-dye on and join the groovy fun at the Forest Fair. Tons of music, dancing, and crafts await your family, and a little parade kicks things off on Saturday. Locals love this event. (www.girdwoodforestfair.com)

Alyeska Resort Blueberry Festival, mid-August. A Southcentral blueberry love-fest, this is a great way to learn more about our favorite local berry. Lots of music, blueberry foods, a pie-eating contest, and kids' games. Oh and don't forget to bring a container to pick berries right outside the resort's back door. (www.alyeskaresort.com)

ANCHORAGE

Fur Rendezvous, end of February. Beat the winter blahs with an outdoor carnival, parade, family footrace, and a popular Running with the Reindeer event. Anchorage pulls out all the stops for this week of winter fun, and it's a wonderful time to visit. (www.furrondy.net)

Iditarod Trail Sled Dog Race, first weekend in March. Catch the ceremonial start to the "Last Great Race" as hundreds of dogs and thousands of people converge on downtown Anchorage. Have kids who love pups? This is the place. Educational information available at a number of venues and trailside viewing is lots of fun. (www.iditarod.com)

Summer Solstice Festival, on or around June 21. Downtown Anchorage's way of embracing the summer sunlight, the Solstice Festival features children's activities and games, a teen skateboard demonstration, a kayak pool, giant sandbox, and lots of music. (www.anchoragedowntown.org)

PALMER

Colony Days, early June. This week of farm-themed fun commemorates the original colonists brought to Alaska by President Roosevelt in the mid-1930s. Parade, rides, music, arts and crafts, and plenty of food to kick of the summer growing season. (www.palmerchamber.org)

Alaska State Fair, two weeks in September. If your kiddos are wowed by animals, giant produce, and carnival rides, this might be the event for you. It's a big affair, with wide appeal for locals, so parking can be a bear. Definitely the place for more rugged strollers, since there will be lots of walking. (www.alaskastatefair.org)

TALKEETNA

New Year's Eve in downtown Talkeetna, December 31. A favorite of our family, this is an old-fashioned, truly traditional way to celebrate the start of a new year. Meet at the Talkeetna Roadhouse (www.talkeetnaroadhouse .com) for a family-style supper, then spend some time watching fireworks on the main street of town or take a midnight snowshoe along the riverside trails. (www.talkeetnachamber.com)

Denali National Park Area

Winterfest, mid-February. Join year-round residents of Denali National Park and the Denali Borough as they beat the wintertime blues. Indoor and outdoor activities for all ages, including dogsled rides, guided snowshoe hikes, a square dance, and free camping at Riley Creek Campground. See the website for other lodging options and a full schedule of events (www .denaliborough.com). Best approached via car, but the Alaska Railroad does stop nearby.

Fairbanks/Interior

Midnight Sun Festival, on or near June 21. Fairbanksans truly love the summer solstice, because it marks nearly 24 hours of daylight after a long, cold winter. Operating from noon to midnight the Saturday nearest solstice, this is a day to get outside and eat, drink, and be merry. Attend the famous Midnight Sun baseball game that begins at 10 p.m., too. (www .downtownfairbanks.com)

Golden Days, mid-/end of July. Over 60 years of Last Frontier fun has residents all in a dither over a gold-themed festival that celebrates the founding of Fairbanks. Grand parade, kids' activities, music, dancing, and tons of history. (www.fairbankschamber.org)

Tanana Valley Fair, mid-August. This is Interior Alaska's time to shine, with tons of produce, livestock, rides, and fair food. We love this fair for its small-town feel. (www.tananavalleystatefair.com)

Ice Alaska/World Ice Art Championships, end of February to end of March. The world's best ice-carving masters converge on Fairbanks every year, and the results are spectacular. Also featured are playgrounds and slides for kids, all made of ice! A fantastic time to bundle up and visit Fairbanks. Take the train, fly, or try a combination of the two. (www .icealaska.com)

INDEX

Note: Italicized page numbers indicate illustrations.